HAMMERED

HEAVY TALES FROM THE HARD-ROCK HIGHWAY

KIRK BLOWS

Plexus, London

Copyright © 2012 by Kirk Blows
Published by Plexus Publishing Limited
25 Mallinson Road
London SW11 1BW
www.plexusbooks.com

British Library Cataloguing in Publication Data

Blows, Kirk.
  Hammered : heavy tales from the hard-rock highway.
  1. Rock musicians–Interviews. 2. Rock music–History and
  criticism.
  I. Title
  781.4'2166'0922-dc23

  ISBN-13: 978-0-85965-485-2

Cover photo by Paul Bergen/Redferns/Getty Images
Cover and book design by Coco Wake-Porter
All interior photographs by Tony Mottram (www.tonymottram.com)
Printed in Great Britain by Bell & Bain Ltd

Acknowledgements
The following adventures and interviews were conducted for: *Metal Hammer* (Paradise Lost,
Alice Cooper, Lynyrd Skynyrd, Iron Maiden, Killing Joke, Dogs D'Amour, Gypsy Queen,
Dumpy's Rusty Nuts), *Metal CD* (Motörhead, Judas Priest, Iron Maiden, Ozzy Osbourne, Black
Crowes, Anthrax, Ace Frehley, Kiss, Def Leppard, Michael Schenker, UFO, Glenn Hughes,
Henry Rollins, Phantom Blue, Sepultura, Quireboys), *RAW* (Ian Gillan, UFO, Status Quo,
Joe Walsh, Pearl Jam, Mick Ronson, Screaming Jets, Dweezil Zappa), *Rock CD* (Brian May,
Lindsey Buckingham), *Music Week* (Yngwie Malmsteen, the Macc Lads, Gamma Ray, Brian
Robertson), *Guitar Magazine* (Def Leppard, Carlos Santana), *What's On* (Hawkwind), *Penthouse*
(Wolfsbane, Steve Vai, Lita Ford, Jim Steinman, Guns N' Roses), *The London Paper* (Metallica).
        Special thanks to: Karen Glaseby, Patricia Laker, Karen, Jessica and Lewis
Blows, David, Jennifer, Helen, John and Rachel Laker, Tony Mottram, Damian Smyth, Jo
Davies, Gary Hawkins, David Powter, Joe Sach, Gerry Levey, John Raven, Ben Sharratt,
Justin Allen, Steven Ball, John Matthews, Matt Butler, Steve Bacon, Steve Blowers, Rob
Newell, Trevor Davies, Iain Liddle, Simon Hayes, Brad Ashton, James Gill, Nick Stocker,
Paul Henderson, Dave Beverley-Jones, plus all the artistes, management, record company
personnel and PRs, writing colleagues, the staff at The Ship, the Marquee Club and the
St Moritz, everybody I've shared a drink with, plus everyone at Plexus Publishing.

CONTENTS

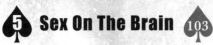

INTRODUCTION

'*H*ell bent, hell bent for leather . . .*' It's Saturday, 23 July 2011 and Judas Priest vocalist Rob Halford is living up to his legendary reputation as the undisputed Liberace of heavy metal by lazing back on a Harley Davidson in an outrageously glittery, studded cape, Village People-style leather cap and dazzling mirrored shades in what seems like his fifteenth costume change of the night.

The veteran, self-declared 'Metal Gods' are headlining the High Voltage Festival in London's Victoria Park and the goatee-chinned Halford – just a month short of his sixtieth birthday – is camping it up big time with a black whip between his teeth as the band cranks out the mighty, metallic riffs of one of their longstanding classics.

He looks, quite frankly, preposterous – and he surely knows it as much as anybody as he sends himself up in one glorious parody. But at least he succeeds in keeping the bike onstage – which is more than he managed on one occasion in the early eighties when he lost control in a fog of dry ice and saw his machine fly off into the photographers' pit. A case of less 'Kerrang!' and more 'Kerrunch!'

Welcome, ladies and gentlemen, to the crazy world of heavy metal . . . Priest might personify the script of a *Carry On . . . Heavy Rocking* movie better than most, but there's no avoiding the fact that the entire genre is difficult to take too seriously at times – as even the most ardent of fans might have to admit.

That's because nothing else comes close to matching heavy rock in terms of accommodating comical characters, exaggerated egos, barmy behaviour, alcoholic excess, backstage bust-ups, hedonistic habits, foolish feuding, self-indulgent stupidity, pompous posturing, sexual shenanigans and downright noisy, er, *naughtiness*.

So perhaps it was more than just the music – enticing though it continues to be – that attracted this author into the world of hard-rock journalism in the early eighties. An administrative role at a record company opened a valuable door for me into the music business, but there was something distinctly unrewarding about peddling disposable, plastic pop. And there was nothing positive to take from that Christmas party spent staggering around in the friendly embrace of former Wham! star Andrew Ridgeley – except, of course, relief that it wasn't George Michael . . .

Access to free music at least provided a regular passport into the Marquee Club, whose DJs were happy to exchange passes for records – Cheap Trick and Ozzy Osbourne yes, Shakin' Stevens no. Fledgling rock acts passed through the club in numbers – Bernie Tormé was always a favourite – and the motivation grew to write about the heavier sounds that were being overlooked by some parts of the music press.

How does one get into rock journalism? 'Find an interesting gig that's off the radar, pay to get in, write a short piece and circulate it to anybody that might publish it,' said work colleague Clive, who had dabbled in some writing and had memorably referred to the 'Dionysian ethos' – as you do – in a review of Whitesnake in concert. They were life-changing words – the advice that is, not the stuff about Dionysus.

The chosen band was called Framed (featuring former Sham 69 guitarist Dave Parsons and Girlschool bassist Enid Williams); the venue the Fulham Greyhound. The less-than-positive review of their debut live outing duly appeared in *Kerrang!* and an important lesson was soon learned – never introduce yourself to a group when you've just rubbished them in print. It stupidly seemed a good idea to say hello to semi-pink-haired vocalist/guitarist Barbara Spitz in the bar of the Marquee. 'You fucking bastard!' she spat (or rather Spitz) before displaying her painfully excellent face-slapping skills and walking off to disappear into European theatre for the rest of her life.

By 1987, the freelance work had led to a full-time position on *Metal Hammer* – a German magazine that launched an English edition to bring more competition to the market. Suddenly it was Meat Loaf for breakfast and sex to the super-speedy sounds of Slayer – frenetic thrills, as anybody might imagine. Indeed, it was like arriving on an exciting new planet, one on which the usual rules of convention and conformity didn't exist.

Soho established itself as the initial home base, with the Marquee, The Ship and the St Moritz – the three Wardour Street watering holes that formed the corner points of London's very own Bermuda Triangle – into which musicians, writers and assorted hangers-on of both sexes disappeared for up to nine hours at a time before finally emerging in a condition that can kindly be described as disorientated. Or drunk.

But rock bands are nothing if not warriors of the road, with scribblers and scribes clinging on to the leather jackets of their subjects in the hope of returning home with some good tour tales. And as the writing continued, for *RAW, Music Week, Metal CD* and the re-launched *Metal Hammer* (the latter two magazines as editor) among other titles, there was no escaping the irresistible attraction of an environment defined by moments of comedy, lunacy and irony – much of it completely unintended – where nobody ever quite knew what was going to happen next.

So one day it's a case of sipping soup with Ozzy; the next it's fending off the menace of Motörhead, chatting with former members of Queen or even sharing a stage with Metallica, with the adventures, conversations and anecdotes that form the backbone of this book stretching from London to Melbourne to Los Angeles, and various stops along the way. Appearances from Priest, Motörhead, Ozzy, Status Quo, Iron Maiden, Guns N' Roses, Kiss, Deep Purple, Alice Cooper, UFO, Yngwie Malmsteen et al. ensure that the fumes of farce are never too far away.

Together, these interview experiences combine to open a window into a wayward world of camaraderie and conflict, riffs and tiffs, vanity and insanity, boozers and losers, obsessions and confessions. Oh . . . and bands breaking and making up when they insist they never will.

Over the past thirty years or so, heavy metal has mutated from its traditional form – thanks to the diverse influences of thrash, indie, pop, rap, punk and funk – into something far more diverse and dynamic. Its relationship with fashion has always been tenuous at best, having been designed to exist in its own orbit. But while its credibility might occasionally have creaked, it has never cracked and, having weathered the major storm of the early nineties, when the changing musical climate threatened to render certain bands redundant, heavy rock has emerged like a phoenix from the flames to become as vital and vibrant as ever.

That's not to suggest, of course, that it's always easy keeping a straight face . . .

Kirk Blows,
London, February 2012

HEADING OUT TO THE HIGHWAY

Backstage bust-ups in Bucharest, sozzled six-stringers in Seville, dirty dames in Detroit, baby-bouncing in Berlin, drugs ditched Down Under . . . Rock music comes to life on the road, and hence there's an inevitable sense of excitement when travelling abroad to link up with a group of musicians, because you just never know what might happen next.

For the bands, as Nick Holmes of Paradise Lost admitted, 'Touring is a fucking terrible strain.' They're living out of a suitcase, isolated from friends and family, while locked in a claustrophobic cocoon with their colleagues. Add in the miles of monotonous motorway, the business bores and pressures of performing and it's little wonder that rock stars need to let their hair down. As Holmes added, 'It's really good flying to a country you've never been to before and getting pissed.'

I couldn't have put it any better myself. Indeed, for me it all began with a first foreign assignment to Dortmund to cover the two-day Rock-Pop Festival at the Westfalenhalle in December 1983. With Iron Maiden, Judas Priest, Ozzy Osbourne, the Scorpions, Def Leppard, the Michael Schenker Group, Quiet Riot and Krokus all battling for supremacy, there was nothing very 'pop' about the event, that's for sure (with even Leppard yet to change their hard-rock spots). Mountains of unconscious bodies – all decked out in dirty denim and lager-stained leather – could be seen in darkened corners as the German locals turned the 16,500-capacity venue into the world's biggest bierkeller.

The quest for alcohol was no less fervent back at the hotel where the bands were staying; meaning lots of hairy men squeezed into tight, stripy trousers and packed into the crowded bar. Photographer George – dubbed 'The Craze' for his bad-boy behaviour – suggested heading to a late-night club, but it was a decision we both regretted when we threw open the rear doors of the taxi to create a perfect symmetry of synchronised sickness.

'Another drink?' suggested George, wiping the vomit from his lips and pointing the way towards the hotel bar. It's no wonder that even rock stars think he's crazy, although the likes of Joe Walsh and Lynyrd Skynyrd would think nothing of it given their lubricated lifestyles – as evidenced in this chapter when they're caught on tour in Seville and Dallas.

For journalists invited to put their passports to use, there's a feeling of heading out on holiday while also wondering what kind of reception awaits. In the case of Alice Cooper it was a surprisingly warm welcome to his nightmare from a man who was back on the rollercoaster after having his sanity seriously shaken during his first bout of fame. And even though by then the veteran preferred chopping other people's heads off to getting *out* of his, there was still a sense of rock'n'roll circus when his entourage rolled into town (all ages invited, it seems).

The same can also be said for the Screaming Jets in Australia, Sepultura in Berlin and the Zappa family in Los Angeles, but no matter how media-friendly the members of a band are, when joining them in their natural habitat – either on the road or in their home environment abroad – there's no escaping the slight suspicion that you're encroaching on their territory or gate-crashing their party, because it's an eventful world that 'normal' people generally struggle to relate to.

Nevertheless, it's always well worth the journey . . .

PARADISE LOST: BUCHAREST BUST-UP

There are hookers in the hotel bar, members of Saxon in the foyer and beggars on the streets outside. It's June 1994 and doom merchants Paradise Lost are in Bucharest, introducing their unique brand of northern charm as this author witnesses the clash of cultures . . .

'Look, I've fucking apologised! What more do you want me to do – get my cock out?'

Paradise Lost might be feeling lost, but there is nothing here that resembles paradise city. Slumped backstage after the band's headlining slot at the Skip Rock Festival in Bucharest's Dinamo Stadium, vocalist Nick Holmes, a man who openly admits to experiencing 'violent mood swings', is starting to feel aggravated. As the scribe invited into the band's inner sanctum tonight, I pray that this is as far as Nick's apology goes – because he's the sort of bloke who might just follow up on his sordid suggestion.

On the floor of the sparse dressing room, bass player Steve Edmondson is laying flat on his back as he draws on a cigarette and reflects on the potentially life-threatening incident that took place onstage just a few minutes earlier. Towards the end of the band's set, Holmes had smashed his microphone stand and hurled it like a javelin across the stage – the missile flying through the air and missing the bassist's face by a matter of inches before embedding itself in the drum-riser and vibrating like an arrow sticking out of a bullseye. *Boing!*

'Just don't fucking do it again!' says Edmondson, feeling no less aggrieved when Holmes insists, 'I missed, didn't I?'

Paradise Lost are touring to promote their *Icon* album, one of the year's musical highlights and by far and away the best release of their career. It's a majestic piece of metal, chiselled from the most gothic stones of hard rock. Leaving their death-metal grunts behind, it's now a case of fewer gargles and more gargoyles.

'I was drinking, so I got fucking ill – very ill.'

– Nick Holmes

As doomy as their music may be, however, the Halifax-based quintet are considerably less gloomy now than when supporting Brazilian outfit Sepultura in Stuttgart several months earlier – despite tonight's altercation.

In Germany the band was still recovering from an exhausting first visit to the United States, which had seen them touring with fellow thrashers Morbid Angel and Kreator. 'There was never a point where you could be on your own,' complained a miserable-looking Holmes to me at that time. 'There were fifteen of us in one tour bus – it was just *bodies*. And I hate that, so I was starting to lose my fucking mind. The tour was necessary for the band, but it wasn't particularly good for my mental health.'

In Bucharest, rhythm guitarist Aaron Aedy concurs that the US trek has been 'mentally quite disturbing', but that spirits – flying microphone stands aside – are now much higher following a decent break. 'I'm ready to fucking do things again,' said Nick the day before the gig. 'It's really good flying out to a country you've never been to before and hanging out with fellow English people and getting pissed. I really enjoy that.'

Backtracking twenty-four hours to the opening night of the festival, Barnsley boys Saxon have been cranking out their heavy-metal thunder to an audience of 3,000 excited Romanians. And Holmes is over the moon when singer Biff Byford comes over to him to offer advice on the perils of the vinyl stage surface. 'Hey, I've just spoken to Biff!' he proudly declares to his bandmates. There's confusion afterwards, however, as the less-than-youthful members of Saxon sit aboard the bus previously allocated to Paradise Lost and wait to be driven the short distance back to their dressing room. Biff says 'fook' a lot before the situation is resolved and wheels (of steel) are eventually provided to take Paradise Lost to the home of Romanian National Radio, where all five members of the band – including lead guitarist Gregor Mackintosh and drummer Matt 'Tuds' Archer – are co-hosting a sixty-minute live show of questions and music presented by MTV VJ Vanessa Warwick.

Once squeezed into the small studio, the band request beers but are handed chocolate, much to their disappointment. As ever when 'on air', everything seems ten times funnier than it usually would, hence a hundred giggles, coughs and farts are suppressed as both Vanessa – a celebrity in her own right out here as a result of her *Headbangers Ball* show – and the band take late-night calls from the public. One caller accuses Holmes of trying to sound like Metallica's James Hetfield, while the band reveal their intention to 'kick arse' to the fans they hope will be 'absolutely rocking'. Meanwhile, Warwick spins records by just about everybody except, peculiarly, Paradise Lost.

The next day offers the band a brief opportunity, as Aedy describes it, 'to play the tourist', although the reality is that the visit to Ceausescu's Palace – former home of the executed Romanian president and the second largest building on the planet – is for the *Metal Hammer* photo-shoot. In keeping with the band's solemn image, however, as they assemble in the huge square outside anything remotely resembling a smile has to be kept strictly off camera. 'I don't really want the general public to see that side of the band,' explains Holmes. And even though it's not particularly sunny, the black shades are most definitely on.

After returning to the Dinamo Stadium for an early soundcheck, the band undertake a press conference at a different hotel where they meet around fifty members of the local media, proving the status they have in this part of the world. It's something of a surprise, to be honest. 'If the metal mania passes, what will you play?' is one particularly comical question thrown the group's way, while Nick is asked if 'sex, drugs and rock'n'roll' are still available. 'Of course!' he says with relish. Yet outside, a female reporter asks the singer why he doesn't like women. 'Because I like sheep!' he replies, leaving her looking rather shocked.

Later, at the Hotel Bucaresti, where the band are residing, there are middle-aged prostitutes in the bar, even older members of Saxon in the foyer and beggars of all ages in the road outside – one of whom has taught her young son how to grip onto the arms of passers-by and cling on until paid to let go. (I am indeed one such victim, but fifty pence thankfully does the trick.) As he swigs a pre-gig Tuborg inside, Holmes views the women on display. 'If you're single this is the best lifestyle you could possibly have,' he says, seemingly not fussy about age, although he admits that touring can be 'a fucking terrible strain' – not least on relationships back home. Just as importantly, the band has learned how to live together on the road. 'We know when to leave each other alone now,' says Aedy. 'That was the thing we had trouble with before.'

'It's not really trouble,' interjects Nick. 'It's just people getting pissed. You get pissed and you start talking shit. Me and Greg are the ones that usually start arguing because we're the ones with the most mouth in the band. But if some major argument crops up you're so used to it now that you realise it's just a load of bollocks and forget about it. But when we were younger and argued we'd think it was the end of the band.'

Asked what the best thing about touring is, Holmes pauses for a moment and says, 'I think probably getting pissed in foreign surroundings. You feel really good when you start getting drunk and if you're somewhere different it's like, "This is great!" To be honest, I don't even feel as if we've got to play tonight. That's the attitude I try to adopt because otherwise I'd just be a fucking nervous wreck. I mean, on the Sepultura tour I just wasn't eating because I was getting so nervous. But I was drinking, so I got fucking ill – *very* ill. I'd have like half a banana a day and be drinking too much fucking whisky.'

Paradise Lost finally hit the boards at 11:25pm. They're an hour late but, given it takes two hours to get a meal in this town, it's hardly the end of the world. While Nick again swigs at a bottle of booze to calm his pre-gig nerves, the 5,000 punters tonight aren't so lucky as this is an alcohol-free event – but what did they expect from a festival sponsored by the makers of a fizzy orange drink?

Vanessa Warwick helps warm things up with an introductory slot that sees her dancing onstage to a Biohazard record while throwing T-shirts into the crowd, and then the band are on. Hoorah! A Paradise Lost banner appears in the middle of the throng, kids sit on their friends' shoulders and the roar of approval between songs proves that Bucharest has truly taken the band to their hearts – despite no product being officially available here and fans having to rely on bootlegs.

For reasons known only to himself, Holmes looks particularly unhappy during 'Your Hand In Mine', and then, of course, there is the incident involving the smashed microphone stand. Guitarist Mackintosh deliberately steps forward when a video cameraman stands immediately in front of him, forcing the guy to step back and plummet a dozen feet into the photographers' pit. Ouch! And there's more conflict after the show – aside from the heated argument in the dressing room, which is where we came in – when the promoter threatens to bill the group for *five* broken microphone stands and several smashed lights; a work of fiction intended to avoid paying the full amount owed to them.

At which point, as the tour manager attempts to resolve the matter, the members of the band consider it an appropriate time to leave in search of a much-needed drink. They certainly find one at the MTV party, towards the end of which I make a complete lemon of myself by falling asleep on the nightclub bar, prompting Holmes and his pals to amuse themselves by sticking drinking straws through my hair and posing for photographs with my unconscious body. It seems that the gentlemen of Paradise Lost, contrary to what they claim, can muster a smile for the camera after all.

JOE WALSH: SOZZLED IN SEVILLE

A guitar legend is boozing for breakfast in October 1991, but the former and soon-to-be-again Eagles member – whose solo career sees him declare that 'Life's Been Good' for good reason – still steals the show as this writer strives to keep both the conversation and alcohol flowing . . .

'Hey, fifty bucks to the one who farts loudest!' Joe Walsh is in a small elevator with five other people, four of whom are also 'Guitar Legends' – or *Leyendas de la Guitarra*, as the title of tonight's televised concert in Seville claims – and one who, rather conspicuously and extremely self-consciously on my part, is nothing of the sort. Queen's Brian May, former Whitesnake man Steve Vai, solo star Joe Satriani and Extreme's Nuno Bettencourt stifle fits of laughter, as well as the temptation to take the grizzled rock veteran up on his generous but inappropriate offer, as they return to their third-floor dressing rooms just moments after leaving the stage. Thankfully, it appears that guitar legends don't break wind, at least not in confined spaces.

It's fair to say that Joe has been drinking . . . seemingly for a very long time. Suitably refreshed in the bar of the Trip Colon Hotel the night before the gig, the man who wakes the Eagles from their natural countrified slumber with his rugged rock'n'roll riffs and zany humour – qualities that have also fuelled a lengthy and successful solo career – treats partygoers to an impromptu *a cappella* rendition of 'Amazing Grace' before shuffling off to bed clutching four bottles of wine, two in each hand. 'What's that, Joe, a nightcap?' enquires Satriani as his pal passes by on the way upstairs. 'Hell no,' says a gruff-voiced Walsh, raising the bottles to eye level. 'This is breakfast!'

The following afternoon, at the 2,500-seater La Cartuja Auditorium, which, like all new buildings in Spain it seems, is unfinished and surrounded by mountains of rubble, Joe ambles onto the stage for the rehearsal session. He's a little worse for wear and the old codger's crumpled demeanour is not helped by the fact he's wearing a shabby grey suit that resembles a London bus conductor's uniform. The band, which aside from the other guitar legends includes established stalwarts such as former Jeff Beck/Rainbow/MSG/ Whitesnake drummer Cozy Powell, Yes keyboard player Rick Wakeman and Free/Bad Company vocalist Paul Rodgers – later to join Queen for one album and tour – among others, run through newly constructed versions of Extreme's 'Get The Funk Out', Free's 'All Right Now' and Queen's 'Now I'm Here'.

Musical co-ordinator May is not happy with the sound, however. 'I can't hear fuck all over here,' he complains from the far side of the stage in a grumpy manner somewhat at odds with his Mr Nice Guy image. Walsh, described by Bettencourt as 'the relief the stage needs to break up the seriousness', then pulls himself together to crank out a crunching version of his solo classic 'Rocky Mountain Way' before the musicians eventually retire to their backstage rooms.

Half an hour later, future Gay Dad visionary Cliff Jones, at this point still a mere rock writer with spots, points me upstairs to where Joe can apparently be found on his own – an opportunity not to be declined. Halfway down the corridor there's an open door on the right, and it leads into Walsh's temporary sanctum. Joe is bizarrely standing in the middle of the room, with his arms behind his back, a tartan bobble hat now perched on his head and a pair of spectacles sliding down his nose. His head is twitching left and right, his eyes peering suspiciously over his glasses even before he detects the gentle knock on the door. Politely, and perhaps a little nervously, I ask if Joe can spare a few minutes to talk to a journalist from London and he drunkenly drawls, 'Well . . . I got a bit of a problem, y'see. But . . . if you come back in fifteen minutes or so . . . I'll see if I can talk to ya!'

A quarter of an hour later, I return to discover that Walsh's room is worryingly empty. But then a commotion can be heard from down the far end of the corridor. An acoustic guitar is being strummed, several pairs of hands are clapping in time to form a beat and Joe's inimitable vocals are delivering a throwaway tune. Walsh, everybody's favourite jester, is indeed holding court and playing the busker, much to the amusement of the likes of May, Bettencourt and Powell, as well as two female backing vocalists, who are whooping and cheering, suggesting that tonight's party has already begun.

Suddenly, as if he has just remembered a pressing engagement, Walsh puts down the guitar and heads to his room. Immediately a minder, who strangely resembles a younger version of his boss, turns to prevent me from following his master through the door. 'No, he's okay,' says Joe, who turns away from his new English friend and starts nibbling at some food he's spied in the corner. More pertinently, however, there's a crate of iced beer on the floor and once Walsh has told me to help myself, it becomes apparent that the longer I can keep the guitarist talking, the more booze I can sink. As the title of his live album suggests, *You Can't Argue With A Sick Mind*, but you can try drinking with one – especially when he's already inebriated. Or that's the feeling as Joe grumbles that fame can be 'a pain in the ass' and sneers, 'You try signing a wet cocktail napkin and see what it looks like five minutes later! It's like somebody's mascara blew up!'

Walsh is clearly still under the influence. His voice is like an elderly rasp, as if the booze has sandpapered his vocal cords. His sentences meander and stagger as if the words themselves have been drowned in whisky and his sozzled speech speeds up and slows down like an old cassette tape caught up in the spools. 'I've never been to Spain before,' he reveals before suddenly starting to croon, 'I kinda like the music . . .'

'You try signing a wet cocktail napkin and see what it looks like five minutes later!'
– Joe Walsh

Yet he's still one of rock's great characters, and is fascinating company as he reflects on being Joe Walsh. He's recently been on the road with Beatles legend Ringo Starr's band and is busying himself with session work on various friends' albums. 'I like to stay behind the scenes and help other people get stuff done. Because if I help *me* too much, I get too fuckin' famous again and then I can't go anywhere!' His voice gets louder. 'I like running away with Ringo because, when I do that, nobody bothers *me*! 'Cos they all want *his* autograph, you know!'

He admits the mega-million-selling Eagles album *Hotel California* represents 'the peak of my career' and claims it 'affected everyone on the planet', but is adamant there's still life left in the old dog. 'I'm not done yet!' he insists. 'It's important that some of us old timers keep going to show the younger guys how you can end up with some brain cells.'

And, no, Joe's not joking, as he reels off his list of immediate ambitions. 'I wanna make a movie called *Life's Been Good* – a day in the life, from when the alarm clock goes off in the morning to the time it goes off again twenty-four hours later,' he says. 'A day in the life of someone who's up against what I'm up against in terms of general reality. And I want to put in all the road stories, all the Keith Moon experiences, everything! The truth, not *Spinal Tap* with the three stooges! I wanna show what's it really like. I'm also writing a book and running for vice-president!'

(The latter of which he does the following year – unsuccessfully, of course.) You see, for all the chaos and craziness of living 'Life In The Fast Lane', as the Eagles song goes, Joe is deeply concerned about the environment. Not for nothing did he name one of his solo albums *Songs For A Dying Planet*. 'I have an

incredible amount of energy,' he says, 'because Uncle Reality has given the whole planet a real hard assignment. Yep! You know what's happening to the environment? I do! There goes the rainforests.'

Or rather *There Goes The Neighborhood*, as yet another Joe Walsh album title would suggest. 'Yeah!' he acknowledges. 'Y'see, when I'm bored, when I got nothing to do, I don't do anything. But right now I'm mad and there's a lot of stuff to do, so I'm busy.'

Sadly, his 'busy' schedule doesn't include venturing to Britain as a solo act. 'Oh heck, who's your promoter?' he asks.

'Er, Harvey Goldsmith?' I offer, grabbing another beer.

'Yeah! I talked to Harvey about it. I'd love to come over but the world is so complex right now with these wars and stuff. The emphasis has come off the arts a little bit. Harvey said, "When it's time I'll call you, but it's a bit risky right now." But I'll come over and sleep in [Pete] Townshend's backyard, I don't care. I'll stay with Eric [Clapton]. Or Ronnie Wood or something, I'll be fine. I just wanna sneak in. I don't wanna headline. Who would wanna headline somewhere like Wembley anyway? I don't play tennis! Er, Wimbledon, sorry. Yeah, I don't play soccer.'

Er, no Joe. So, anyway, is he looking forward to tonight's gig?

'As Thomas Petty says, the waiting is the hardest part.'

On this occasion, he says this without resorting to singing the line of the song he's referring to. 'But it's kinda special,' he says. 'I've known a lot of these guys for a long time, but we never get the chance to play. We always see each other at airports, y'know? The other thing is that it's not for some stupid fund-raising cause that costs too much.'

Walsh is as 'old school' as they come. So can he relate to relatively modern guitarists such as Vai (later described by May onstage as 'the genius and master of the space-age guitar' for his futuristic work with Frank Zappa and solo efforts) and Satriani, who he will soon have to play with?

'Sure! I have the highest amount of respect for them,' he insists. 'It's getting me off being around these young guys, 'cos they're smart asses and it's getting them off being around me. They stole a lot of my licks learning how to play guitar, y'know. So it's a fair trade. The thing I like is that nobody is afraid of me. What stinks, what is no fun at all, is to have somebody else playing guitar who looks up because I'm me. I'm just me. What's the big deal?'

So does Joe have any idea – if he can actually remember, given the state he's in – of how well structured tonight's show will be?

'Well, we know what ain't gonna happen – and that's all ya gotta know,' he says. 'It doesn't matter what happens, as long as you know what *ain't* gonna happen. If we knew what was gonna happen, it wouldn't be any fun, y'know? Er, I gotta run downstairs.'

It's surprising he doesn't fall down them. But in what seems like no time at all, Walsh is onstage with bandana around head and trusty Gibson in hand. The band, which features a continuous turnover of personnel throughout the evening, get their heads down for a two-hour show that delivers twenty-one songs – solos excluded – and allows all the guitar heroes to hog the limelight at different times. Bettencourt embarrasses himself with a rendition of 'Flight Of The Bumblebee' that sounds more like the theme from *The Twilight Zone*, before May introduces Walsh as 'a man who is a guitar hero to all us guitar heroes'.

Incredibly, amazingly, unbelievably and despite the fact that his intake of alcohol in recent days has surely surpassed all the other guitarists put together by some distance, Walsh transforms himself to blow the competition off the stage as he conjures up stomping versions of 'Funk #49' and 'Rocky Mountain Way', relying on adrenaline and natural charisma to steal the show. 'Amazing Grace' is aired 'in loving memory of Stevie Ray Vaughan' and after the whole sensational shebang is eventually closed by a Rodgers-fronted encore of 'Hey Joe' – in tribute to Jimi Hendrix rather than Walsh, of course – one of rock's favourite nutters is piggy-backed off the stage by the rather more sober and sensible Satriani.

'You just go "wow" when he plugs in,' says Satriani as he reflects on Walsh's performance when everybody has returned to the hotel bar. 'It's personality, that's what it is,' he adds.

Strangely, one of the blonde co-vocalists comes over and requests my help in the impossible task of splitting her headache pill in two. And that's *before* Joe gets his guitar out again . . .

SCREAMING JETS: AUSSIES RULE

Roadblocks! Drugs! Condoms! Swear words! Girls dancing around handbags! It's the summer of 1991 and Australian rockers the Screaming Jets kindly extend a generous invitation to join them on the road Down Under to watch, er, some men at work . . .

It's raining cats, dogs and kangaroos as the two Toyota Taragos hurtle along Highway One through the South Australian wilderness towards the small steel-refining town of Whyalla. The raucous sounds of Aussie aggro-merchants Rose Tattoo are blasting from the cassette player and a few 'tinnies' of Victoria beer are being necked as Screaming Jets guitarist Richard Lara, who's taking his turn at the wheel of the second vehicle, is warned by the band's tour manager that a police roadblock lays in wait ahead.

Fellow guitarist Grant Walmsley looks nervous. 'Is it because they know we're coming?' he enquires, to nobody in particular. No risks are taken and the vehicle suddenly screeches to a halt before the band's 'excess baggage' is hastily ejected through a window. Thankfully so, because the large articulated truck that is parked across the highway suggests the cops are not mucking about tonight, although they would appear to have far bigger fish to fry than a rock band with a few dodgy substances in their luggage. Nevertheless, there's a feeling of tension in our Tarago as we negotiate a series of police cars, uniforms and flashing lights without attracting undue attention to ourselves.

The Whyalla locals are somewhat bemused when the Screaming Jets eventually arrive in town. Indeed, it's a case of 'Why-the-Alla would anyone ever want to come here?' because even the Sydney-based band, whose never-ending tour adventures have extended to some 800 dates, have yet to venture into this particular neck of the woods.

Conveniently, tonight's gig takes place at the Westland Hotel where the band are staying and the townsfolk are so grateful for any kind of chart act to pay a visit that it seems as if everybody under the age of thirty has bought a ticket, irrespective of their musical tastes. So there's a mixture of genuine fans at the front of the auditorium, a gaggle of giggling girls dancing around their handbags in the middle and the dedicated drinkers at the back. But the show doesn't start until 1:00am, by which time pretty much everybody is well and truly pissed anyway.

Rolling Stone magazine admits the Jets' highly enjoyable but fairly predictable musical offerings 'may not break much creative ground but they prove that meat 'n' potatoes rock can still excite lots of Australians'. Indeed it does, with the band playing their latest *All For One* album – a Number Two success in their homeland and their first to be released in the UK – in its entirety. 'D'ya know what makes me puke?' asks a bare-chested David Gleeson as he strolls across the stage. 'This does!' says the vocalist, before sticking his fingers down his throat. Next he's slagging off heterosexuals who condone gay behaviour and hanging upside down from the rafters while bandmate Paul Woseen blows up a condom and sticks it over his head. As you do.

The bassist certainly needs something to protect his cranium the following day as he struggles with a hangover while the beers are shared out once again. He later admits his alcohol consumption is somewhat excessive as a result of his efforts to recover from a drug problem.

The Jets' convoy is heading back towards Adelaide when the band starts to reflect on the previous evening's performance in Whyalla. 'It was like a radio town,' says Gleeson. 'And you could tell that only about ten people had the album.' Walmsley adds, 'We've done plenty of country gigs before but not this far out. This is like the desert!'

The conversation turns to a song called 'FRC' – otherwise known as 'Fat Rich Cunts' – the band's notorious diatribe against political corruption that was reportedly the cause of them being thrown off a tour with fellow Aussie rockers the Divinyls after just one date.

But Gleeson reveals another theory. 'We had a few people getting into the song and the bouncers were making them all stay in their seats,' he recalls. 'So I said, "What are you here for, a rock'n'roll show or a tasteful flash of vagina?" And [Divinyls lead singer] Chrissie Amphlett was standing there at the side of the stage. She was not amused.'

'We've always said we won't play the song at under-eighteen gigs, but after the main set they're all yelling out for it, so it's like . . . er, all right! So we just go on and play it and let the kids sing the "cunt" bit. That was my angry young man song . . . Look at those emus!'

He excitedly points out of the Toyota's window before exclaiming, 'I've never seen an emu out in the wilds in my whole life!' I'm tempted to say I've never seen one without Rod Hull's hand up its arse, but the singer probably wouldn't understand the joke unless he's strangely familiar with the British entertainer of the 1970s and '80s. Yet everybody in the vehicle sees the funny side when a huge signpost for a town called Iron Knob comes into view, prompting the band to exploit a rare photo opportunity and behave like tourists in their home country by posing for the camera with big childish grins on their faces.

'What are you here for, a rock'n'roll show or a tasteful flash of vagina?'
– David Gleeson

Back in the van, Grant admits the endless touring – the only way an Aussie hard-rock band can prove they really have what it takes – can take its toll on the group's members. 'The last couple of months have been really fucking hard playing every night,' he confides to me. 'The gig does fuck you but it's the travelling as well. Having said that, the harder we tour the closer we get as friends. It's rare that we have a row and if we do it's usually about trivial shit.' Gleeson adds, 'Me and Grant have probably seen each other every day for the last twelve years. But that's why this band worked in the first place, because of the chemistry.'

With that, the vehicle is soon skidding to a halt again amid a cloud of dust. This region of Australia may be uncharted territory for the Screaming Jets to explore but there's one landmark they instantly recognise when they see it – and that's where they offloaded their contraband the previous day. Remarkably, the bags of stuff are exactly where they landed by the side of the road, and the band are quickly on their way and ready to rock again that evening when they arrive in Adelaide.

This may be the City of Churches – a place with such an antiquated atmosphere that I was told by one Australian to put my watch 'back about twenty years' – but the Old Lion Hotel, where the band are playing tonight, appears to be the most popular place of worship, with its 1,200-strong crowd making full use of the two bars that stretch the length of the venue and pouring vast quantities of Foster's and Coopers Sparkling down their greedy gullets.

The Jets are far more at home in this hot and sweaty atmosphere than they were in Whyalla and they pull out all the stops with the likes of 'C'Mon', 'Blue Sashes' and 'Starting Out', whipping the crowd up into a frenzy. 'It has come to the attention of the Screaming Jets,' announces Gleeson from the stage, 'that the world is full of shit! And we're still fucking buying it!'

The man is clearly one of the world's great philosophers. 'That was more like it, a mega gig!' he beams after the show, and a few celebratory beers are duly enjoyed back at the hotel despite the next morning's early flight to Melbourne, where the band will play to around 6,000 fans at the Festival Hall.

'We actually played to *nobody* once,' admits Lara the following afternoon as he reflects on how the Jets' fortunes have improved of late. The band have been posing for photographs in the district of St Kilda – appropriately described by the group's (rather attractive) female PR as 'the Blackpool of Victoria' – and the sea is lapping at the sandy beach. 'We were in this club out in Muswellbrook – a real coal-mining valley – and we were told to be onstage at 9:30pm. But there was a pub across the road and people had no intention of entering our place until that one had closed. But we had to go on and the place was fuckin' empty!'

Gleeson adds, 'I actually dropped my pants down to my ankles, just so that I could say I played a gig with no clothes on!'

Of course, it's easier to get away with lewd behaviour if nobody is watching, especially in a country where people accept most things on a literal basis.

'I remember when Faith No More played a gig in the western suburbs of Sydney,' Lara says, 'and Mike Patton came out and said, "We're really all gay!" And the crowd didn't get the joke. Out here, if you say you're gay, they're gonna believe you!'

The band are less than pleased to discover they're on stage at 9:25pm. 'Oh well, my voice will be like a sack of shit then,' complains Woseen, who'd been hoping to catch up on some serious sleep. Furthermore, it turns out that the Festival Hall is a dry gig, meaning there will be no alcohol on sale before or during the show, which is hardly in keeping with the Australian way of life – or that of the Screaming Jets, for that matter.

Everybody goes their separate ways for an hour or so during the afternoon and *RAW* magazine photographer Tony and I are sitting in the foyer of Melbourne's Cosmopolitan Motor Inn, with drinks in hand, when Gleeson furtively sneaks in with a suspicious package under his arm. The corkscrew-haired vocalist is clutching a brown-and-white striped paper bag that, for reasons that should perhaps remain undisclosed, is instantly recognised by the pair of us as having been obtained from the nearby sex shop. It's impossible to resist the temptation to tell him that he's been rumbled.

'Er, David, we know where *you've* been . . .' I say.

'Hey, lads,' he says, nodding towards the elevator. 'Come upstairs with me.'

The mind boggles as to what kind of devious act the excited Australian is hoping to indulge in when he arrives at his room. He feverishly rips the bag open and thrusts a plastic cylindrical object into view. 'Where the hell are you going to stick that?' I ask.

'In yer mouth,' he replies, before explaining that the item in question is known as a bong – from which much smoking of illegal substances must now promptly be done. The room is soon clogged up with claustrophobic clouds and its inhabitants – now including several members of Gleeson's group – recline in a suitably relaxed mood. Indeed, everyone is virtually comatose – which is an interesting state of affairs considering that the Jets are scheduled to be soundchecking in no time at all.

Not surprisingly, they eventually appear onstage – as is traditional in rock'n'roll – somewhat later than advertised. 'This is not a song about sex and drugs,' says Gleeson, as he introduces 'Starting Out' to the crowd, just to avoid any confusion. 'It's about a subject we can all relate to – masturbation!' It's perhaps no wonder that he does his shopping in sex shops.

The crowd laps up a set of tunes delivered in a rich, metallic coating, with Gleeson throwing himself to the stage floor with, er, Glee-ful abandon. 'Sister Tease' comes across as a hybrid of old rock'n'roll standard 'Good Golly Miss Molly' and AC/DC's 'Whole Lotta Rosie' and the song – and indeed the regular set – climaxes with the sight of Walmsley playing guitar with his legs wrapped around his singer's neck while being swung up and down. It looks, as you would imagine, rather ridiculous.

Afterwards, the band retire to Melbourne's Cathouse club, where some serious drinking takes place in the company of assorted Aussie rockers – including former members of the legendary Cold Chisel – and an endless supply of gorgeous girls (or groupies, depending on your point of view).

After barely a few hours' sleep, it's time for the band to bid an emotional farewell at Melbourne Airport before flying back to Sydney, while London beckons for Tony and I. 'It's been a blast,' says Woseen, the bleary-eyed bassist, while shaking hands. 'We really dunno how you guys do it,' he adds. We emphasise that it was simply a case of trying to hang on to the group's coat-tails, prompting Woseen to respond with a look of surprise. 'But we were just trying to keep up with *you* . . .'

ALICE COOPER: SCHOOL'S OUT IN DETROIT

It's 'Detroit Rock City' but the only 'Kiss' on offer is from a pair of young schoolgirls (well, 'School's Out', after all) as Vince Furnier's pantomine alter ego enjoys a comeback in 1987, while this writer wipes off the bloodstains, fends off the fans and tries to lure Alice away from the TV . . .

Alice Cooper is a Jekyll and Hyde sort of guy. One minute, rock's most theatrical figure is beheading a seven-foot nurse on stage, resulting in pints of 'blood' spurting from the neck of the female's staggering body across the front rows of the crowd in Detroit's Joe Louis Arena; the next he is generously offering me a ride back to the hotel on his tour bus – a kind invitation that is gratefully accepted, of course.

When the vehicle finally arrives at the Omni, there's a sea of Alice Cooper fans waiting outside for their hero – and it's a struggle to get through the excited crowd as bodies surge forward and hands grab at any part of anybody who is part of the singer's entourage. It feels like being in the middle of Beatlemania. Well, almost. 'Can I have your autograph?' asks one young guy, just inside the hotel's doorway.

'Er, not really. I'm not actually in the band,' I admit. Curiously, he demands a signature regardless and my name is embarrassingly squiggled on a crumpled piece of paper. I don't exactly look like a rock star (not enough hair). Nevertheless, inside the expansive and expensive foyer, two attractive young blondes make their approach. 'Hey, can we come up to your room?' asks one, looking a picture of innocence but hardly acting like one. 'Erm, well, how *old* are you?' I ask. With no hesitation, she boasts, 'We're both fourteen!' I splutter some excuses about needing to interview Alice's guitarist Kane Roberts (which is sort of true) and the girls look elsewhere for accommodating interest – it can be assumed with some success.

Early the next morning, Alice – or rather Vincent Damon Furnier, the man who invented the pantomime figure that represents his alter ego – is sitting in his suite, eyes glued to the television. Alice has been written off countless times but, just when you think the guillotine's blade has dropped for the final time, he returns from the dead to continue his trail of terror – a bit like Freddy Krueger from the *Nightmare On Elm Street* movies. Fittingly, last night's show coincided with Halloween, but it's no accident that Alice was performing in his hometown at this very time. 'He's back *every* Halloween,' said the cab driver on the way to the venue, grateful for the extra business if nothing else.

Cooper is enjoying one of his more spectacular comebacks. But it's been a long time since his seventies heyday, when Alice began to lose the tug-of-war with Vince that saw both characters nearly suffer a grisly end. Vince ended up in an institution after losing his long-running battle with alcohol and Alice faded from public view after a series of dismal albums that deservedly finished up in the bargain bin. 'The four years between *Dada* and *Constrictor*, I was really trying to straighten out my whole physical act,' he confesses, still keeping one eye on the TV. 'I was really in a state where I physically couldn't go on stage and perform anymore. I couldn't think straight. When I think back to *Zipper Catches Skin*, I really wish I could re-record some of those songs. But when I consider the state I was in, I really can't imagine how we ever got the album done at all.'

'Sex, death and money are the things I write about.'
– Alice Cooper

Alice's commercial decline coincided with a loss of credibility with his original hard-rock audience as a result of a number of successful ballads such as 'Only Women Bleed' and 'How You Gonna See Me Now' – great songs in their own right but not what his true fans really wanted to hear. 'I'd say, "No, don't make *that one* the single or people will start thinking I'm a crooner." A lot of my audience really thought I was going to [Las] Vegas,' he laughs. 'Every time I had another hit ballad, it was another pile of soil in my grave.'

But Alice, or Vince for that matter, didn't die. For this is a cleaned-up Vince talking – sometimes about himself, sometimes about Alice. Indeed, the latter is constantly referred to in the third person. Asked if he has a greater licence to shock than he did in the old days, he says, 'I don't think Alice needs to say "fuck" every two minutes.'

The television in front of him is showing nothing of particular interest. Yet Alice – sorry, Vince – seems unable to allow his eye to rove too far from the screen, despite happily speaking at length about the philosophy of the present-day Alice Cooper. 'Most of our violence is based on fantasy – an erotic fantasy, an erotic violence and erotic blood lust,' he explains. 'Alice is involved in the human perversion side of things. Sex, death and money are the things I write about. They are the three things that people relate to. I like to bring these things into the open and laugh at them but, at the same time, people also take it fairly seriously. If you look at the character in "Chop, Chop, Chop", "Gail" and "Roses On White Lace", this guy is a total maniac, a real psychopath. But he also has different sides to his character. He only kills girls called Gail. He dresses them in wedding gowns after he kills them and he doesn't see blood, he sees roses. He's very romantic.'

Er, that's lovely. So, how does Vince manage to juggle his two roles in life? 'I just kind of tag along,' he shrugs. 'What I'll be doing over the next few days is setting up what Alice does, what this character is going to be doing. He's just pulling me along. I look upon him as a separate character. Alice has a whole different attitude about everything. He's so arrogant. He looks at the audience and says, "You're my world now; I own you." His idea of a love affair is to rape them – and the audience *wants* to be raped.'

Vince/Alice can't help but name-drop as he admits there's an obligation to shoehorn old material into his set-list despite the new show being based on a specific theme of gory stories. 'I remember talking to Jimi Hendrix all those years ago,' he says. 'And he told me that if he had to go onstage and play "Foxy Lady" again, he was gonna kill himself. I sat there and thought, "If he doesn't play 'Foxy Lady', I'll be really pissed off." It's the same with "Eighteen", "Billion Dollar Babies" and "School's Out", when I think "not again", but when we go ahead and do the show I know the reaction is gonna be amazing. When you've got 17,000 people singing the lyrics to your songs, you never get tired of that.'

So why is Alice not playing 'Elected' in the current show? 'We inserted "Freedom" into the set in place of "Elected", which is basically the same kind of song,' he admits. 'But a lot of people like that song – I remember it was always John Lennon's favourite. He used to come down to see us in New York and I know he really loved that record.'

The thought of the ex-Beatle raising his fist and yelling to the Cooper-man's classic is perhaps a difficult one to conjure. But Vince has a strong affection for Lennon and he is grateful for the loyalty and support shown by his audience in the murdered singer's home country as he enjoys his renaissance. 'Everything is looking great again for me now, particularly in England,' he declares. 'England has always stuck up for the underdog. They always want the guy who's been knocked around a bit to bounce back. I've been up and down a few times and the alcohol knocked me back down again. But now I'm fighting back.'

The conversation is over. And Alice – sorry, Vince – once again focuses on the television.

LYNYRD SKYNYRD: DALLAS COWBOYS

Forget the weeping, legendary southern-rock hedonists Lynyrd Skynyrd are whooping it up as their 1987 US reunion tour reaches its climax . . .

Lynyrd Skynyrd are in Dallas, Texas, playing the thirty-second and final date of their 'Tribute' tour across the United States. Tonight's gig is at the 20,000-capacity Reunion Arena – an appropriate choice of venue given that the highly revered outlaw rockers are playing again for the first time since original singer Ronnie Van Zant and guitarist Steve Gaines were among six people killed when the band's plane crashed in Mississippi in 1977.

Founding member Allen Collins, who co-wrote the band's southern-rock epic 'Freebird', survived the air tragedy but is now paralysed from the waist down following a car smash in which his girlfriend was killed – and that he was deemed to be responsible for, having been driving under the influence of alcohol. Part of the former guitarist's plea bargain to avoid jail was to promise to address fans at concerts to educate them about the perils of drinking and driving. And Collins is duly wheeled onstage near the end of the band's set tonight – which feels like a homecoming despite their Jacksonville, Florida roots – to deliver some words of wisdom. Yet his physical condition is such that

> **'My life was nearly ruined by drugs twelve years ago until God helped me see the light.'**
> **– Ed King**

he can barely manage to speak at all, although he does, after much coughing, spluttering and throat-clearing, eventually succeed in croaking a message to the audience: 'YOU'RE ALL . . . A BUNCH . . . OF MUTHAFUCKERS!'

Embarrassed-looking guitarist Randall Hall quickly approaches his microphone and says, 'Allen Collins – we know he's gonna be back onstage for you real soon.' Well, how could he know that his friend would die of chronic pneumonia little more than two years later?

It's left to returning six-stringer Ed King to warn the Dallas crowd about the dangers of substance abuse. 'My life was nearly ruined by drugs twelve years ago,' he confesses, 'until God helped me see the light and change my ways. Listen to the lyrics on these two songs.'

Current vocalist Johnny Van Zant (amusingly, older brother Donnie is also available if Johnny tires of succeeding Ronnie) duly delivers the words of 'The Needle And The Spoon' and 'That Smell' as Confederate flags are waved in the crowd but, as the climax of the gig approaches, it's time for everybody's favourite Skynyrd tune.

'It's been a real pleasure singing my brother's songs for you,' he drawls, 'but there's one song tonight I can't sing . . .'

It is, inevitably, 'Freebird' and the responsibility for crooning the lyrics is passed over to the audience as the band synchronises their music with the famous footage of Skynyrd's appearance at Knebworth in 1976, which is being aired on three giant video screens. Meanwhile, as a final gesture, one of Ronnie's old hats is perched on a lonely mic-stand at the front of the stage.

Forget the beers, it's tears that are forming rivers in the toilets as the two-hour show finally ends in hanky-hugging style. 'Man, that was more emotional than when the band's plane came down all those years ago,' blubs one fan to his mate as they stand alongside each other at the urinals.

The outpouring of emotion is indeed overwhelming but, while the crowds are still weeping, the band are whooping it up in the bar of the luxurious Embassy Suites Hotel, having seemingly broken all land-speed records to begin their end-of-tour party. Yeehaw! The late Ronnie, it can be assumed, would surely have been proud of their efforts as the revelling continues until the small hours. Pretty soon, Texas is not the only 'state' many of the touring entourage are in, given the amount of alcohol consumed.

Legendary producer Tom Dowd can be seen, as well as an elderly man with a white beard by the name of Lacy Van Zant. 'I'm proud of my sons,' he says to me, while drummer Artimus Pyle, looking nothing like his hirsute former self, declares, 'We're just one big family really.' Somewhat surprisingly, he reveals that he's been living in Jerusalem while studying Judaism and has a rabbi travelling on the road with him. So maybe that's water he's drinking . . .

At lunchtime the next day, Billy Powell, the man who plinks and plonks the piano for Skynyrd, is lurking near the bar and only too happy to join me for a rather large alcoholic beverage or two – despite his wallet remaining conspicuous by its absence throughout. He claims that doctors are still investigating the cause of his old friend Collins's paralysis, as his spinal cord is apparently undamaged, which comes as something of a surprise.

'I've loved every second of this tour,' insists Powell, who will later join Ronnie Van Zant, Gaines, Collins and bassist Leon Wilkeson in a reunion of deceased former Skynyrd members for a great gig in the sky after suffering a heart attack in 2009. 'It may have been thirty-two dates, but it's seemed like a week-and-a half. I wouldn't have missed it for the world.'

He raises his glass. 'Yeah,' he says, pausing only to knock back another double. 'It's been emotional.'

GAMMA RAY: HELLO HAMBURG

Former Helloween guitarist Kai Hansen is playing a live date with his new outfit Gamma Ray at the Hamburg Docks in September 1990 and, for this particular journalist, it's a routine one-night trip that becomes rather more eventful than anticipated . . .

Jerry, a fellow rock journalist, thinks it's a good idea to meet for a quick drink in the centre of London before heading to Heathrow. This proves ill-advised when, three or four pints later, it becomes a race against the clock for the pair of us to catch the flight to Hamburg, where former Helloween guitarist Kai Hansen is playing tonight under the guise of Gamma Ray, his new power-metal quartet.

Indeed, with less than forty-five minutes until departure time remaining as we exit the Tube, we have little choice but to sprint down the moving walkway into the airport terminal. Ahead, a man is holding his trolley but there's plenty of room for me to squeeze past him – or so it seems.

CLANG! The bloke and his set of wheels are clattered against the metal guardrail . . . and it quickly becomes apparent that it's not a trolley full of luggage he's pushing but an old-age pensioner in a wheelchair. 'Oops, sorry!' I shout, hoping his passenger is okay. The real worry, however, is that we still need to collect the flight tickets from the check-in desk, where the world's

> **'I always wanted to be a funny asshole.'**
> **– Michael Weikath**

longest queue of people has formed. In the end, there's only one thing for it – to nip in at the front and plead for urgent attention, otherwise it's goodnight Vienna – or at least Hamburg.

'I can serve you, but only if the people in line don't mind,' says the female check-in clerk.

'Sorry?'

'I'll let you jump in, but only if the other passengers don't mind,' she says. At which point I undertake a sudden transformation into a Basil Fawlty-like character and start shouting at the crowd of people behind me.

'EXCUSE ME! Our plane leaves in a few minutes and if we don't collect our tickets now we've had it. So, DOES ANYBODY MIND?'

People drop their heads and stare at their shoes, clearly with a huge sense of embarrassment, as they seek to avoid making eye contact with the fruitcake in front of them. Except for one man, whose efforts to avoid being picked out are rather sluggish, and he ends up paying the price. I point a finger directly at him.

'You, sir! DO YOU MIND?' I ask.

The guy casually shrugs his shoulders as if to suggest he really couldn't be less bothered either way.

'That's it!' I declare. 'He doesn't mind! We've asked the people and they really, *really* don't mind!'

Thankfully, the attendant promptly hands over the tickets before the next hurdle arrives in the form of passport control. Again, there is a huge queue of people waiting to show their documents before they fly to European destinations. But there's another desk available for those travelling to Tel Aviv – and it's a free run. Our appeals to the weary-looking middle-aged guy who is manning the desk fall on deaf ears, however, as we're clearly not Israel-bound, so we're sent to the back of the queue . . . until he eventually takes pity and relents. 'Okay, you two,' he says. 'Come through here.'

The flight leaves in just ten minutes and so we make a desperate dash to the departure lounge, where a female writer by the name of Chris is waiting for her two hapless/hopeless colleagues. She hears the stampede of feet and sees a blur of denim and leather as the pair of us run past her, believing we've probably missed the boarding of our flight. Through a big window to the left, Jerry spots a plane parked a few hundred metres away on the tarmac.

'There's our flight! Look, we can still catch it!' he shouts, before leading the way down some stairs, at which point Chris picks up a bag in each hand and frantically gives chase. As the three of us rush towards the plane, the flight captain suddenly emerges from his cockpit at the top of the mobile staircase. Strangely, Jerry appears to think he's running for the bus. 'Excuse me! Does this go to Hamburg?' he asks. 'No, it doesn't,' says the stern-looking pilot. 'And you're coming with me – this is a major breach of airport security.'

As the figure of officialdom herds the trio of trespassers back towards the terminal, it transpires that the other passengers – all of whom have been patiently waiting for the flight, which has apparently been delayed – have got their heads and hands pressed up against the window of the departure lounge, wondering what the hell is going on. Thankfully, the captain is content to just push the three of us back into the crowded room and let us scrape the egg off each other's faces without further action being taken.

The plane eventually departs an hour later and, despite the delay, there's still enough time in Hamburg for us to be introduced to Hansen at tonight's venue, The Docks, before the gig gets underway. Kai is friendly and cheerful as he mingles with the various strangers in his dressing room. 'And *you* are?' enquires Chris, surprisingly oblivious to the fact that she is shaking hands with the very musician she's been sent all the way to Germany to review.

'Ha ha! That's Kai Hansen!' guffaws Jerry, as if Chris hasn't already suffered enough embarrassment for one day. The fact that she is not an authority on the music of the German guitarist becomes even more apparent when, during the gig, she asks for help from her journalist colleagues. 'Oh, this is a brand new one,' I deviously misinform her as Kai dips into Helloween's distant speed-metal past with 'Ride The Sky'. 'And this is an old classic,' Jerry misleadingly claims as Hansen plucks a track off his brand new *Heading For Tomorrow* opus. God only knows what a mess her review is going to be.

Backstage, some of Kai's former bandmates are chilling out in the best way they know how and there are wafts of suspicious smoke hanging in the air. Michael Weikath is in particularly sociable mood. 'I always wanted to be a funny asshole,' says the guitarist before revealing, '"Heavy Metal Hamsters" [one of Helloween's album tracks] actually became a serious lyric.' And to think that some people suggest that Germans haven't got a sense of humour . . .

Much later, in the red light district of the town, prostitutes in basques, knickers, stockings and suspenders cling to the concrete pillars of an underground car park. Nice young ladies, but thankfully the memory is beginning to fade.

The next day is a hellish experience, even ignoring the hangover. If the journey to Hamburg proved problematic, it's nothing compared to our efforts to return home, with the airline claiming the flight is already full with more than an hour to go before departure. 'THAT . . . IS . . . CRAP!' booms Jerry, not realising that those three words are set to become a catchphrase he's unable to shake off for many years to come.

The bad news is that the next flight is another four hours away. If there's any good news, it's that the bar is less than four minutes away.

THE ZAPPAS: AT HOME IN HOLLYWOOD

'Blow me, I don't give a fuck!' says Dweezil Zappa as he invites the author into his family home in 1991 and proves he shares certain characteristics with his father Frank, one of rock's most intellectually creative forces, who – it is revealed in unusual circumstances – never did learn to drive . . .

The yellow sun pierces the bright blue Los Angeles sky as the taxi twists and turns its way through the Hollywood Hills. Eventually, the car pulls up outside a mysterious, unnumbered house in Laurel Canyon. There's an eerie feeling as the heavens suddenly darken, the trees shrouding the building start to shake in the whistling wind and the idea of bats circling the roof as streaks of lightning bolt down from the sky becomes terrifyingly easy to imagine.

It feels like a scene from *The Addams Family*, but it's no work of fiction, with this being the house where the Zappas live. After a short wait, Gail Zappa – wife of eccentric musical genius Frank and mother of Dweezil, Ahmet Roden, Diva Muffin and Moon Unit – emerges behind a small iron gate which produces a logical squeaking as opposed to the anticipated creaking that would seem more appropriate given the arcane environment.

And then we – *RAW* photographer Tony and I – are introduced to Dweezil, who appears from nowhere wearing a bright white T-shirt featuring the smiling faces and gleaming teeth of Donny and Marie Osmond. Bizarrely, it's Donny who provides lead vocals on Zappa junior's new version of the Bee Gees' *Saturday Night Fever* classic 'Stayin' Alive', so perhaps Dweezil's choice of attire is not as unlikely as it might seem. 'I came up with a bunch of people who I thought would be good to sing the song,' says the Dweez, taking a seat in the small studio complex built into the side of the house, before explaining that an original version featuring the voice of Ozzy Osbourne had to be shelved.

'His record label gave me some big lie about how it would interfere with his own product, which is total bullshit,' he says. 'It's political stupidity because there's this special message in the record which I direct towards record company fools like the people who represent Mr Osbourne and also some people in television. It's a message directed to all those individuals who I particularly loathe that says, "Blow me, I don't give a fuck!"'

Meanwhile, a mature, moustachioed gentleman can be seen through a window into the adjoining control room as he works diligently at some kind of computer terminal. Needless to say, it's father Frank composing his new album – quite possibly his 174th given his incredible productivity since the mid-sixties – on the Synclavier, a piece of technology that relies on computer programming.

'It's a message that says, "Blow me, I don't give a fuck!"'
– Dweezil Zappa

At this point, Tony elects to visit the toilet before exploring the local area in the spare time he now has available this afternoon, as Dweezil has bizarrely decided he's not in the mood to have his picture taken – despite his record company spending a fortune flying somebody over from England to do just that. 'It's through there on the right,' says Dweezil, who becomes alarmed a few minutes later when he sees Tony emerging from the toilet and knocking on the door of the small room in which his dad is busy writing. 'Oh no, he shouldn't be doing *that*,' he mutters nervously. 'My father never likes being disturbed.'

Sensing that an alien intruder is about to penetrate his inner sanctum, Frank spins around in his chair as Tony's head appears round the door. Both men jump back in shock, Frank wondering who the hell has had the audacity to disturb his concentration and trespass on his private territory, and Tony not realising that the back of the head belongs to one of the world's biggest – and scariest – rock legends. At which point, Tony fractures the silence by asking, 'Er, you haven't got a street-map of LA by any chance, have you?'

'No,' says Frank in that famous deep voice of his. 'I don't drive.'

Dweezil breathes a sigh of relief as Tony emerges from the confrontation with nothing more serious than a red face, but Zappa junior's mood doesn't improve when the subject of his former record company Chrysalis is raised.

Alice Cooper, aka Vincent Damon Furnier, proved to be something of a Jekyll and Hyde in his hometown of Detroit, where we talked 'romance' and 'rape' while, er, watching the television.

Above: Anyone know the way to Iron Knob? The Screaming Jets (from left to right: Paul Woseen, Brad Heaney, Richard Lara, David Gleeson and Grant Walmsley) on a debauched tour of their Australian homeland. The trail of condoms, illicit substances and empty beer cans they left in their wake is not in shot . . .

Left: Gregor Mackintosh and his gloomy, doomy colleagues in Paradise Lost took their majestic brand of metal to Bucharest and found several reasons to smile – not that you'd be able to tell from this photograph.

*Above: Outlaw rockers Lynyrd
Skynyrd, featuring duelling axe-
heroes Ed King (left) and Gary
Rossington (right), were in party
mood on the final date of their
Reunion tour in Dallas, breaking all
known land-speed records to hit their
hotel bar within minutes of leaving
the stage. Yeehaw!*

*Right: 'Everybody has got this
attitude that I'm some sort of spoilt
kid,' said Dweezil Zappa, the son
of Frank, when interviewed at his
family home in the Hollywood hills.
He also found time to denounce his
former record label as 'total retards'.*

Above: Bruce Dickinson vowed he'd never leave Iron Maiden
. . . and then suggested he'd never return. The vocalist did both,
of course, admitting a certain 'difference in philosophy' between
himself and founding member Steve Harris. 'We fought like cat
and dog,' he said.

Left: Seething with rage and demanding to see me, Lemmy
bears a worrying resemblance to the beast they call **ursus arctos
horribilis**. 'Nothing in this business has ever hurt me so much,'
he insisted of my candid interview with Motörhead guitarist
Würzel in 1992.

Members of Judas Priest were on bitchy form following the departure of vocalist Rob Halford (left), who communicated his leaving by, er, fax machine. 'Maybe he's trying to hold onto his youth,' they speculated, before the band (including guitarist Glenn Tipton, right) eventually kissed and made up with their former frontman.

'Lick it up': Gene Simmons of Kiss proves that size does matter, though this author has apparently surpassed the notorious cock-rocker in at least one other crucial department . . .

Above left: Swedish guitarist Yngwie J. Malmsteen provided an afternoon of vanity and insanity with drunken tales of his recent trip behind the Iron Curtain. He told how thousands of Russian women had spent their lives waiting for him to 'hit town' – to hear his music, of course . . .

Above right: Ever-sociable Quireboys vocalist Spike was forced to admit that all the gigging and ligging had finally caught up with him during one confessional conversation at the peak of the band's success. 'I was just a fucking mess,' he confided over a rare non-alcoholic beverage.

Right: Dumpy, who fronts the Rusty Nuts, is not a man you want scribbling on your backside if it can be avoided. But that's what happens when you keep the good man waiting for several hours, tell him his new album is 'shit' and then fall asleep during the interview.

'They did absolutely nothing with my first two albums and are total idiot losers,' he says. 'In fact, I call them Syphilis Records. They're total retards.'

It's reassuring to hear that Dweezil – who recorded his first album at the age of fifteen – has inherited his father's well-known disdain for the corporate side of the music industry, although being rejected by every major label in the United States might also have something to do with it. 'I think it's because they have no taste and they're absolute bloody idiots,' he offers. 'But that's just my personal opinion.'

Dweezil's new album, *Confessions Of A Deprived Youth*, which features the traditional Zappa trademarks of satire and unpredictability, is released on his father's Barking Pumpkin label, and it would be natural to assume that Frank has been the single biggest influence on the youngster's career. Not so apparently. 'Eddie Van Halen is actually the main reason I started playing guitar,' he declares. Indeed, it was Eddie who produced Dweezil's first single, 'My Mother Is A Space Cadet', which he wrote at the age of thirteen with guitarist Steve Vai, who was then a member of Frank's band.

'I was never exposed to anything other than my dad's music until I was about twelve-and-a-half,' he adds. 'I'd gotten a guitar when I was five or six but never played it. I messed around with the drums but I was terrible, 'cos I have the worst sense of rhythm on the face of the earth. Which is why my songs have really odd rhythms, because that's what's natural to me. I only played my father this record when the whole thing was done. He gave it ten out of ten, so that was good enough for me.'

Not that the Zappa surname has done much to help Dweezil's musical career so far. 'If I'd been anybody else there would be a lot more people ready to help me out,' he suggests. 'Nobody goes out of their way to help me at all. Everybody has got this attitude that I'm some sort of spoilt kid who has got everything I ever wanted . . .'

A few days later, the Zappas are having a family outing. Well, most of them that is. Frank's deteriorating health – he's been diagnosed with the terminal prostate cancer that will sadly claim his life in December 1993 – is such that evenings at the Roxy Theatre on West Sunset Boulevard are not best advised, even if eldest son Dweezil is playing one of his first gigs and sixteen-year-old Ahmet is guesting on vocals.

Mum Gail has rounded up the rest of the clan, however, and Dweezil is guaranteed a rousing reception, not least when he guides his band – which includes several former members of his father's live entourage – through a medley of around 130 (!) different segments of seventies songs. It needs to be seen to be believed – as does the scene when actress Beverly D'Angelo takes the microphone. 'I can't fuck without falling in love,' she croons romantically to an appreciative audience. Yes, we all know the feeling.

PHANTOM BLUE: LA WOMEN

Four Californian cuties (a description that fits only three according to their producer) are set to be interviewed in a Los Angeles studio in May 1993 – when their English visitors have finished drinking, that is . . .

The barmaid's breasts are quivering as she shakes up the latest in a long line of cocktails in the West Hollywood branch of Barney's Beanery on Santa Monica Boulevard. There's an interview with female rockers Phantom Blue set for this afternoon, but the forty-minute drive to the studio, in which the band is currently working, will have to wait a little longer while the next drink is prepared for photographer Mick and I, especially as one of the locals – a middle-aged chap who looks as if he's spent most of his life in this very seat at the bar – insists on buying the next round. And the one after.

We are therefore required to make serious excuses when eventually being introduced to the members of Phantom Blue more than an hour later than scheduled. After all, these Skip Saylor Studios are difficult to locate when you're not familiar with the roads of Los Angeles (well, that's our excuse and we're sticking to it). 'Hi there,' says blonde vocalist Gigi Hangach, whose ample cleavage is still highly memorable from the sleeve of the band's self-titled debut album, released four years previously. Meanwhile, guitarist Michelle Meldrum looks fully prepared for the afternoon's photo-shoot with her cut-off jeans, fishnet tights and dual Metallica/Raven T-shirt perfectly cropped to expose her stomach.

> **'The record company wanted us to be like a female Def Leppard.'**
> – Michelle Meldrum

Who wants to interview legendary Who guitarist Pete Townshend in Twickenham – as I'd previously been scheduled to do – when there's a chance to meet four Californian babes in their heavy-metal homeland, whether they sell any records or not? Not that Los Angeles holds the attraction it once did for bassist Kim Nielsen, at least in terms of the music scene. 'People still curiously come here to see what's going on,' she says, begging the question of just whom she might be referring to, 'but it's not as happening as it used to be.'

The girls insist they were massively misrepresented on their debut album sleeve, with their musical integrity being lost amid a blur of hair lacquer, lip gloss and blush powder. 'It was all too frou-frou with all that wavy hair and that kind of shit,' admits Kim. 'It's not really us.'

'The record company wanted us to be like a female Def Leppard,' adds

Michelle. 'We didn't have any leverage at that point in time so we just did what we had to do. The music business is a pain in the rump.'

We're chatting with English producer Max Norman outside the building later when Kim approaches him about a certain little social gathering he's organising for the weekend. 'Hey, Max,' she says. 'Can I bring my boyfriend to the party on Saturday?'

'Of course you can, love,' he says, before turning to Mick and I and, when she's out of earshot, adding, 'With a face like that she's fucking lucky to have one . . .'

SEPULTURA: BRUTAL BRAZILIANS IN BERLIN

Babies are being bounced in Berlin as Brazilian thrashers Sepultura throw open the doors of their dressing room to discuss life on the road in November 1993, with frontman Max Cavalera warning that 'shit can get really ugly' . . .

With their past Satanic symbolism, Sepultura look as if they should be eating babies rather than spawning them. So it's perhaps a surprise to see frontman Max Cavalera carrying his young son Zyon in his arms as he appears in the dressing room at Huxley's Neue Welt in Berlin, especially as it's now gone midnight.

Nothing has gone according to schedule today. Sepultura had planned to spend the afternoon at their Hilton Hotel, but with the engine of their tour bus deciding to drop its guts all over the autobahn *en route* from Hamburg, the band have lost not only an opportunity to snatch a few hours' rest but to swap phone numbers with the one and only Cliff Richard, who is also residing on the east side of Brandenburg Gate.

There's a reason why touring rhymes with boring and, although Sepultura have long been aware there's a lot of hanging around involved in being on the road, they don't enjoy spending several hours waiting *on the road* itself.

The brutal Brazilians have taken huge strides forward with albums such as *Arise* and *Chaos A.D.*, yet it wasn't long ago that Max was quoted as saying, 'There are still things about Sepultura that I think are shit.' But although nobody is happy that the new tour bus proves just as unreliable as the old van, Max doesn't want everything around the band to become too slick an operation.

'When I said some things are shit, it's like these are the things that we're working on to get better, but not that much better because it's gonna get boring if we get so fucking professional,' he tells me, appearing way beyond his twenty-four years of age due to the rigours of the road. He looks tired, hairy and overweight, but that's perhaps par for the course. 'We don't want to get too fucking serious, you know. We still wanna have fun like we did ten years ago. Which is why we like interviews that are more like pub talk. We don't want to get bored and turn this into a job.'

The beers are thankfully out so the dressing room is indeed a pub in all but name. And the fact that the booze is free. Max's American wife Gloria, who manages the band, looks after the baby (who can be forgiven for dozing off) while the other members – brother Igor, bassist Paulo Jr and comically monickered guitarist Andreas Kisser – try to relax after a relentless set of ruffian riffs. Cavalera is pleased that the Berlin crowd displayed an attitude more in keeping with 'old punk than metal' and which gave tonight's show 'a different vibe'. Certainly, the band now sings about social issues far removed from the lyrical approach of the early days, when the devil danced about on their artwork.

'It was about aggression,' explains Max. 'I really don't believe in all that Satanic stuff, but I don't have a religion and there was a lot of anger going on. We'd play those songs live and it was fucking crazy, man. I remember when we opened for Venom – it was fucking wild and it was with that material. It's about releasing what's inside of you.

'I hate the fucking Church,' he adds. 'And when people come to your shows in America – like when we were on the Ozzy [Osbourne] tour – to fucking preach to you, it was like, "Fuck you, man, with your religion bullshit." That's still how I feel about it, but now I've got other stuff to talk about. We're now more focused on what we think is important. We criticise the bad shit about Brazil and the rest of the world, but when it comes to shit about the police and stuff, you can't be nice. It's all fucked up.'

It's appropriate that 'shit about the police' is mentioned given that Max and Gloria were recently arrested in Phoenix, where Sepultura are now based. According to the lead singer, they were nicked for throwing a rock, having been attacked by a gang with iron bars. 'We were victims so there's nothing to be afraid of,' he insists. 'We have a real good lawyer so maybe we're gonna be suing those cops and laughing about the whole thing. They do that shit and they think they're winning, but what goes around comes around and let's see who's laughing in the end. I believe in fucking karma, man. Those pigs were fucking us big time that night, but I told a cop, "Think about what you're doing, 'cos shit can get really ugly." I ended up in the jail sitting around talking to people, but it was still better than it would have been in Brazil, where they fucking rape you and sometimes kill you. So I was thinking I was kind of lucky.'

There's always been a determined sense of drive in Sepultura's music. The

Cavalera brothers have not had it easy after losing their father when they were young boys, but the band have made a major international breakthrough and it's now just a case of keeping the juggernaut on course. So it was no surprise when their vocalist recently said it would take a death in the band to break the unit up. 'When I say that,' explains Max, 'it's like, nobody in this band is showing one drop of unhappiness. Everybody is really, really into it, more than we've ever been before. So I really feel that the only thing that *would* split up this band is somebody fucking dying.'

Bands have said similar things before, of course, yet still continued following a change of personnel. But Andreas shares his singer's viewpoint. 'Those bands were never the same,' he says. 'Never.'

Despite not 'fucking dying', Max Cavalera makes just one more album with Sepultura after the other members of the band decide to dispense with the management services of his wife. Max, who avoids police charges, forms Soulfly and continues to be represented by Gloria, while Sepultura, to quote Andreas, are indeed 'never the same . . . never'.

HEADING OUT TO THE HIGHWAY

FEUDS AND FALL-OUTS

Feuds, fights and fall-outs in the world of hard rock are as inevitable as Gibson guitars, lousy lyrics and drawn-out drum solos. Whether it's the strains and stresses of the lifestyle creating internal tensions, the clash of enormous egos, rows over women or 'wonga', or good old-fashioned musical differences, there's no shortage of reasons why relationships within heavy metal are rarely of a harmonious nature. Groups are combustible entities and not for nothing have Black Sabbath had twenty-five members and Deep Purple split and reformed more times than most people have cared to keep count of.

As Lemmy of Motörhead said, 'Bands are very sensitive things.' So fragile, it seems, that his own warship was nearly torpedoed as a direct result of my in-depth interview with Würzel, in which the guitarist unleashed an emotion-fuelled and unprecedented assault on his leader because of fears over Motörhead's direction and ailing fortunes. 'You could have broken up the band,' said Lemmy. 'You nearly despatched Würzel into the wilderness.'

It's difficult to believe my feature could have halted the journey of a vehicle that has motored on through numerous changes of personnel, lost record deals, management rip-offs, court injunctions, financial hardships and undulating popularity. But it reflects the communication breakdown that had taken place within the group that one member felt compelled to use the press as a medium to convey a vital message to another. And whether such a ploy ultimately causes more problems or helps solve them depends very much on your point of view.

Ian Gillan certainly knows a thing or two about troubled relationships after his experiences with Purple, Sabbath and his own outfit over the past four decades, not least with temperamental guitarist Ritchie Blackmore. 'He was such an arsehole,' said the vocalist as he threatened physical violence against his former colleague in the unlikely event that he should join us for a cup of coffee.

Groups are like marriages and the members of Judas Priest felt somewhat jilted after vocalist Rob Halford decided he'd rather get friendly with some younger musicians than the ones he'd fronted for twenty years. 'Maybe he's trying to hold onto his youth,' suggested bass player Ian Hill during my conversation with the band after being dumped. But conflicts aren't confined to within individual bands, and it should surprise nobody that the competitive nature of touring, trying to outsell other outfits heading down the same musical highway and generating bigger acclaim and fame sometimes fuels the kind of rivalry that's liable to spill over into outright acrimony. Such is the case with Priest and Iron Maiden, with guitarist K.K. Downing describing the latter as 'minging old fucking grannies' when I dare to mention their name. Ouch!

Of course, Maiden themselves have had personnel problems over the years and it was fascinating to discuss the departure of Bruce Dickinson with both the vocalist himself and founding member Steve Harris as the changing climate of metal caused storm clouds to brew over the band's future in the early nineties. Yet while heavy-metal musical chairs continues to be played, history proves that, despite the number of supposedly burned bridges, bands have a funny habit of rebuilding them when circumstances dictate that it might prove (financially) beneficial . . .

MOTÖRHEAD: LEMMY'S IRON FIST

The mighty metal machine that is Motörhead has marched on mercilessly through the years, but it's in danger of being stopped in its tracks at the end of 1992, as guitarist Würzel breaks ranks to launch an unprecedented attack on main man Lemmy, who consequently issues a summons to find out why a certain journalist is trying to destroy one of Great Britain's most influential and iconic musical entities . . .

The ground tremors, the light fittings swing and assorted decorative ornaments begin to rattle, as the thudding footsteps grow disturbingly louder. It feels as if Godzilla is approaching, menacingly eating up the snazzy hotel carpet with every thundering step. When Ian 'Lemmy' Kilmister eventually turns the corner to finally appear in view, he's not a pretty sight –

not that he's ever been described as such – and it's apparent that my increasing sense of anxiety and apprehension is fully justified.

Lemmy is the face of Motörhead and today that face resembles a particularly disgruntled grizzly bear's – an ursus arctos horribilis in all its threatening glory. His eyes are bulging, his teeth are bared and he can smell fear just feet away. He's clearly in the mood to attack.

The veteran frontman feels he has good reason to as well, having just re-read the recent *Metal CD* article in which long-time guitarist Würzel, fuelled by alcohol and anguish, breaks ranks to complain about, among other things, the influence of Lemmy's defection to the United States of America and the unfamiliar highways – or rather *freeways* – the group is now heading down.

After decades on the road, Motörhead's laundry is dirtier than most – and it was now being unceremoniously washed in public. This, in Lemmy's view, is an act of such treason and treachery that it justifies summoning the journalist responsible to his hotel, fittingly just minutes away from the Odeon venue that spawned the band's legendary Number One album *No Sleep 'Til Hammersmith*.

'Your fucking piece moved me to tears,' he says after dictating that we take seats in the lounge bar. 'I sat in front of Würzel and wept in front of him. I couldn't believe he said what he did and I couldn't believe you printed it. Nothing in this business has ever hurt me so much.'

I respond by saying that's not something that brings me any pleasure – not that it improves his mood.

'Good,' he responds, 'because if I thought it did I'd smack you in the fucking mouth.'

And as Lemmy looks into my eyes, there is absolutely no doubt that he means it, too.

Less than a month earlier, Würzel had felt compelled to contradict a record company statement that the band's British tour to promote the recent *March ör Die* album had been scrapped at short notice due to 'time constraints and scheduling conflicts'.

Sitting in an Islington pub by the name of Mulligans, Würzel – born Michael Burston, his haggard features proving that his years in Motörhead have taken their toll – is desperate to put the record straight. It looks like he's been there for several hours and, as the tape begins to roll, it quickly becomes obvious that there are things he wants to get off his chest.

'The real reason was because we hadn't sold enough tickets,' he admits. 'It's pissed me off enormously us having to cancel this tour. I think this is gonna do us a lot of damage and I'm really wild about it. The fans are not stupid and you shouldn't treat them as if they are. We've cancelled shows before – the London Town & Country Club was once fucking pulled because Lemmy said it's not a prestigious enough gig! I said, "You cunts, it's fucking sold out, it's a wonderful place to play." But we haven't been doing well in the UK for the last few years – ever since "His Godhead" went to live in LA – because we've concentrated so much on America.'

The 'Motörhead England' slogan is as much of a trademark as the Snaggletooth image that has adorned the millions of T-shirts sold since the band's inception in 1975. With their fast 'n' furious, 'everything louder than everyone else' philosophy, the band's early grime-infested offerings such as *Overkill*, *Bomber* and *Ace Of Spades* spread the germ that created thrash metal and were unmistakeably British in flavour. Motörhead was always intended to be a filthy beast, not a slick animal. But *March ör Die*, the successor to the highly impressive *1916* album, marking the band's signing to Epic Records and Lemmy's move to Los Angeles, was very much a compromise pandering to the American market in Würzel's eyes and ears.

'I'm going to be really honest,' he says, slurping at his pint of Guinness, 'I'm a little disappointed with the new album – it's not as good as *1916*. We found it really difficult this time with *March ör Die*. I hate the title track so much. I fuckin' hate bullshit. I don't like it being fed to me and I don't like feeding it to other people. I've had it up to here with flags and war.'

Würzel is particularly unhappy with the 'I Ain't No Nice Guy' single – a ballad which sees Lemmy share vocals with Ozzy Osbourne while Slash of Guns N' Roses guests on guitar. 'Slash and Ozzy are our mates, but those bastards [at the record company] turn the whole thing around and I personally wouldn't market the band that way. Motörhead is not like any other band – it's an institution. And if I were a fan, I'd be pretty pissed off to hear us doing ballads. I don't want to see another ballad on the next album and we could have some confrontation about that.'

Yet for all his reservations about some of the *March ör Die* material, Würzel believes that he and fellow guitarist Phil Campbell have been denied the credit they deserve for their creative input. 'We're the ones who initiate albums now,' he says. 'We take the songs over [to the USA] and Lem writes all the words and chucks in a few things here and there. The majority of the work is definitely done by Campbell and me – but he [Lemmy] is getting all the glory.

'Lemmy formed the band and is Mr Motörhead; I'll admit that any time and would never take that away from him. We're not trying to take the fucking thing over, but let's have a bit of justice here and there. He gets in all the papers and big magazines – and the rest of us get the fanzines. We've got a readership of 200 while he's got a readership of two million and he doesn't even talk about the band. It would be great if he said "that solo was by so-and-so" and "they wrote that bit". But all he talks about is his fucking communal swimming pool and how hot it is in LA. Who wants to know about that? Our audience isn't made up of doctors and professional people; the majority of them are couriers and people on the dole, saving all their money to come to our shows. They don't want to read about somebody sitting by their poxy swimming pool and drinking Jack Daniel's.'

The guitarist is particularly upset with what he perceives to be a change of outlook on Lemmy's part since he became part of the LA social scene. He says: 'Lemmy has associated with so many strange people in the Rainbow [Bar & Grill]. They always tell you what you wanna fucking here over there. Fair play, Lemmy has wanted to live in LA all his life, but we never expected him to pick up an LA attitude. I suppose it's difficult when you're living in a place like that, which is rock city, but it's very fucking shallow. I can't relate to people out there.

'I can't find good conversation in LA,' he continues. 'If you live out there you don't think anywhere else exists. They don't even know where fucking Europe is. I'll give you a good example – I was in a club with [drummer] Mikkey Dee and a chick asked where he's from. He told her Stockholm and she said, "Where?" And he said, "Sweden, it's in Scandinavia." And she said, "Gee, how many countries are you from?" And I'm thinking, "Oh, for fuck's sake!" That's not to say there aren't intelligent people out there, but the people we seem to attract aren't that fucking bright. And what pisses me off more than anything is that we don't have an intelligent team around us.'

A feeling endorsed by the experience of the recent US tour which saw Motörhead support Ozzy Osbourne and join the Guns N' Roses/Metallica package as well as playing their own club dates. 'The American end of things was fucking chaos,' says Würzel. 'It was the worst American tour I've ever done. The organisation was *awful*, absolutely terrible. We've concentrated far too much over there – it's time to do it here. But Lemmy has slagged off the UK so badly in the press. You don't slag down the country that has supported you for so many years.

'Lem has lost touch with this country. He will give you a lot of good reasons why he went to America and they are very valid. But I can't live a lie; if it's not "Motörhead England" any more then I don't really want to know. I'd rather go and do something else. I know I won't be as successful, but I just can't live this way.'

It's shocking to hear Würzel talk this way. Yeah, he's had a few, but that doesn't mean he doesn't mean what he says, if you know what I mean. I ask if the perception of Lemmy being a dictator is the wrong one for people to have, but he insists not. 'Not these days it's not, no. I know this sounds dreadful because it looks like I'm giving him shit behind his back, but it's not meant that way because we've been friends for a long time. I do want to do another album – *lots* of albums – with Motörhead, but I want no more ballads and no more flags and war. I want a rock'n'roll album that kicks some serious arse.'

Würzel guzzles the remains of his Guinness as his heart slides down his sleeve. 'I love this band so much, I love it fucking dearly,' he says. 'To me, the concept of Motörhead is fucking fantastic. I believe it's unique and I'm really proud to be part of that. But I can't stand to see us losing it and Lemmy doesn't fucking see what's happening to us.'

I know this is dynamite stuff and, of course, it's inevitable that there will be serious recriminations. It's difficult to remember if any rock musician has publicly criticised a colleague – especially the leader of his band – to such a degree while still an active member. But Würzel had volunteered his views and, while I can't deny there's a sense of excitement over the exclusive, a journalist's job is to provide a platform for what people have to say. Nevertheless, there's a sense of a fuse being lit and wondering when the bomb is going to explode.

When the time comes, the telephone command is predictably curt. 'Lemmy wants to see you tomorrow,' says Joe the press officer. 'The Novotel in Hammersmith. Two o'clock. Don't be late.' When the main man of Motörhead eventually appears, all his legendary trademarks are there – the unbuttoned black shirt,

'If I were a fan, I'd be pissed off to hear us doing ballads.'
– Würzel

the bullet belt wrapped around the waist of his tight black jeans and, of course, the white boots. His face is bright red, the veins in his neck are visible as he speaks and there's hurt and anger in his eyes.

'The geezer was upset and had a beef with me,' admits Lemmy as he reflects on Würzel's complaints, well aware that a tape recorder has been placed on the table in front of us and switched on. 'But that's something that is internal – you don't write about things like that in public. It was irresponsible on your part because printing something like that might break up a band. I don't think you've helped us and I don't thank you for it. I've never been anything other than co-operative with the press, so why should you do a fucking hatchet job on me like that?'

Indeed this is true. From taking reporters on the road to sharing wine discreetly hidden in teapots in dodgy Chinese restaurants off Wardour Street after the St Moritz has closed for the night – as he did during one of our very earliest encounters – Lemmy has been nothing but accommodating to writers, irrespective of their experience. However, I argue that the feature in question accurately reflects what Würzel had to say, with no hidden agenda on the magazine's part.

Yet Lemmy is having none of it as he enters into a conversational contest about the rights and wrongs of publishing the article. 'We've always been honest and he was being honest with you. But there was no reason to write things down verbatim,' he insists. 'You could have thought, "Obviously there are factions in the band, let's hope they fall out of it because they've been decent to us, so let's not fucking put the knife in any further since they're going through a troubled period." But no . . .'

'But Würzel had been keen to make certain points,' I insist.

'It's just a lack of communication, that's all it is,' he says.

'Because you're living in LA and Würzel is in London?'

'Yeah, but we never saw each other much between tours when I was living in England anyway. It just happens that I live 6,000 miles away instead of two miles away, but we see each other as much as we did before.'

'Do you think living in LA has changed you?'

'No, I don't.'

'What about Würzel's claim that you've developed an LA attitude?'

'Rubbish! If I had an LA attitude, I'd be suing you instead of talking to you.'

'Why do you think the UK tour tickets sold so badly?' I ask.

'Because England, as usual, has turned its back on Motörhead. It's done it before.'

'Würzel seems to think it's because Motörhead has turned its back on England,' I explain.

'We haven't turned our back on England,' he insists. 'We still *wanted* to tour the country; that's why we booked the dates. But we discovered that it would cost us one hundred grand to tour England and we don't have one hundred grand.'

'Does it hurt you that the band's position in England is not what it should be?'

'I don't care anymore, I'm used to it.'

'Würzel is obviously very disappointed . . .'

'I know, because he's a very fiercely English man. I'm not; I don't give a shit about England. I don't give a shit about any country, come to think of it. I consider myself a citizen of the world. I've been around it too many times to become anchored to one patch of ground.

'I paid taxes every year [in England] and the one time I tried to get assistance they wouldn't give me any because I didn't have the right stamps on my card. So what do I owe anyone? They had us at Number One for one fucking year and then dumped us. And we stayed here and worked like beavers. The last album before I moved to America spent one week at Number 79, so what the fuck do I owe them?'

'When you have a dig at England, a lot of people will think you're having a go at your fans . . .' I suggest.

'No, I'm not,' he retorts. 'I love our fans, from wherever they come from. I love our German fans, I love our French fans, I love our English fans. I've always gone out of my way to look after them. We're an old band and we've been around a very long time. Kids at the record-buying age no longer see Motörhead as part of their gang. The new bands are gonna be their gang –

it's very important when you're seventeen to twenty years of age to have your gang and I understand that.

'But only in England do the press immediately jump in like fucking rats when there's a crack showing. You guys would love to see us break up, wouldn't you? It would make great copy. A thing that's been going for so many years and through a lot of terrible fucking difficulties but has always held itself together. It would be nice for somebody to say, "Fucking Motörhead are excellent, they've been trying hard for so long, we should take our hats off to them." Nobody ever writes an article saying everything is great with Motörhead.'

'But Würzel didn't say everything was great with Motörhead, did he? So are there problems in the band?'

'Nothing that can't be handled.'

'Is Motörhead a democracy?'

'Yes. I've said it before – I never want a dictatorship. If I feel really strongly about something then I will use the power of veto, but in almost all things we are a democracy and always will be. And that was the thing I fought for the most. I've been in bands that were dictatorships and I didn't like it, so I swore that I would never do that. But occasionally, because I'm at the nerve centre of everything, because we're with an American record company whose headquarters are in Los Angeles where I live, I have to make a decision.

'When I was living in London we would never have got nominated for a Grammy [for the *Hellraiser* soundtrack] – the same album could have been made and they would never have noticed us. So there are advantages to me living out there.'

'What about Würzel's comments about the people you're mixing with out there?' I ask.

'He doesn't know who I mix with. That's just pure bitch. He doesn't like the obvious American backslapper, but neither do I. And he never went to the Rainbow when he was there – him and Phil always used to go to the Cat & Fiddle.'

'Nevertheless, Würzel definitely seems upset about the direction the band is going in.'

'Actually, it's none of your business what direction the band is going in – that's *our* business.'

'The public might believe it's their business as they're the ones who buy the records,' I offer.

'It's not their business either,' he insists. 'It's their business to either like or dislike the records at their discretion. We make the records but never with a view to public consumption. We made them because we like them. Got it?'

'Er, how about accusations that the last album, *March ör Die*, was very Americanised?' I ask.

'Bullshit!'

'You don't acknowledge that at all?'

'No, I don't, because I'm not American. All the lyrics I wrote for that album are in English, not American.'

'What about Würzel's complaints about flags and war on the album?'

'There are no flags on the album. And how many tracks are there about war?'

'Well, "March ör Die" for a start . . .' I suggest.

'Not completely; it's also about ecology.'

'Würzel was very critical of the title track,' I state.

'Too bad.'

'Did he express his reservations at the time of recording?'

'Yeah. But when you have to get the fucking album out, you have to get it finished. I've said this before; the title track was never finished to our satisfaction. We tried mixing the fucking thing about nine times, but the point is that it was the *best* that we could do in the time allowed. I still think it's one of the best things I've ever written. It's a valid statement.'

'How about the fact that Motörhead are now doing ballads?'

'What the fuck is wrong with that?'

'Würzel obviously doesn't like the idea. He doesn't think a song like "I Ain't No Nice Guy" is what Motörhead are about.'

'Well, Phil Campbell likes it, Mikkey Dee likes it and I like it. So if it's a democracy, he's voted down, isn't he?'

'Once upon a time, though, a ballad would not have made it onto a Motörhead album, would it?'

'Yeah, but that's when we were trying to give the people what we thought they wanted – and what they *said* they wanted. And what *you* said they wanted. And nobody bought it. And anyway, I was brought up on the fucking Beatles and the Ronettes and all those bands in the 1960s. I've got a bigger history than just da-da-da-dum, which is what you think we should be fucking playing all the time. Well, I'm sorry, I'm not gonna do what you think we should be playing all the time, I'm doing what I think we should do, what *we* think we should do.'

'Do you think *March ör Die* is better or as good as *1916*?'

'As good as, easily,' he insists. 'I think it's a fucking excellent album.'

'How about Würzel's claim that the majority of the writing is done by him and Phil Campbell?' I ask.

'Well, that's smart given that I've got three songs on that album with just my credit. How do you figure that then? That's not true, that's just bitch, you know. It depends on who writes the riff. And since they've been in the band, they've always written a lot of the riffs. And it's me who tidies them up, puts them into context, arranges bridges, writes all the words and fucking half-produces them.'

'I started the band, employed Würzel and gave him a vote. And on everything until the last album, a quarter of all songs I wrote on my own. I wrote "Orgasmatron" alone and gave him his share of a four-way split. Nobody ever mentions the good side of the fucking dictator, do they? Do you see David Coverdale [of Whitesnake] doing that?'

It's a rhetorical question so I don't answer it – and throw another enquiry Lemmy's way. 'What's your relationship with Würzel like now?'

'It's gradually climbing back,' he concedes. 'You really didn't help the band get through a bad patch. You almost despatched Würzel into the wilderness.'

'He insisted there was nothing in that article that he hadn't already told you himself.'

'That's not true. And that's not what he said to me on the bus two days ago.'

'What did Würzel say to you on the bus two days ago?' I ask.

'He said that he stands by some of it but some of it was a terrible mistake.'

'Did he blame me?'

'Partly, yeah,' he says. 'I'm only partly blaming you. To print it was irresponsible – you can see that it might kill a band. Bands are very sensitive things.'

'They might be,' I respond, 'but if an article like that is going to cause a band to break up, the relationships must be hanging by a thread anyway . . .'

'No man, that's not fair,' he says. 'That's not fucking realistic. A band is a conglomeration of individuals who are not held together by family ties, only by ties of music. And when a band has been going for as long as we have without any financial reward . . . Würzel has been in the band for nine years and still got no money. We're always living on the edge, hand to mouth. And we've always been one hundred per cent.

'I don't recall a single year when Motörhead didn't put an album out or do a tour of England. I wouldn't say we've turned our back on England as much as, say, Ozzy Osbourne, who doesn't tour here for seven years and never gets a fucking brickbat in the press at all.

'We're the only band that gets this shit. And you know why? It's because familiarity breeds contempt, because we're too good to you. And we get shit for it, because they think, "Ah, old Motörhead, yeah, they're easy, they're always friendly." What idiots! I mean, people like fuckin' Ozzy and Coverdale, or people who have deserted England completely to the point of never touring the country at all, are treated as heroes!

'I don't know what I'm supposed to do for fucking England. What's it done for me? Give me success then turn its back on me for eight years. You'd all rather I stayed here and slowly starved to fucking death, wouldn't you? The year before I went to America, we'd have had to give up or go under.'

'It's not the press who are speaking out against you being in LA,' I submit.

'Isn't it? You're the ones asking if I've deserted England.'

'Only because Würzel seems to think you have.'

'Jesus Christ! Can't you see through that?'

'Well, why does Würzel feel that there are major problems in the band?'

'I don't know.'

'You don't know?'

'Well, I do now, because we've talked it out.'

Now I feel we might be getting somewhere. 'Right, so maybe something *has* been achieved by Würzel speaking out in the way he did?' I suggest.

'No, it hasn't,' he says, 'because that sort of thing has opened up a hole between him and me that will never be filled again, not completely. It can never be exactly the same relationship as before because it was done in public. We can come to blows in private and they can be forgotten. But you can't forget a thing like this. And *he'll* never forget it.'

'Has communication between the two of you improved now?'

'Yes, but it didn't need a hammer blow like that. Anybody less strong than me would have fired him, if I'd been an arsehole. I don't see that you should take it upon yourself to act as a go-between for a member of my band and me. You could have broken up the band.'

'Your fucking piece moved me to tears . . . I sat in front of Würzel and wept in front of him.'

– Lemmy

'We don't see it that way,' I state.

'No, you wouldn't, would you? That would be a terrible responsibility. If he had been fired on this tour, would you have thought that was all right? Würzel was easy to get, wasn't he? Pissed off and moaning, like everybody gets now and again.'

'Do you consider it unprofessional of him?'

'Mmmm . . . Yeah.'

'Do you think it was naive of him?'

'Naive of him and unprofessional, yeah.'

'Are there *any* points that you are prepared to concede that Würzel might be right about?'

'Yes,' says Lemmy. 'I would concede that I have become removed to an extent because I'm working very hard in Los Angeles for the band. I know how it might seem over here, that I don't give a fuck about him or England. But I was always doing that amount of work when I was in the UK. There just wasn't that much more to do here because nobody gave a shit. I finally got tired of being sold cheap. I mean, only in England is there a record company that puts out four compilations on four different labels at the same time. That's great!

'I just don't see why I should be hunted all the time for deserting England, because England deserted us long before I moved to Los Angeles. I made no money in this country. I went through three record labels and three managers, one of which – an Englishman – robbed us of every penny we made. We couldn't do anything else but relocate – and in the event two people didn't. That's not my fault.

'I've always been the same and I'm not going to change now. The only reason Motörhead has survived this long is because I'm a strong character. And *I* preserved it. I will be a strong character and if people can't take it, that's tough – because Motörhead will survive, as long as I'm it. It certainly couldn't survive without me.'

'What is the future of Motörhead?'

'The future of Motörhead is that we'll still try the best we can to make the best records we can and tour as best we can.'

'How far into the future are you looking?'

'I don't. I take it day by day. I haven't got enough money to plan. I've never made any money out of rock'n'roll, but it's had my life out of me.'

'Do you ever feel like giving up?'

'No, I've never thought about giving up. Never. I told you, I'm a strong character.'

'What's your motivation? What drives you on?'

'I know I'm good. I know I'm worth it,' he insists. 'If I didn't exist it would have been necessary to invent me. You need a whipping boy that won't go down. You need somebody who lines up and says, "Fuck you!" And I will!'

And that's exactly what I fear he's going to do when the phone rings at home one evening several weeks later and the unmistakeable voice of Lemmy is heard on the line. An edited version of our conversation has been published in the latest issue of *Metal CD* and Mr Motörhead was quick to make sure he saw a copy. 'I've just seen the new piece you did,' he says, doing little to remove the suspicion that his wrath has been incurred yet again. After all, it's not an argument that he convincingly won – not in my eyes, at least. But Lemmy is full of surprises. 'I just wanted to say . . . thanks. You let me have my say.'

Which is, of course, the very thing that Würzel had been allowed to do in the first place. But I decide it's best not to go there, with the beast having seemingly been tamed.

Würzel records just two more albums with Motörhead before leaving the band because of 'personal issues'. Having maintained a low profile since his departure, Michael Burston, sixty-one, pours himself a pint of Guinness on 9 July 2011 and in doing so suffers a heart attack and dies. Lemmy describes him as 'my friend and my brother' before adding, in acknowledgement of the beer, 'At least we know he went with a smile . . .'

IAN GILLAN AND DEEP PURPLE: VIOLENT IMPULSES

Ian Gillan seems a placid kind of guy as we sit down for a coffee in a Kensal Rise brasserie in October 1991, but maybe the caffeine takes command as the legendary singer declares his desire to destroy former colleague Ritchie Blackmore's face, calls his old Gillan bandmates 'lazy bastards' and declares he'll never rejoin Deep Purple again . . . Oops!

Ian Gillan is in a violent mood, not least when the name of old sparring partner Ritchie Blackmore crops up in conversation. 'I'd take a four-by-two across his nose if he walked in here now. I have this primitive desire to mangle his face,' warns one of rock's greatest singers of one of rock's greatest guitarists. 'It's not an irrational thing to say I want to do that,' he insists. 'He put a plate of spaghetti in my face and gave me a black eye, for no good reason one day, just because he wanted to. And I owe him one for that!'

There's nothing quite like heavy metal for producing a great feud, and the disputes between the key members of Deep Purple – one of the cornerstones of British rock, who have suffered numerous changes in personnel and repeatedly split up and reformed – are up there with the best of them. It's two years since Gillan was forced out of the legendary band for a second time and, as the vocalist sits opposite me in a noisy London brasserie and stirs his coffee, he is still trying to work out precisely why. 'I think what they recently said was that I didn't write any words for what turned out to be *Slaves And Masters*,' he scoffs. 'I mean, listen to it! I certainly couldn't be inspired to. It's crap, utter crap! It's embarrassing.

'The guitar player [Blackmore] just wanted Purple to be a vehicle for his own ideas. I don't think there was a more destructive element in the band. He wanted to close down every other major input. I'd be at writing sessions and John [Lord, keyboards], Ian [Paice, drums] and Roger [Glover, bass] would be jamming through something. Then Blackmore would turn up, plug in and go up to ten. It was so arrogant and rude it was unbelievable. And they kowtowed to it. It used to drive me crazy because he was such an arsehole.'

It's perhaps ironic that Ian uses such a term given that's exactly how his former bandmates from Gillan – or certainly bassist John McCoy and keyboard player Mick Underwood – would probably describe their old singer. Especially after he disbanded the unit – formed five years after leaving Purple the first time around – on the advice of a doctor fearing for Gillan's deteriorating voice, only to then join Black Sabbath (a somewhat unlikely move whatever the circumstances) within a matter of months. You'd think he would concur that his old colleagues might have a genuine grievance, but Ian is having none of it. 'No, fuck it, I don't!' he retorts when I suggest such a thing, stirring his coffee ever more furiously. 'I was fucking pissed off with the lazy bastards, expecting the benefits of employment and the privileges of partnership – and moaning like bitches all the time.

'The Gillan band was an equal split in every way, shape and form. The band [members] were on fixed income, with guaranteed advances against equal share of the profits. The accounts are in the office, open for anyone to examine. You can publish the damn things if you want, I don't care. Now, in order to keep everyone's income up we had to tour. And all I was getting was, "Oh no, not another fucking tour!" So I'd say, "Let's take six months off." And then it was, "What are we gonna do for money?" The atmosphere was pretty bad. I remember having screaming slagging matches with John and Mick about money and I didn't need it. A few years later, I sent a message to Mick through a mutual friend saying Happy Christmas. I saw the guy a few months later and he told me Mick had said, "Tell Gillan to stick Christmas up his arse!"'

> **'I was fucking pissed off with the lazy bastards.'**
> – Ian Gillan

Gillan is supposed to be promoting his new solo album as we speak, but he's far too busy reflecting on a career that certainly invites *This Is Spinal Tap* comparisons. '[After splitting up Gillan] I had no plans whatsoever but one night I went out and got drunk with Tony Iommi and Geezer Butler – and apparently I joined Black Sabbath. Which I only found about the next day! And then all the flak and abuse started flying around,' he says. 'But it was a great year [in which *Born Again* was recorded] and I enjoyed every minute of it. It was a mistake, but that's one of the things I'm really good at – making big mistakes!'

It's fascinating listening to Ian as he discusses the personal politics of the bands he's been part of. He admits he 'totally misread the Purple situation the second time around' and insists there is absolutely no chance of getting together with the notoriously temperamental Blackmore ever again. Nor has he the desire to still be singing the likes of 'Child In Time', 'Highway Star' and 'Speed King' when he's approaching retirement age. 'If you're diametrically opposed to somebody, you're not gonna just meet in the middle,' he says. 'It's just not possible and I don't think I can enjoy my life working under a cloud. I'd much rather be unemployed or be a carpenter. And I don't want to be yelling and screaming and running around the stage when I'm sixty.'

One year later, reports emerge that suggest Gillan has in fact opened negotiations to rejoin Deep Purple. I ring the good man's home and his wife Bron picks up the phone in his absence. 'I can tell you now, I'm his wife and he's *not* rejoining Deep Purple,' insists Mrs Gillan. 'I believe Ian made a statement last year saying he'd get a lot more pleasure cutting his own throat. There's no way he is going to reform with the band, not with Ritchie Blackmore in it.'

Within months, Ian Gillan reunites with Ritchie Blackmore for the recording of a brand new Deep Purple album. And more than forty years after its inception, Gillan continues to front the band — albeit without his old foe on guitar — well into his mid-sixties.

FLEETWOOD MAC: DODGY RUMOURS

A jetlagged Lindsey Buckingham has set his heart on promoting his new solo album as he sits down in a Holland Park hotel in June 1992, but this writer is more interested in finding out if the key Fleetwood Mac member really did do nasty things to former partner Stevie Nicks . . .

'Then it got physical. Lindsey grabbed Stevie and slapped her and bent her backwards over the hood of his car. Was he going to hit her? He'd done it before . . .'
Mick Fleetwood, from *Fleetwood: My Life And Adventures With Fleetwood Mac*

It's not easy asking a bloke if he is a 'wife-beater'. It's even harder when it's Lindsey Buckingham of Fleetwood Mac and the woman in question is Stevie Nicks, whose light sandpaper tones are the most distinguishing and appealing feature of a band that have sold an estimated 120 million albums since the American couple joined its British nucleus in the mid-1970s.

Buckingham is a little jetlagged as he sits in his suite at London's Halcyon Hotel after arriving from the United States, so it's fair to assume he's not really in the mood to be dealing with questions about alleged violence towards his former partner — with whom he's sharing neither a bed nor a band at this point in his life. Not that it would be the most diplomatic way of opening a conversation at the best of times.

I therefore consider it prudent to warm Lindsey up by getting him to concentrate his thoughts on his latest solo project (*Out Of The Cradle*), which is really why he wants to talk in the first place. Of course, it's impossible for Buckingham to discuss the new album without placing it in the context of his work with Fleetwood Mac, which is really why everybody wants to talk to him in the first place. And it's not about bringing up the name of Nicks but that of founding member Mick Fleetwood who, after all, is the one making the allegations. And making a vague reference to the drummer's autobiography is all I need to do to prompt Lindsey into believing it's all *his* idea when he touches upon a sensitive topic.

'There were things in Mick's book that were hurtful to everyone in the group,' he states. 'There was one specific thing about when I had gone over to Christine [McVie]'s and told them that I wasn't going to tour. And he had written in there that something had happened and that Stevie ran out screaming at me – which she *did* – and that I'd slapped her, which I *didn't*. And I thought, "Jesus . . ." And then, like three months later, Stevie came up to me and was apologising for him having written that. That kind of thing is very hurtful. I can't say I read the whole book but I skimmed through it. I don't think I could have brought myself to read it because it was trashy and it didn't dignify the name [of Fleetwood Mac] at all.'

'I never bought cocaine in my life and I don't even drink.'
– Lindsey Buckingham

So that would be a denial, then. But why would Mick take such an approach in his autobiography? Lindsey has his theories. 'The reason the book was the way it was is that he had – and this is only my opinion – a "hack" for a [ghost-]writer, the guy who did the Led Zeppelin biography,' he says. 'I don't think he's a good writer. Mick didn't take enough responsibility for the editing process and this guy was up at his house every night. They'd probably have a few drinks – free-associating night after night – and a lot of it is the product of that.'

A journalist and a musician allowing the flow of alcohol to influence their work? Who would have thought it? But who's interested in booze when there's a conversation to be had about drugs? Even when Fleetwood Mac's party was in full swing, there was always a matrimonial dispute in one corner – the forty-million-selling *Rumours* album provided the soft-rock soundtrack to the break-up of Buckingham and Nicks as a couple, as well as the marriage of John and Christine McVie – and another argument in the kitchen, not to mention somebody hogging the bathroom for all the wrong reasons. So, are all the, er, 'rumours' of Stevie's cocaine problems to be believed?

'Well, I don't know . . .' says Lindsey, looking a little uneasy. 'Even if I knew, I probably wouldn't comment on it, but . . . everybody had a problem at one time or another. If you want to spend your money, that's a good way to spend it . . . well, not a *good* way to spend it but an *effective* way of losing it. I never bought cocaine in my life – that was never part of my thing – and I don't even drink anymore. It just wasn't productive.

'But in the seventies everybody was doing that, that was the way to go.

Everybody when they're young has their time for being wild and hopefully you grow out of it. But that was part of the problem, you know. Maybe in 1977 that made sense; in 1987 it didn't.'

I suggest that the five-year gap between the Mac's only two 1980s studio albums, *Mirage* and *Tango In The Night*, reflected the growing distance between the band's members at that point in time. 'We were never one of those bands who hung out together and went to the same restaurants . . . two couples breaking up has a little to do with that,' says Buckingham. 'There was a certain formality there. I mean, I never hung out with John ever. At the time, maybe *off the record*, I was smoking a lot of pot and he was already an alcoholic [McVie allegedly once threw a glass of vodka into Buckingham's face], you know, so . . . please don't print that.'

As *if* . . . 'As you pointed out, or were so perceptive to *surmise*,' Lindsey adds, with a vague hint of sarcasm, 'the band was never made up of Siamese twins. If we were off the road it wasn't like I would hang out at Mick's house.'

He admits to having 'some serious monthly mortgage payments' but denies he'll ever be tempted to return to the band he left after the *Tango In The Night* album. 'I can't see the sense in it,' he says. 'There are so many things I still want to look into that excite me.'

Needless to say, Lindsey Buckingham rejoins Fleetwood Mac in the late-1990s and he remains a member – alongside Mick Fleetwood, Stevie Nicks and John McVie – to the present day.

JUDAS PRIEST: SCREAMING FOR VENGEANCE

The relationship between the members of Judas Priest is considered as strong as British Steel until vocalist Rob Halford announces his departure . . . by fax. It's March 1993 and the singer's former partners are feeling somewhat betrayed as they sit in a London hotel and discuss how they're going to pick up the pieces . . .

This particular studded leather belt – a genuine Judas Priest trademark – has probably been hugging K.K. Downing's hips since the late 1970s. It would be rude for me to ask, though. He's wearing the rock star leather pants with shirt and jacket – all black, of course. Sitting alongside him in the lounge of London's Swiss Cottage Holiday Inn is trusty Judas Priest bass player Ian Hill – the quiet one who rarely emerges from the shadows engulfing his stack of Marshall amps.

Priest are still reeling from the defection of charismatic vocalist Rob

Halford, feeling bitter at the breakdown in communication (for which they blame Halford), as their old friend seeks to launch his new solo project. 'He doesn't wanna be involved with us anymore, it's history now,' shrugs K.K.. 'Rob has secured his [record] deal with Epic and literally the day after that he sent us a fax saying he's not gonna be involved in the band anymore.'

Halford had initially announced his intention to jump ship at a press conference for his new band Fight, which seems a strange way to inform your old mates that a twenty-year relationship is over. 'I dunno, maybe he fooled us all those years,' says K.K. of the singer's apparent disdain for the rest of Priest. Hill introduces some pragmatic wisdom into the discussion in the manner you'd expect from pipe-smoking Spinal Tap bassist Derek Smalls. 'I think he's also been got at by third parties as well,' he offers. 'I've got to be careful what I say, obviously, because it's all supposition.'

'It's the *way* he's gone about it,' complains K.K. 'The norm would have been for Rob to do his own thing and by the time we say, "Hey, Rob, we've got an album's worth of stuff that needs singing on," he only needs to come in for a couple of days to lay his tracks down – and he'd make himself a few bob as well. But he wanted to cut himself off from the Judas Priest machinery as well – such as the management and co-ordinators – and it's now gone to lawyers and accountants and so he's isolated himself totally now.'

'There's no reason on earth why we still couldn't have been friends,' insists Hill. 'But the way things have happened and developed, it's gonna be impossible for us to do that now.'

K.K. and Ian admit there had been signs that Halford and the rest of the band had been growing apart, but these had mostly been in a musical sense with the singer developing a taste for more extreme metal. 'He's been getting more and more into Pantera and all sorts of thrash stuff,' says K.K., screwing his face up. 'He's just totally covered with tattoos and all that sort of stuff. And if he wants it more radical, there is nothing we can do about that – *Painkiller* is really as far as we go down that line.'

Ian: 'Maybe he thinks the direction he's going in now is the future of heavy metal. But the rest of us don't necessarily feel that way.'

K.K.: 'In Priest we like to pride ourselves on being *leaders* rather than followers and the direction Rob has taken is kind of following all the younger bands.'

Ian: 'Maybe he's trying to hold onto his youth.'

K.K.: 'As a band we like to think we've been pretty picky and choosy and none of us has gone off and bastardised ourselves. But Rob's been out there singing with Skid Row, Ugly Kid Joe, Black Sabbath . . . It brings the image of the band down because Priest have got our stature to think about. I think he's been jacking about.'

Ian nods sagely. 'It all kind of cheapens things a bit,' he says.

K.K.: 'It's almost like the feeling you got when Kiss unmasked themselves; it's like Rob has unmasked himself.'

Fellow Priest guitarist Glenn Tipton had previously told me that 'if one of the four [long-term members – i.e. anyone apart from the drummer] leaves the band there's no point in continuing' – but this noble principle appears to have been abandoned. Yet K.K. attempts to explain the band's apparent U-turn. 'I don't think any one of us would be having somebody else determine when we stop, through what *he* chooses to do,' he says in reference to Halford.

'It's in our blood,' declares Ian, before adding, 'What are we gonna do, become bus drivers or something?'

I take the liberty of pointing out that Priest's fans hardly want to hear that these metal gods are continuing simply because they're not capable of doing anything else. 'No, that's *not* what I'm saying at all,' responds Ian. "There's a lot of good mileage left in Judas Priest, we've got a hell of a lot to offer. We're not just doing it for ourselves; we've also got a commitment to the fans. We're not the only band to lose vocalists or key members and carry on, you know.'

> **'What a load of minging old fucking grannies they were!'**
> **– K.K. Downing on Iron Maiden**

The big question is whether Priest would ever take Halford back if his solo ventures prove unsuccessful. 'You never know what's gonna happen,' says K.K. 'But at this point in time there's no reason why we shouldn't write, get the concept for a new album together and find ourselves a red-hot vocalist who's hungry and capable.'

I joke that Bruce Dickinson, singer with bitter rivals Iron Maiden, will soon become available. 'He might be hungry, but he's not *capable*,' grins Ian, looking across at his guitarist. 'That's right!' says K.K. 'He ain't capable! He's definitely a bit lacking on the high notes.'

Tim 'Ripper' Owens eventually lands the job of fronting Priest and after several albums by both parties fail to seriously trouble the charts, Rob Halford announces in 2003 that he is rejoining Judas Priest, whom he continues to sing with to this day (although the 2011-2012 Epitaph tour does indeed threaten to be their last).

The ageing priest looks down on the young maiden and offers a leg-up, so to speak, only to become angered by a lack of respect and succumb to the overwhelming urge to impale the body in view. A true story, no less, but there are no elderly vicars or fresh-faced females involved – although maybe that's just as well. Because this is yet another example of what happens when guitars and egos clash in the world of heavy metal, which is famous for producing fantastic feuds and rivalries.

Needless to say, Judas Priest's ongoing row with fellow British legends Iron Maiden is up there with the best of them. Forget Spinal Tap's comical complaint that one of their support acts was so bad that the crowd was 'still booing 'em when *we* were on', Priest's lingering anger with former tour colleagues Maiden prompts a far more furious response. Guitarist K.K. Downing is reflecting on the band's early days during our conversation in a London hotel in 1993 when I throw a hand grenade into the room simply by mentioning Iron Maiden's name . . .

'They antagonised us no end with all sorts of things,' complains the Brummie of the Londoners. 'They pulled just about every stroke in the book to try and dethrone us. We were just about to embark on the *British Steel* tour [of 1980] together and the first thing we know is that they're telling the press, "Oh yeah, we're gonna blow the bollocks off Judas Priest, because we're this, we're that . . ." So I went to our manager and said, "Get 'em off the tour, there are so many bands that need a tour and would *really* appreciate it."

'But the manager says, "Oh, don't worry about it, just go out there and show 'em who's boss. And anyway, if you throw 'em off the tour now, it will only get back to the press that you're scared of them."

'I said, "Don't give me that crap, get 'em off, they're arseholes." Anyway, they stayed set for the tour and we were rehearsing down in some cinema in London. We were on the stage when they walked in off the street, sat down in the seats and started taking snapshots. So, of course, I said, "Who are these geezers?" And somebody says it's the support band. I said, "It's Iron Maiden, is it? Get 'em out! Now!" As you would. I mean, they've quoted all this stuff in the press, we've heard nothing back from their management to say sorry and they just walk in like that! The thing is, they did the tour, they died a fuckin' death and nobody said nothing!'

K.K. has got the bit between his teeth now. 'Later, when we went to America, they applied for the gig to support us,' he remembers. 'This was after [Maiden vocalist Paul] Di'Anno [left], some years on. So they came over there with us, which was a pain in the arse because they broke on the back of us in Europe and then fucking broke on the back of us in the States. And they gave us so much fuckin' shit: "We wanna do this, we want more this, we want smoke . . ." They were moaning that they hadn't got enough room onstage, then they wanted to build a stage on top of our stage! It was getting ridiculous. One night they went on and go, "We won't be appearing tomorrow night in Chicago because of certain restrictions by the headlining act." What a load of minging old fucking grannies they were! I flew into the dressing room and grabbed the fucking manager by the fucking throat. I was gonna fuckin' impale him!'

Indeed, K.K. looks as if he's in the mood to punch somebody's lights out. And he's still not quite finished . . . 'And,' he adds, 'another reason I don't like 'em is that all their song titles are fucking movies or books. Any joker can do that! Where's the media? They've never had a slagging in their lives!'

And with that, K.K. leaves the room in a right proper huff.

IRON MAIDEN: BRUCE ON THE LOOSE

One of Britain's great institutions proves it's not immune to internal conflict and U-turns, as this writer discovers when speaking to departing vocalist Bruce Dickinson and founding member Steve Harris during the early nineties, when their relationship appears to have broken down for good . . .

It's the spring of 1990 and Bruce Dickinson has just released *Tattooed Millionaire*, his first solo album, but don't dare suggest the singer is thinking of leaving Iron Maiden. 'The point is that Maiden is the thing that has built the credibility and given me the opportunity to do this,' the vocalist tells me as we speak at his management's offices in London. 'This is my personal game that I'm playing with rock music, but if people are gonna push me into a corner and stick a gun to my head and say, "Iron Maiden or your solo career?" I'd have to say Iron Maiden.'

Bruce Dickinson duly leaves Iron Maiden in 1993 to pursue a solo career.

Steve Harris is feeling just a little bit miffed. As if it wasn't bad enough having vocalist Bruce Dickinson announce that the recent summer of 1993 tour would be his last with Iron Maiden, the bassist was forced to persevere with what he believed to be distinctly below-par performances from his departing frontman. 'He just wasn't giving one hundred per cent, in the vocal department or performance-wise,' he sighs, during a conversation at his Essex home in which he is supposed to be promoting the band's new live album, the perhaps aptly-titled *A Real Dead One*. 'We all felt it and were very annoyed by it, although it's understandable to a certain degree if he's not gonna be there anymore. But he could perform well when he wanted to, such as the last show [filmed for TV at Pinewood] because he knew it was his last gig and that it was going out to millions of people. I felt he could have done that on more nights but he chose not to.'

Anybody who has listened to 'Mission From 'Arry', a recorded argument that can be found on the twelve-inch version of the 'Two Minutes To Midnight' single, knows that Maiden are not immune to backstage bust-ups. Yet Harris reveals that the rest of the band surprisingly tolerated Dickinson's performances for fear of exacerbating the situation. 'We thought that if we ended up having a big row, the tour could just fold up there and then,' he explains. 'Or Bruce might perform even *worse*. So it was decided amongst ourselves to just grit our teeth and get on with it. That was a very, very hard thing for us to do because we're usually very open about things. But we didn't want an ugly situation. As much as your instincts are telling you the opposite, sometimes you've just gotta stand back from a situation and be cool.'

Good advice, indeed . . .

It's a sweltering day in the summer of 1994 as Bruce Dickinson bounces around his management company's offices in London and sings the praises of his latest solo album, *Balls To Picasso*. 'It's good, innit?' he boasts as a copy of said opus is waved around. 'It's a serious, modern heavy-metal record for human beings,' he declares with not a hint of modesty. Not that the album is necessarily what we want to hear about, with the singer's recent departure from Iron Maiden offering far more potential for interesting discussion.

Thankfully, the ever-articulate Bruce just can't stop talking – especially when seated – and once he makes reference to an unspecified intimate song he wrote about his father, there's no need for me to ask him why he decided to leave Maiden because he heads down that highway all by himself.

'It was the only song I had ever written that really made me . . .' he says, taking a moment to pause, before explaining: 'It was the *truth*. It's not released, but it's a very angry song. I'm not sure it's the truth now necessarily, but at the time I thought it was and it affected all the guys who were in the studio. Maybe I was only supposed to write one song like that in my life, but I thought that if I don't try [to write another] I'll never find out. And I'll never find out if I stay in Iron Maiden and try to have it both ways. So that was one of the big catalysts that made me leave.

'The idea that I might quit the band first happened in 1985, when Maiden was at its biggest and we did the *Somewhere In Time* album. I was on record as saying I wasn't particularly happy with it and at that point I thought, "Sod it, I'll bugger off." I was very pissed off with the way I thought things were being run. But I thought, "Hang on a second; what's my real motivation here? Is this just a very pissed-off ego getting annoyed here? In which case, this is not the right reason to leave." So I stuck with it and thought, "Well, okay, what's my role within the whole situation?" It seemed to me that my role was to try and help in trying to re-invent the band with every album, because it was obvious to me that the band in general was pretty conservative – they didn't want to make grand gestures and take big risks. It just wasn't that sort of band, so I thought, "Well, I'll have to try and introduce stuff in there as much as possible that tries to stretch the envelope a bit."

'So anyhow, we trucked along,' he continues, much to my fascination. 'And when we did *Fear Of The Dark*, it kind of got misconstrued, my idea of going back to the original core kind of concept, which was really in-yer-face stuff, the kind of stuff that Soundgarden and the grunge bands were doing. Not to re-live the days of *The Number Of The Beast*, but to re-invent it, using modern influences and also to upgrade the sound of the band. Particularly because I thought the production of the previous records – especially *No Prayer For The Dying* – was really shitty and I think everybody generally agreed with that. And we went with it and *Fear Of The Dark* was not a bad record.

'As we were doing the tour, I was at the same time doing these different solo things [a first album, writing a book etc.] and was obviously doing a lot of travelling and wandering around and talking to people about music and everything outside the band. And that's when it suddenly struck me that the writing was potentially seriously on the wall, not so much for me leaving Iron Maiden, more for *Iron Maiden itself*. Not as a financial institution, because Maiden fans have always been notably loyal and this band still sells a lot of records, but it struck me as an artist – and this was one of the first times in the last four or five years that I actually thought of myself as that. And I was starting to think, "Well, I'd better have a serious word with the chaps and find out how far they are prepared to go to take a chance with the band's reputation in order to try and do something artistically that's really, really new."

'So I had big chats with Nicko [McBrain, drums], Dave [Murray, guitars] and Janick [Gers, guitars] and was basically just playing devil's advocate the whole time, saying the world is really changing – not like a bit but a *lot*. It's not like a haircut anymore and Deep Purple will never sell another platinum record. Those days are really gone. Rap music is not a fad; these things are fundamental changes. It's not quite the death of traditional heavy metal by any means, but it's really going to have to adapt and change; it's going to have to pull on board all those attitudes in order to survive. If it stays rooted in conservatism and tradition and sterility, nobody's going to give it the time of day. Why the fuck should they? Anyhow, it just seemed to me that they [the other Maiden members] were very content in being pretty much where they were and for me to try and pull things in any more radical a direction was going to cause a personality complex.'

It seems logical to suspect that this difference in musical philosophies might have put distance between Dickinson and the other band members – particularly bassist and founding member Steve Harris – on a personal level. But Bruce reveals that he and Harris never really bonded anyway during their time together. 'I think there was always a distance between me and Steve, right from the word go,' he admits, much to my surprise. 'There was always a difference in philosophy between me and Steve. And we used to argue and fight like cat and dog for the first couple of albums after I joined the band [*The Number Of The Beast* and *Piece Of Mind*], which were arguably the best two that we made. And then after the *Live After Death* tour I didn't like getting up in the morning and spending the whole day head-butting myself against a brick wall. Life's too short for that bollocks. So I just thought, "Sit back and enjoy it." And I guess we *all* sat back and enjoyed it. And that was one of the reasons why I made the decision to leave.'

Indeed, it was Harris who was critical of Dickinson's final performances with Iron Maiden and I reveal what Steve has said about his singer on the last tour. 'Well, yeah, I expected some kind of bitterness,' smiles Bruce. 'If you wanted an example of some kind of philosophical difference between me and Steve, there it is. I would never expect him to understand that it was emotionally difficult for me to go

> ## 'I'm not interested in spending my life living off Iron Maiden royalties.'
> – Bruce Dickinson

onstage, because it's never emotionally difficult for Steve to go onstage, like it's never difficult emotionally for him to kick the ball into the back of the net. That's how he sees music and I think that's pretty much how he sees life – in very black and white terms. In many ways, he is *Roy Of The Rovers* and I think he casts himself in that mould. It's not for nothing that everything is West Ham United and soccer and there's nothing that matters more than your mates and all the rest of it. That's his view of the world. And that's okay; I'm not going to challenge it.

'And when it came to doing those last shows, I thought, "Well, in line with trying to be straight about things and not submerging myself under the collective umbrella anymore, I don't have to do that. I've left the band and everybody knows that." If I run around onstage like a fool, pulling funny faces and acting like nothing has happened, then one, I'm gonna feel like a complete fake, and two, there's going to be some people in the audience who are going to think, "Who's this guy trying to fool?" So I thought, "What I'll do is if I really feel like running around like a maniac I will, but if I don't I'll just go on and sing my bollocks off. And if I feel like I'm wandering around onstage and I feel really odd, I'll walk offstage and at least you know I'm not going to be there after August." I was aware that it might get misinterpreted but, as far as I was concerned, it was better to be honest and be misinterpreted and talk about it after the fact than it was to run around like a fake and a complete tosser.'

He denies that *Balls To Picasso* is therefore a more sincere offering than anything he recorded with Maiden, it's just sincere in a different way. 'Iron Maiden records were sincere as far as they went,' he offers, 'but they were sincere in black and white. This one is sincere in colour.'

Of course, Bruce has the luxury of knowing that if his solo career fails, he could always live off the royalties of Maiden records for many years to come . . . not that he likes the idea when I put it to him. 'That's not a career,' he retorts, 'that's *retirement*. I'm absolutely not interested in spending the rest of my life wheeling pushchairs up and down the high street and living off Iron Maiden royalties. It's not the way I want to live my life, living off the scraps falling off of someone else's table. That's absolute bollocks. The only thing you have as an artist is your creativity and your credibility. And once you lose either of those two things, you won't exist anymore.

'I suppose I see the last six or seven years of my life as like a hiatus. I did an awful lot of things, from getting divorced to getting married again, to having two kids, to having a third kid and setting up a house, and doing various side projects and finally leaving the thing that for the last twelve years has been my bread and butter and made me mega-famous and not short of the price of a pint. And now I'm sitting here with a record that feels to me like a new beginning. It feels to me like now I can start maybe moving forward.'

With the cold winds of Nirvana and the grunge scene bringing a chill to the heavy-metal climate, Iron Maiden are beginning to look just a little bit rusty in the early part of the nineties. So they seem the ideal candidates to throw some really difficult questions at, especially as they are currently without a singer following the departure of Bruce Dickinson. Good sport that he is, bass player Steve Harris agrees to step into the line of fire, although it's not certain if he knows just what he's letting himself in for as we settle down for a conversation at his Essex home.

So, Steve, what does Iron Maiden have left to say that's not already been said over their lengthy back catalogue? 'We still feel we've got a lot more to offer,' he insists. 'We've talked a lot about the rights and wrongs of carrying on and whether we should knock it on the head while we're still on top. And we thought, "No, sod it, why should we give up just because Bruce has gone?" We're enjoying it too much.'

Sure, but aren't Maiden looking rather old-fashioned in today's hard-rock climate? 'Yeah,' admits Steve, 'but you've got to remember we were considered old-fashioned when we first started. We've *always* been unfashionable. Whenever you get these big changes, everybody feels they've gotta go that way just to still be fashionable or seen to be credible. That's why you've had loads of bands trying to sound American. People forget that they've just got to be true to themselves.

'What's been happening in recent years has probably affected everybody a bit,' he adds. 'In some ways it's good because it shakes the whole scene up a bit, but the Seattle grunge thing is very much about fashion, whereas when thrash happened it was just about the music. It will change soon because people will get fed up with having to look a certain way and feeling they've got to listen to certain things. Some of the new bands might last but they'll have to change to do that.'

I ask Steve what Iron Maiden would do if they lost their major record deal with EMI – lose face by signing to an independent label or decide to call it a day? He doesn't look entirely happy with the negative tone of my questions, but perseveres regardless. 'I've got my own studio so if we found ourselves without a deal, or even if the band wasn't together anymore, I could still record an album here and put it out myself,' he says. 'We're in a lucky situation in that we're not gonna be held to ransom by anybody because we can just do what we want. So the answer is yeah, we *would* make another album if we felt it relevant to do so and there'd be no shame in putting it out on an independent label.'

What would be Maiden's response if EMI said they would only renew the band's contract if original vocalist Paul Di'Anno – who was fired after two albums – was re-hired? I know it would never happen but it's worth asking just for the hell of it. 'It's not a question of Paul Di'Anno himself,' says Harris. 'It would be the principle of the fact that they're trying to tell us what to do with our music. And they would be told to fuck off – in capital letters. Because they don't tell us what to do with the band and we don't tell them how to sell it.'

Iron Maiden are hardly the most diverse of bands musically so don't the members feel straight-jacketed by their established rigid formula? 'Not at all,' insists Steve, beginning to bristle just a little bit. 'I've never felt the need to go off and do a solo album or anything like that. We've all been doing what we want to do and Bruce has found some other stuff he wants to do, so he's gone off to do it.'

Would Wolfsbane's Blaze Bayley make a suitable frontman for Iron Maiden? 'I think he'd make an excellent front man for Maiden,' declares Harris. 'He's got a great voice, too, but whether it would suit Maiden, I dunno. You could get the most probable man in the world for the job and he might not fit. I think he's got what it takes but unless he auditions for us I wouldn't know if he would suit the band.'

Would Maiden consider reuniting with Bruce Dickinson in the future if both parties' careers fail to hit the heights independently? 'I very much doubt it,' says Steve. 'I think the next album will probably do well purely because people will be interested to see what's going on. If people don't accept it, or the new singer, it might be the following album that's the problem. But I really don't think that Bruce would come back anyway – and I don't think we'd want him back. If he has left because the passion has gone, then why is the passion going to come back in a few years' time? Is it because he misses us all and misses the music – or because of money?'

Blaze Bayley does indeed join Maiden for two studio albums, the second of which, *Virtual XI*, is the poorest selling of the band's career. Despite everything said, Bruce Dickinson returns to Iron Maiden in 1999 and they continue to record albums for EMI until the present day.

ANTHRAX: CAUGHT IN A MOSH

It's the spring of 1993 and John Bush takes time out before getting horribly drunk to explain why he had to succeed Anthrax vocalist Joey Belladonna, who, according to guitarist Scott Ian, just wasn't up to the job of fronting the New York thrash quintet (until he returns, leaves and returns again) . . .

Anthrax vocalist John Bush is good at drinking. Good at knocking it back rather than handling it, that is. Tonight he is sitting at the round table in the St Moritz club in London's Wardour Street, but his face is barely visible as he gradually slides down his seat until he is virtually horizontal. It's well past his bedtime and he's had a few, you see.

Earlier in the day, he'd been speaking about adjusting to his new life after succeeding Joey Belladonna as Anthrax's new frontman for the band's *Sound Of White Noise* album – an emphatic statement of intent for the revitalised quintet. He and guitarist Scott Ian are asked to approve the new cut of their video for 'Only' – which features Frank Silva, who plays evil spirit Bob in *Twin Peaks* – at an impromptu screening on the second floor of their record company offices in Kensington High Street. 'That's the best one,' says Scott as he emerges from the small room. 'With the last edit Charlie [Benante] was complaining that he wasn't in it enough.' Drummers, huh?

The guitarist, who formed the New York band – which fused thrash, hardcore and rap – in the early 1980s, insists Bush was the only man considered to replace Belladonna, who appeared on big-selling albums such as *Among The Living* and *State Of Euphoria*. 'We knew we wanted John,' he says. 'It's weird because people always ask the question, "Why did Joey leave the band?" I always joke and say, "Because we *asked* him to." We just wanted to get a singer who was gonna be part of the band creatively.

'I was writing all the lyrics, [bassist] Frankie [Bello] and I were coming up with all the vocal ideas and it just got to the point where we really needed a singer who was gonna be able to come in with his own personality and express himself. Never once did Joey come in with a word on a piece of paper and say, "I have this idea I would like to try." It just got to the point where we said, "We can't do this anymore." But John's arrival has opened us up musically and it's almost like I'm not listening to my own band now.'

Bush candidly reveals it wasn't easy acclimatising to his new environment after fronting Los Angeles power-metal outfit Armored Saint for his entire singing career. Indeed, he once spurned Metallica to stay with his old school buddies. 'I needed to make the adjustment but at times I was letting fears get in my way,' he confides. 'It's human nature when there's a drastic change in your life, a lot of fears rise up. Looking back, I laugh and think, "C'mon, are you a fucking woman or what?" If I had never done this I'd be the dunce of the fucking century.'

> **'Never once did Joey come in and say, "I have this idea."'**
> – Scott Ian

Scott adds, 'I don't want people to think, "Oh, all that other shit was a waste of time." But I wrote the lyrics to those songs and I know how I heard them in my head. For me, something would get lost in translation. I always heard a much heavier version and Joey just didn't have that vocal style or attitude that I would have when I would sing it. It's the way I wish it could have been in the past.'

In 2005, Joey Belladonna rejoins Anthrax for a reunion tour of the *Among The Living* line-up. Bush insists he can *never* return to the band, but rejoins in 2009 for several live dates, only for Belladonna to return yet again the following year. But as we've learned, in heavy metal you should just never say never again . . .

FEUDS AND FALL-OUTS

BOYS ON THE BOOZE

I t seems pointless denying that alcohol is as much an intrinsic part of the heavy-metal scene as denim and leather – if for no other reason than rockers like letting their (long) hair down. It flows through the various levels of the rock industry, soaking everything in its wake and allowing few participants to escape the reek of its intoxicating influence. It exists as a form of oxygen for bands on the road, is used by record companies and publicity agents to encourage favourable support, is seen by journalists as a major perk of the lifestyle and is guzzled by the gallon by fans who admire and aspire to the hedonism of their heroes.

It's in the pubs, it's in the clubs, it's at the gigs, it's at the ligs. Consumed in excess (which it generally is, of course), it prompts hilarious and hysterical but also horrendous behaviour and guarantees a headache or hangover. There's romanticism about alcohol, but it can also have tragic consequences. As Def Leppard's Phil Collen admitted when reflecting on former guitar partner Steve Clark's dependency on booze following his death, 'Steve worked in the music business where drink is really easily accessible and there's a myth attached to it.'

Consequently, and perhaps inevitably, the smell of booze is never going to be too far away as any rock journalist goes to work. Bands are either going to be drunk or reflecting on the days when they used to be; the bottle being seen as a friend or an enemy. Either way, it's always going to produce a range of fascinating experiences – funny, farcical or philosophical.

They say you should never meet your heroes because they will frequently disappoint, but there's something reassuring about the fact that UFO vocalist Phil Mogg was pissed when we first met – even though it made interviewing him a little problematic. It's certainly difficult to imagine him saying 'do you like a wank?' under any other circumstances.

Trying to get much sense out of Yngwie Malmsteen turned out to be something of a forlorn hope following the Swedish guitarist's return from Russia – back in the days when the Iron Curtain was virtually made of metal – but it was laughable listening to the man's ego run riot as a result of his well-oiled state when we met up for what was supposed to be a serious chat. 'All these women in Russia have spent their whole lives just waiting for Yngwie to hit town,' he drunkenly declared after boasting of his sexual conquests on tour.

The lubricated lifestyle might be celebrated by bands such as the Dogs D'Amour – 'people are talking more about the drinks than the music', complained bassist Steve James as lead singer Tyla did just that – but, while admitting that they enjoyed the excesses of their heydays, such veteran acts as UFO and former Thin Lizzy guitarist Brian Robertson still recognise that their careers were ultimately undermined by the distractions of drinking.

That's certainly the case for Kiss guitarist Ace Frehley, whose alcoholism cost him his place in the band in the eighties and has continued to sporadically plague him, as I discovered when venturing backstage in Detroit on one occasion. 'It's tough to be sober on tour because the lifestyle is so insane,' he admitted.

But there's no denying that's part of the attraction and, for many, heavy rock will always represent a platform to party . . .

YNGWIE MALMSTEEN: FROM RUSSIA WITH LOVE (STORIES)

Beers are flowing and peanuts are flying as the noisy narcissist that is Yngwie J. Malmsteen deigns to meet in April 1989 to reflect on his recent groundbreaking visit to Russia and, after much consideration, drunkenly declares: 'It's a fucked up country . . . but the girls were great!'

Yngwie Johan Malmsteen is drinking. In fact, the Swedish 'neo-classical' guitarist is three sheets to the wind, if the truth be known. So much so that, after spying his reflection in the mirror opposite and pausing to flick his fingers through his permed hair in self-adulation, he fails to notice – or negotiate – the coffee table right in front of him as he tries to head to the toilets and promptly falls arse over tit to send beers, peanuts and cigarette stubs flying everywhere.

The noisy narcissist is enjoying a brief stay at the Holiday Inn in London's Marble Arch after returning from a groundbreaking string of dates in communist Russia. And after several drinks in the lounge bar, he issues orders to his personal assistant to perform an errand that will improve his mood even further – only for the guy to eventually return empty-handed.

'I'm sorry, Yngwie, but there's nothing doing,' he says apologetically. 'I've had no luck at all.'

Malmsteen is not happy. '*How* much do I pay you?' he whines as he refuses to be denied. 'C'mon, go and try again.'

The man, who once sold out London's Marquee Club only for the fact that a herd of dumb Bruce Springsteen fans assumed 'The Boss' was playing a secret gig under a pseudonym based on an anagram of his name (!), begins telling me about his experiences behind the Iron Curtain.

'The human race is egotistical, self-centred, self-indulgent, very greedy and very violent.'
– Yngwie Malmsteen

'The girls were great!' he says excitedly, in an interesting accent that meanders between Swedish, Cockney and American. 'I fucked some of them and they were just so wet, y'know?'

I nod, as if I've been there myself. 'And then it occurred to me,' he continues, 'that all these women in Russia have spent their whole lives just waiting for Yngwie to hit town!'

I struggle not to laugh. Of course, Yngwie's adventures should not imply that he doesn't have a long-term partner back home. So, I feel compelled to ask, does that mean he is happy for his other half to see other men while he is away, enjoying himself on tour?

'No way!' he responds. 'If she touches another man she's dead!'

Er, does that not represent a little hypocrisy on his part?

'There's one thing you have to understand about men and women,' he tells me. 'Men are *men*. And women are *women*. And hypocrisy,' he says, 'is when women want to act like men!'

It fails to occur to Yngwie that if all women behaved in the way he wanted them to, there wouldn't be many available for him to take advantage of. But returning to the main topic of debate – which would be helpful given this interview is for serious trade magazine *Music Week* – Malmsteen claims he was inspired to play in Russia after his father, who apparently was 'in the Swedish military', made a discovery while away on business.

'He's very involved in the ministry of culture and all that shit,' says Yngwie. 'And he was in Moscow when this Russian opera singer, just out of the blue, took this record out and said, "You gotta check this out. It's been Number One for seven months. It's the hardest shit." And my father looked at him and went, "That's my son!" And the singer went, "Yeah, *right*." Anyway, it all derived from that.'

In keeping with Russia being a throwback to the past, that album turned out not to be Malmsteen's most recent effort *Odyssey* but its predecessor *Trilogy*, which, according to Yngwie, shifted '50,000 copies in one day after the first show in Moscow'. But Yngwie is not the best when it comes to figures, as evidenced by his claim that 'eleven concerts in Moscow with 14,000 people each night, then nine shows in Leningrad with 18,000 each night' amounted to '250,000 tickets' sold. It's tempting to ask the guitarist what happened to the extra 66,000 tickets that went missing, but he's too busy talking about why his loud licks were lapped up by the locals.

'My music is so different to regular so-called heavy metal,' he declares. 'It's extremely melodic yet very heavy; the classical influence is undeniable. If you look at television in Russia, they use classical music all the fucking time, so when I play Albinoni's 'Adagio' or Paganini's '24th Caprice' they know it. Hey, barman! Another two bottles of Elephant, please. Thanks.'

Few western European rock artists have set foot to play in Russia at the time of Yngwie speaking. And it's fair to say he wasn't overly impressed by what he saw outside the concert venues. 'Now, let's start talking about fucking Russia!' he says, before necking back more beer. 'That whole society is so desperately out of line. It's amazingly bad!' he adds before laughing, 'It truly is horrible! There's nothing to buy, there's nothing to eat, there's nothing to drink. It's a completely fucked up country in every way you could possibly imagine.

'I truly feel sorry for the Russian people. All the propaganda on television and everything just tells them that the Russian society is the most amazing way to live. And they would show bums on the streets of New York and shit and say . . . Western, y'know, capitalism and . . . y'know . . . what's that word . . . ?'

'Er, democracy?' I offer.

'No, not democracy, er . . . *imperialism*,' he eventually responds. 'They tell everybody the western world is fucked and show them some MiG-15s or whatever.'

Which brings Malmsteen onto the specifics of communist ideology. 'I just happen to have a little bit of education when it comes to communism,' he proudly boasts. 'The truth is that the society in Russia is as far away from communism as you can actually get. Communism means to share all and everybody is equal; it's an idealistic society that's impossible to put into reality. The human race is egotistical, self-centred, self-indulgent, very greedy and very violent and so it will never, ever happen.'

Despite the alcohol flowing through his system, Yngwie is finally beginning to talk some sense at last. 'In other words, the only society that could possibly work is one where everybody is given an equal *opportunity* to do what they really want to do. Not to be told what to do, that you've got to share everything, but just to do exactly what the fuck you want to. And the strong will survive and the weak will die. That's why there are lions and fuck-all rabbits, you know?

'The only society I can think of . . . I'm not trying to say the United States is perfect, but truly, the closest thing to Utopia, the closest thing to the true essence of the word "land of opportunity", or sentence or whatever, is America – because you can have a shop if you want to, whereas in Russia you can't have a shop. You can be great or whatever, it's like "get in your factory and work" and that's the way it is.

'The thing is, when people say, "I hate communism, I hate communists," they don't really know what they're fucking talking about. Because communism, in essence, is the same thing that Jesus preached: love your neighbour, everybody is equal, whether you have long hair, short hair, are rich or poor. Russia has nothing to do with fucking communism, although it's *called* communism. What it is, is a dictatorship, it's bureaucracy and it's *extrrrreeeeeemely* corrupt.'

It's not too long before Malmsteen's assistant returns to the bar, somewhat sheepishly. 'No joy, I'm afraid,' he concedes, sending his Swedish employer apoplectic. '*How much do I fucking pay you?* It's not good enough,' he shouts. 'But it's Sunday, Yngwie, we've just hit town and there's nobody about,' says the poor guy, hoping his master will show some reason. But there's not much chance of that and off the bloke goes again, tail between legs, on his increasingly desperate mission.

I suggest to Malmsteen that some of the Russian fans might be feeling a little exploited and starting to resent western bands for using their trips behind the Iron Curtain as nothing more than a PR exercise. After all, it's not as if anybody can take Soviet currency back home with them. 'Ah, yeah, I dig, I dig! I definitely see that,' he concurs. 'People should not underestimate the intellectuality of the Russian kids. These kids know what the shit is. I mean, a lot of people just go, "This is just a bunch of fucking peasants." But they're not. They're a very educated audience.'

Slightly more so than the Russian musicians who are somewhat behind the times, it seems, as they attempt to adopt the heavy-metal clichés. 'I feel sorry for them,' says Yngwie. 'They're not bad, some of them, it's just that they're so uneducated. You look at pictures of these guys and you'd think it's 1976 or 1977, with their cheapo studded belts and T-shirts with white and red stripes, like zebras and shit. And they actually think that stuff is hot.'

Our conversation eventually returns to Yngwie's own music – which is appropriate, as the guitarist loves nothing more than talking up his own talents. *Odyssey* was his first – and final – studio collaboration with former Rainbow vocalist Joe Lynn Turner. And while some considered it appropriate for Malmsteen to link up with the American who had previously worked with Deep Purple legend Ritchie Blackmore – whose guitar sound Malmsteen himself has occasionally been accused of cloning – it was hard to imagine the tug-of-war for the spotlight lasting for very long.

'Well, we're not sleeping together anymore,' admits Yngwie, when I ask about his current relationship with Turner. 'He is a brilliant singer and nobody can deny that, but I got slightly irritated by the guy. Our personalities began to clash a bit.'

The pair certainly appeared to be pulling in different directions while on stage together, yet the marriage somehow seemed to work on record. It's a mistake, however, for me to suggest the album is a product of anything approaching an equal partnership, despite the shared songwriting credits. 'I wrote all these songs *long* before Joe was here, I'd like to point that out,' he insists. 'He had no influence on those songs. None. He just sings what I wrote.'

The radio-friendly 'Hold On' track sounds as if Turner has brought something substantial to the table, I suggest, but Yngwie is having none of it. 'No fucking way, man! It's about ten percent him. That's the truth.

'Let me just inform you about something that really blew my mind when I found it out. Rainbow, worldwide, never really sold that much. The only album that really sold a lot of records was the one with 'Since You Been Gone' on it. That was the only one. *Odyssey* sold more copies worldwide than any other record that Joe Lynn Turner ever fucking played on. Let's face it – this is Yngwie Malmsteen's solo career. I'm a solo artist. My albums sell between 400,000 and 500,000 records in America. Joe Lynn Turner's solo album sold 40,000 copies in America. I don't wanna be an asshole, but let's face the fucking facts. You see, the thing is, I don't just play guitar; I'm a composer. I compose music; I don't just write a fucking riff. I compose *everything*.'

Malmsteen is building up a head of steam now. 'Joe seems to have this idea of thinking that this is a conceptual format; that once you're generic enough you will sell records,' he says. 'Unfortunately, that's not the way it is. Just look at Guns N' Roses; Guns N' Roses are as far away from my music as anything can get, yet I really like them because they're true, they're honest. They're not plastic.

'Then there's Iron Maiden. I think Iron Maiden is the most pathetic fuckin' attempt at trying to be intellectually musical in the world. They should play at the same level as AC/DC or Guns N' Roses because their musical abilities are not beyond that. I can't stand hearing their fucking music, because they're making an attempt to be musical and complex and sophisticated. And they can't! They're pathetic!

'Listen, I don't give a shit about fuckin' [Maiden vocalist] Bruce Dickinson or fuckin' [manager] Rod Smallwood. I know both those guys and they already hate me, so fuck them! I love AC/DC, I fuckin' love ZZ Top, I love these bands because they're not *pretentious*. And then there's fuckin' Iron Maiden. It just makes me fucking puke.'

After returning from the toilets and inadvertently treading peanuts into the carpet, Yngwie sits himself down only for his floundering assistant to re-appear empty-handed yet again and spark the guitarist into another rage. 'HOW MUCH DO I FUCKING PAY YOU?!!' can be heard from well outside the bar as more than one member of the public considers it prudent to stay out of harm's way.

Several years later, Yngwie Johan Malmsteen confirms that he no longer drinks alcohol.

ACE FREHLEY AND KISS: ACE OFF HIS FACE

The former Kiss guitarist is drunk in Detroit and his girlfriend asks for help. Staying sober is a constant battle for Ace Frehley, as he admits himself in 1993, while old colleagues Gene Simmons and Paul Stanley find it hard to imagine working with him again (oops!) . . .

Ace Frehley's girlfriend is backstage at Detroit's Joe Louis Arena and she's in tears. 'It's Ace,' she sobs. 'He's drunk again.' In his dressing room, Frehley cuts a desolate figure. Pointing him in the right direction home is no easy matter and not something I feel particularly equipped to do (especially as I've had a few beers myself). Earlier in the day, the former Kiss guitarist had been drinking nothing stronger than coke when I recognised him in the bar of the downtown Omni Hotel (which isn't easy given his years in 'Spaceman' make-up) and asked for an interview. 'I hope I'm a rock legend over there,' he'd said of his status in Great Britain, before emitting a wild cackle of laughter.

A few hours on, he seemed in naturally ebullient spirits as he welcomed guests into his inner sanctum following his new Frehley's Comet outfit's successful slot supporting Alice Cooper. But it then becomes obvious that it isn't just the adrenaline that's been flowing (later it might be a case of Frehley's Vomit rather than Frehley's Comet) and, with the show now over, all the friends, band members and hangers-on have long since disappeared – as has any close association with his old Kiss colleagues. Ace left the band in confusing and controversial circumstances in the early eighties, officially as a result of 'musical differences', yet there was always a strong suspicion that the six-stringer's excessive lifestyle had finally caught up with him. Singer and bass player Gene Simmons certainly blames Frehley's alcohol abuse for the erratic behaviour and lack of commitment that apparently led to

> **'It's tough to be sober on tour because the lifestyle is so insane.'**
> **– Ace Frehley**

his initial departure. Indeed, he goes so far as to claim the problems became evident as early as the mid-seventies when the band's first live album saw them become huge stars.

'It was the most depressing thing,' he sighs when the matter of Frehley's fall from grace is raised during one conversation between us. 'After *Alive* came out, we exploded and became overnight sensations. And this cocksucker . . . We were in the studio for our next record and he actually had the audacity to come in one day and say, "Look, I don't really feel like playing this solo, I've got a card game at seven o'clock, do you mind if I split early?" And I just couldn't fucking believe it. There were some solos on that record [*Destroyer*] that he never even played on – "Beth", "Sweet Pain" and a couple of others – because he had card games and drinking. That was more important to him.

'And I was so hurt. I'm still hurt to this day that he would choose that meaningless, fucking smelly can of beer over being a member of Kiss. But he's paid his price. I do not feel sorry for anybody who chooses a lifestyle, because it's their choice. Ace is a good guy, with not a mean bone in his body, but he chooses to do this.

'While he was in the band we kept getting doctors. Trust me, his friends have all tried to get him help. But the problem is not about drinking or drugs, there's some other loose screw. We all have our loose screws – I'm not saying I'm totally normal and Ace and [former drummer] Peter [Criss] are fucked up. But there's something else inside them that makes them drink and get high.'

Co-frontman Paul Stanley, when quizzed by me at another time, concurs with his partner about Frehley's demise. 'I wish Ace all the best,' he says, 'but when he left us he was barely functioning in the band. I run into him in New York and he always wants to know when we're gonna get the original band back together. I say, "It's been great seeing you and I'm in your corner."'

Six years after the Detroit debacle, in August 1993, it appears that Ace has cleaned his act up somewhat. He admits he fell off the wagon when hitting the road with Frehley's Comet, but denies getting platform-booted out of Kiss – whose motto is, after all, to 'rock and roll all nite and party every day' – because of his boozing and that he is still hankering for a reunion of the original line-up.

'I'm in a much better frame of mind these days,' he says from his home in New York. 'Getting sober helps. After Kiss I kind of got into it [drink] even worse. For my first album I cleaned up but then I slipped back into it again. Being on the road . . . it's tough to be sober on tour because the lifestyle is so insane. It's just as hard now, but there is a support group that I use and people that I call and travel with that help me out. It's a constant battle, but I've been winning it over the past year or so.'

He confesses to drinking throughout his years with Kiss, but insists he left the band because of the direction Simmons and Stanley were taking it in. 'I've read articles where they say they fired me, which is the biggest crock of shit. I was drinking [from] the day I joined that group to the day I left and I always showed up and did my job. I quit the band because I wasn't happy working with Paul and Gene.'

He admits he'd consider rejoining Kiss if he was 'offered a fair deal' but adds, 'It's not something I'm holding my breath for. I've bumped into Paul twice in New York and both times I've never even mentioned any type of reunion.' Yet Ace insists it's the very thing Kiss needs after becoming just another formulaic hard-rock band since losing two original members and removing their make-up in the early 1980s.

'I don't think their records are bad, but they're never gonna recapture the magic they had with me and Peter Criss,' he declares. 'It's not that Peter and I were the greatest musicians, but there was a chemistry between the four of us. [Eventual replacement] Bruce [Kulick] is a very good guitar player, but he's limited in what he does. He doesn't have the spunk that Ace Frehley has.

'I admire them for their ability to continue – they're workaholics. I sometimes wish I had the drive they have. But they have a problem dealing with the reality that the original band was more exciting and charismatic. It's something they've been fighting ever since they took the make-up off.'

Within two years of this particular conversation, Ace Frehley and Peter Criss are invited to 'Kiss and make-up' with their former partners for a world tour that will eventually take in nearly 200 dates and gross more than $43.6 million. Criss would leave, return and depart again, while Frehley bails out in 2002 after what was labelled a farewell tour. A solo album, *Anomaly*, is released on 15 September 2009, reportedly to commemorate the third anniversary of his getting sober (again). Meanwhile, a new Kiss, without Ace, continues to play on in their face paint and exploit the band's legendary trademarks.

THE QUIREBOYS: SPIKE DRIES OUT

All the gigging and ligging eventually catches up with ultra-sociable Quireboys singer and Soho scenester Spike, as he confesses in February 1993 after sinking his final drink (for the time being) . . .

It's another frenzied night in Los Angeles at the Cathouse . . . or the Pussyhouse or House of Pussy or whatever it might be called. And it's somewhat appropriate – for a band that reek of the alcohol-soaked flavour of 1970s good-time geezers the Faces – that the Quireboys are yet again propping up the bar. Yet it's still a surprise for me to view the reflections of singer Spike and ragamuffin riffmeister Guy Bailey in the

> **'I can't just have one drink, that's the thing.'**
> **– Spike**

mirror between the bottles of spirits while fighting for another drink – if only because the Londoners personify the Soho scene to such an extent that it's rare to see them so far away from their natural habitat.

The Quireboys could always be found in The Ship . . . or the Marquee Club (whether playing or not) . . . or the St Moritz, the three watering holes that represent the cornerstones of Wardour Street's very own Bermuda Triangle. Members of the capital's rock fraternity would disappear into the zone as normal human beings during the early evening . . . only to finally emerge in the small hours of the night in zombie-like fashion and remembering very little about the experience. Indeed, when Spike throws open his arms to provide a welcoming embrace in LA, it suggests that perhaps far too much time has been spent in his company over the years because it's all been on the razz.

A few months later, in the spring of 1993, the Newcastle-born frontman has decided he's had enough of a hedonistic lifestyle that was beginning to take its toll, proving you really can have too much of *A Bit Of What You Fancy* – the title of the band's debut EMI album. 'I'm just fuckin' sick of it,' he confides with a familiar rasp over a distinctly non-alcoholic beverage when back on home turf. 'I just wanna get my life back in order. I was just a fuckin' mess. I'm not saying I've given up drinking for good or anything, but I was hanging out with low-life types of people and I don't wanna do that anymore.

'The thing is,' he says, 'nobody was taking any notice of me anymore. It was just like, "Here's the drunken Geordie again." I was speaking to a lad the other day and he said, "I was really upset the last time I saw you after a gig; you were just sitting there shaking." Even when I was in America, everybody was talking about half the shit I was getting up to. I'd be speaking to people and thinking, "How the fuck did they know about that?" And hearing these stories about being a fuckin' heroin addict and all that type of stuff, which wasn't true.

'But I can't just have one drink, that's the thing. I was in Los Angeles and I just decided to stop, because physically I was a nervous wreck and really ill. I was having really bad blackouts and waking up not knowing where I was. And there would be all these weird people around us. So I just thought, "I've got to stop this." I moved in with a mate who hasn't had a drink for three years. He said, "Do you want to go for a meeting?" On New Year's Day it was. I went to AA every day for three weeks in LA and I'm going to meetings here in London. I recommend that everyone [with a problem] does it.'

Of course, as is later revealed on an acoustic outing recorded with fellow partner-in-grime Tyla (of the Dogs D'Amour), Spike's temporary abstinence proves to be all too *Bitter Sweet & Twisted* – the title of his band's second, and final, EMI album . . .

UFO: ON ANOTHER PLANET

Phil Mogg and Pete Way, two of heavy rock's heroic hedonists, went their separate ways in the early eighties, but nearly ten years later they're back together again to launch a new version of UFO. The only problem is that Mogg is both pissed and pissed off at the same time. 'I feel like wrenching your head off your fucking neck,' he says . . .

The definitive UFO line-up, with German guitarist Michael Schenker at the peak of his powers, produced some of hard rock's most majestic moments, as displayed on their magnificent double live album of 1979, *Strangers In The Night* (a Number Seven hit in the UK, no less). Few could deny that the likes of 'Doctor Doctor', 'Only You Can Rock Me', 'Lights Out', 'Love To Love' and 'Rock Bottom' are essential listening for any discerning rocker. Needless to say, the classy combination of melody and muscle seemed magical for a teenager such as myself when first discovering the British band and witnessing a brace of special fan club-only dates at London's Marquee. But those days are, as suggested in the title of another of their songs, 'Long Gone', with founder member and bassist Pete Way quitting to form his own outfit [Waysted] and UFO crashing to earth in spectacular fashion in the early eighties as the band's hedonistic habits finally took their toll.

Many years later, in the early part of 1992, Way and singer Phil Mogg are somehow back together again as they set about re-launching a new version of the band (with guitarist Laurence Archer and drummer Clive Edwards). But old habits die hard and a tired-sounding Mogg is not entirely sober as he sits in a London hotel room and attempts to discuss the group's reformation. 'It's just fucking around,' he says lazily of the new project, much to Way's embarrassment.

Schenker, perhaps not surprisingly, is not involved in this particular reunion and Way admits that 'the whole thing would probably fall apart' if the erratic/eccentric six-stringer was brought back into the fold. 'We've been through the wibbly wobbly phase,' says Mogg, not entirely constructively, before declaring, 'He divvies around. He's playing stuff that's got nothing to do with songs.' At which point he starts humming something that resembles the theme tune of *Hawaii Five-0*. 'It's a real shame,' he adds, 'because Michael is a really good guitar player. He's just a bit lost.'

I naturally ask about the other former members of UFO who have not been invited to join the new party – such as Schenker's original replacement, Paul 'Tonka' Chapman. 'No, we don't like him very much,' says Mogg of the Welshman. 'He used to nip out to the blood-donor bank; he used to draw off your blood. And he never used to wash or change [clothes] either. He used to change into his spandex in the toilet . . . and then still

> '**Being drunk for so many years, you don't make rational decisions.**'
> – Pete Way

be wearing it two days later.' Way adds, 'He didn't influence the band. Michael would say [adopts German accent], "Poor thing, he could never play my licks."'

The name of rhythm guitarist/keyboard player Paul Raymond is then thrown into the conversation, just for good measure. 'I think I'll pass on that one,' responds Mogg, before performing a U-turn. 'He's got this huge chip on his shoulder. He's got like a permanent period.' And last but not least is drummer Andy 'no neck' Parker. 'Well,' says Phil, 'it would take a lifetime for us to sit here and talk about Andy.' And he's clearly in no mood to do that.

It feels good to be in the presence of two personal heroes such as Mogg and Way, even if the former is a little inebriated and less than enamoured by my presence. I ask why the band cracked up in its heyday and Mogg takes a dislike to the terminology used. 'Have you never had a job where you've said, "Excuse me, I've had enough?" If that's cracking up then fine.' I rudely point out that he soon found the motivation to resurrect the name with a brand-new line-up, but he plays down his influence. 'As far as I'm concerned, I'm just the singer,' he shrugs.

It's logical to assume that with Mogg being the only original member of the band in the mid-eighties – when the line-up included guitarist Atomik Tommy M and former Damned bassist Paul Gray – he must surely have guided UFO's course at that time. But again the vocalist is reluctant to accept responsibility. 'No, I wasn't guiding its course,' he insists. 'It was a fucking pain in the arse. I just like singing . . . you can do what you want around it. You can go-go dance . . .'

Er, yes, well, is Phil at least prepared to admit he's difficult to work with? 'No, just difficult to interview,' he deadpans.

'It's not easy,' interjects Way. 'I had it when I formed Waysted; you have to listen to twaddle that other people talk. There's so much twaddle.'

'We don't have any twaddle,' adds Mogg.

'It's true, though,' says Way. 'It's always this twaddle, that twaddle, that twaddle and it isn't you. It's because you happen to be different.'

Mogg: 'I'm the one who goes, "Am I really listening to this?"'

Way: 'Some people are real arseholes.'

Not least his singer today, many would think. A few minutes later, the cassette machine clicks off with Pete in full flow about the band's current plans. After a new tape is eventually found and inserted, I joke that I've forgotten the original question, but Mogg pretends to save the day. 'Do you like a *wank*?' he suggests.

The new UFO are set to return to the road, which can prove an expensive operation. 'The thing is,' says Way. 'You've got to re-invest in the band if you believe in what you do.'

Mogg: 'You sound like John Major.'

Way: 'The travelling is the only thing that can be a pain.'

Mogg: 'Especially if the hotel's too far from the gig.'

Is the band confident that their new record company can shift some albums? 'Okay, let's touch your arse and fucking let's go to the gigs,' says Mogg. 'That's the bottom line. What the fuck?'

The frontman of UFO has seemingly landed on another planet. I suggest that Phil doesn't always appear to be in the right frame of mind for an extended period on the road. 'You've made me want to do these gigs now,' he says, before adding, 'I feel like wrenching your head off your fucking neck.'

At this point, it seems appropriate to terminate the conversation. Way offers some sort of apology for Mogg's mental state and suggests we get together again within a couple of days. Thankfully, Mogg is in a far friendlier mood when he agrees to meet again to smooth things over – and hopefully talk more sense. Pete is reassuringly also in tow as the streets of Victoria are roamed in search of a pub that has a pool table. 'My nipples are really sore,' moans Phil. 'You know what's it like when they get really cold and rub against your shirt?'

Sadly, yes. When later seated with beer in hand, Mogg admits that UFO 'touched the twilight zone' at the peak of their wild days. 'It was extremely excessive,' he says, already showing far more co-operation, 'although not me personally, of course. I just watched!' Way elaborates by explaining how the rigours of 'non-stop touring' resulted in the band members becoming 'a bit messed up'. He explains UFO's downward flight-path by admitting, 'Being drunk for so many years, you don't make rational decisions.'

But there's no doubting the band's long-held philosophy of trying to 'have a good time, all the time' – as Spinal Tap keyboard player Viv Savage once famously put it. As Way says, 'You're stuck in Iowa or somewhere and what do you do, walk around the shops in the snow or find out if some guy's gonna pop down with a couple of grams and sit in the bar? We're not the type of people who sit down and read a book, you know. We always wanted to enjoy ourselves – even down to the German part of the band. Michael was quite funny, because he got it down to a fine art. It was like [cue German accent again], "It's five o'clock, I haf to haf one beer now, two beers at six and then two Valium . . ." It was like organised excess!'

The mention of their former guitarist's name makes Mogg laugh. 'I loved the article where Schenker said that we drove him mad,' he says. 'I couldn't believe that, when it was *him* who drove *us* fucking mad! I'll always remember him being arrested in Kentucky and doing this Sieg Heil thing!' Yet crazy behaviour was the norm, according to Way. 'Nobody questioned what we did,' he sighs. 'I wish somebody had said, "Why have you stayed up all night and spent £500 on cocaine when you could have had a good night's sleep?" Not naming names, but we had a manager who was doing more drugs than we were! Somebody should have said, "Look, take two months off and stop drinking for a few days. What do you need those drugs for?" We really needed a break.'

And with that, another round of drinks is ordered. Before another. And then another.

DUMPY'S RUSTY NUTS: SLEEPING ON THE JOB

Dumpy, he of the Rusty Nuts, is delighted to be interviewed in October 1987, but the bearded biker is less happy when kept waiting for four hours only to be drunkenly told that his new album is 'shit' . . .

It's probably not the best way of commencing an interview. 'Tell me about your new album; I think it's shit.' But having been drinking for the best part of the day (thanks to a *Metal Hammer* 'editorial meeting' in the pub) that's what happens. Poor Dumpy Dunnell – leader of perennial Marquee Club favourites Dumpy's Rusty Nuts – responds in predictably blunt fashion about his latest vinyl offering. 'It's black, it's round and it's got a fuckin' hole in the middle.'

Not that the crusty veteran is in the best of moods anyway, having been waiting several hours for this inebriated interrogator to arrive at the offices of

Razor Records – in vain, as it transpires. 'I'm the only one left in the building,' he complains over the phone as day slowly passes into night. 'Well, just me and the cleaner.' He suggests a meeting at The Ship on Wardour Street, adding, 'I can at least have a pint while I'm waiting – in case you're late.'

Needless to say, the interview doesn't exactly get off to a flying start. Dumpy does, however, admit that the production of *Get Out On The Road* – a routine slab of heavy biker rock – is not quite what it might be because of a paucity of funds. 'The thing is,' he says, 'you've got to go with what you've got . . . and we've got fuck all!'

Shona, the editor's secretary at *Metal Hammer*, has come along for the ride and her sunglasses sit temptingly on the bar. Dumpy's greying beard – not quite in ZZ Top's league but gradually getting there – appears far too bright for these eyes and so it seems only logical to stick the shades on before asking him about the semi-comic rockers appearing to take a more serious approach to their recent shows. The tubby entertainer begins to waffle on about the band's humour being misunderstood – for what seems an eternity.

'I would never have thought I could say "bum" onstage, let alone "fuck off, you wanker".'
– Dumpy Dunnell

'I guess you could call me sexist,' he admits, 'but I'm not anti-gay, which is something I have been accused of a few times. We get the things that embarrass people and bring them out into the open. I would never have thought I could say "bum" onstage, let alone things like "fuck off, you wanker". As long as our fans enjoy us, everyone else can get fucked.'

Ten minutes later he's still rabbiting away, completely oblivious to the fact that his tired and weary interviewer has eventually succumbed to sleep behind his sunglasses. Hence there's a lengthy silence when Dumpy eventually finishes talking.

'Oi!' He looks across at Shona. 'Here, I think he's asleep!' At which point, my right elbow slips off the bar to prompt a sudden return to consciousness. 'Er, yeah, where were we?' I say. 'That's right, yes. Er, Dumpy, you seem to have been taking a more serious approach to your recent shows . . .'

'You've just fucking asked me that!' he spits through his beard.

And with that, the interview is terminated on the grounds that I'm in no fit state to hold a decent conversation. The memory may be vague, but the cassette machine records everything . . . including what half the customers in the pub have ordered to drink that night due to its position on the bar. 'Two pints of lager and a packet of crisps, please.'

But Dumpy soon has an opportunity to win the last laugh after a late-night drinking session at our hotel during the Reading Festival. Indeed, my trousers and pants are down by my knees while the Dumpster and a young girl play noughts and crosses on my backside (as you do). There's a rare glee in Dumpy's eye as he drags the black marker pen across the pair of naked white buttocks staring up at him from the sofa in the bar – and not just because he thinks he's winning.

This is his chance for revenge for that ridiculous interview, he thinks, delighted that somebody else's rusty nuts are on display for once. The ink is a bugger to remove, of course, as the young lady later discovers upstairs . . .

DOGS D'AMOUR: FEELING RUFF

'You drink, you fucking fall over, you fall asleep,' says Tyla, leader of wrecked rockers the Dogs D'Amour, as he explains his daily routine (when not visiting the hospital) in early 1989 . . .

The Dogs D'Amour's set at the Astoria Theatre in London is about to reach its climax when an idea enters the head of Tyla, the man responsible for the gypsy rogue romanticism of this Muttley crew. He grips the neck – not that of his Gretsch Chet Atkins guitar but the litre of wine which has proved an equally reliable companion during his performance – and smashes the bottle against the drum riser behind him. With the jagged remains in his right hand, he drags the glass across his naked ribs, causing a river of blood to run from the gaping five-inch wound. Some members of the crowd laugh, others are shocked and horrified. For Tyla and the Dogs, it's just another gig.

A short while later, presumably after a painful visit to hospital to get stitched up, Tyla is sitting with me in a Kensal Rise brasserie trying to justify his appetite for (self) destruction. 'It shows how real we are,' he insists. 'We're not like Alice Cooper, playing about with false blood or anything. There was no real reason for that. I just felt like it and when I want to do something I do it.'

What next – a cover version of 'The First Cut Is The Deepest'? Tyla gets rather upset when I put it to him that some people suggest that the band's drink-till-we-drop image is anything less than one hundred percent genuine. 'I feel like saying, "Come back to my place and I'll take you through a week." Some people would be on the verge of a mental breakdown,' he claims, before unleashing a great rock'n'roll quote. 'A lot of people have died around this band.'

'Lots of people hang around us because they want to pretend to be something they're not,' continues Tyla, pouring himself another stiff one. 'It's taken me ten years to get where I am now and I know how much I can drink.

Some guy from a Sunday paper interviewed me the other day and I was telling him how people slag me off because I can drink more than them. And he said, "All right, I'll take you up on that. I've just been with Keith Richards and he can drink." We ended up having six Jim Beams and he had to leave.'

Not that Tyla is the competitive type. 'If someone comes up to me now and says, "I can drink more than you, let's have a drinking contest," I'll just tell them to fuck off. These people who want to beat someone at drinking – that's not enjoying yourself; it's not a game. Why don't they grow up? We drink this much because we drink. We don't do it to impress anyone.'

With that, Tyla suddenly walks off – not the first time this afternoon, it should be added, much to my annoyance. 'It's getting a bit out of hand because people are talking more about the drinks

> ## 'A lot of people have died around this band.'
> ### – Tyla

than the music,' admits bassist Steve James in his singer's absence. Well, that's what you get when Jack Daniel's is presumed to be the fifth member of the band (due to its presence in all the publicity photographs) that has staggered and swaggered its way to success with, er, a dogged determination for debauchery. After all, their most recent album was called *A Graveyard Of Empty Bottles* . . .

'If people want to talk to me about drinks, I'll talk about drinks,' says Tyla upon his return, although he looks pretty disgusted when I ask him if he ever has to pace himself. 'There's no such thing as pacing yourself,' he retorts. 'We just carry on. If you feel a bit sick, you feel a bit sick and that's it. Everybody has a tolerance; you drink so much, you fucking fall over, you fall asleep. Everyone looks after you; making sure you're in the right position [to avoid doing a Jimi Hendrix/John Bonham/Bon Scott] and then you carry on.'

He wanders off once again . . . in the direction of the bar.

DEF LEPPARD: TRAGIC TIMES

Def Leppard have never been portrayed as party animals, so it's somewhat ironic that they have suffered so heavily as a result of alcohol abuse, with one guitarist losing his place in the band and another losing his life, as Phil Collen and Joe Elliott reflect in the early nineties . . .

Stephen Maynard Clark had everything to live for after Def Leppard roared out of Sheffield in the eighties and conquered the world with highly commercial albums such as *Pyromania* and the twenty-million-selling *Hysteria*. Instead, he drank himself to death, with the fatal evening arriving on 8 January 1991 when he mixed alcohol, painkillers and anti-depressants at his London home.

One year later, Phil Collen, his former guitar colleague and sometime drinking partner, takes time out to reflect on the untimely passing of his good friend at the age of thirty. 'Obviously I'm very upset on a personal level that Steve died,' he says, 'but also because we had developed something *musically* very special between us.'

Collen, a Londoner who joined the band in 1982 as a replacement for Pete Willis, who also suffered alcohol problems, relaxes with me on the sofa at his mum's house in Holland Park as he remembers when Clark's drinking seriously began to destroy his long-term prospects with Def Leppard. 'We started work on the *Adrenalize* album [the follow-up to 1987's *Hysteria*] and that's when things started getting really bad,' he reveals. 'It became pretty obvious that Steve's performance was really suffering with the alcohol thing.

'He'd come in [to the studio] and his playing would be really sloppy and he wouldn't be into it. For me it was like, "Okay, I'll do all the stuff, you go and get your head together." He'd come back and say, "I think I feel a bit better now." But he didn't, he had all these problems and would be drinking even more. That's when we said, "Look, you really gotta go somewhere." Which he did until the day he died.'

Def Leppard had already experienced the trauma of seeing drummer Rick Allen lose an arm in a car crash in 1984 before embracing him back into their fold with a specially adapted kit. And once again with Clark, the members of the band did everything within their power to help one of their colleagues overcome his troubles. 'It was only the alcohol problem that fucked him up,' says Collen. 'Steve was a lovely guy; he was fucking *great* and a real sweetheart. He wasn't a weirdo or a flake; in fact he was the most normal person I've ever met. But he had this normal problem and it can happen to bakers, plumbers or anyone. Unfortunately, Steve worked in the music business where drink is really easily accessible and there's a myth attached to it and all that bollocks. But it's an illness and he really needed help.

'I think you can trace it back to childhood. When we went to see Steve [in hospital] I'd talk to his doctors about alcoholism and what they'd tell you was pretty eye-opening stuff. It's a physical thing and is almost like a disease. We learned a lot about it and I'm really glad we did, because we didn't fully understand initially. I just knew he was fucking unhappy and miserable – and he needn't have been.

'I know there was pressure because we'd had the biggest-selling hard-rock album [*Hysteria*] and all that, but everyone else was bearing up to it. But with an alcoholic, they get that slight bit of pressure and they turn to the booze.'

It's hugely ironic, of course, that had original member Willis not been ejected for his excessive alcohol abuse, Collen would not have been given his opportunity to join the band as they prepared to build on the platform of their first two albums. 'Yeah,' remembers Phil. '[Vocalist] Joe Elliott phoned me and said, "We've got problems with Pete; when he has a drink he turns into a different person. Can you learn sixteen songs in two days?"

'"Yeah, *of course*," I lied.'

Another year on from the conversation with Collen, in May 1993, Elliott himself is on the phone and the frontman is in a candid mood as he remembers Clark. 'He was funny, shy, erm, moody . . . and I *miss* him.

'But time heals,' admits the vocalist. 'I don't think about it at all, it's too depressing. I accept it's part of our history, it happened and it comes up in conversation now and again. But it's normally something funny. Steve didn't live the lifestyle like the stereotype you may think he was, but he definitely enjoyed indulging in what was available, whether it was females or alcohol or whatever. It's a shame that he's taken so many great ideas with him.'

'With an alcoholic, they get that slight bit of pressure and they turn to the booze.'

– Phil Collen

Clark's death, at such a young age, represented the lowest moment of Leppard's career as a band, but Allen losing his left arm certainly came close. 'At least Rick's still around,' says Joe, although he adds, 'It's very hard, when you're around Rick, to moan about a little cut on your finger or a headache when this guy's surviving with one arm. His other shoulder is all fucked up, too. When he got thrown out of the car's sunroof, he kind of trashed both his arms but only one of them got torn off. He can't lift his arm properly but still manages to play the drums.'

In many respects it's incredible that Leppard have achieved their level of worldwide success considering the number of serious setbacks they have faced. One of the earliest of those came in the shape of Clark's original guitar partner Willis.

'We had a *lot* of arguments when Pete was in the band,' says Elliott, 'because when he got pissed he was a nasty person. When Steve got pissed he was just sad; but all you'd wanna do with Willis was throw him out of the window. I almost threw a bottle in his face once but I smashed it against the shower wall instead. He went onstage pissed out of his head – somewhere in the States when we were supporting Ozzy Osbourne – and I didn't think it was fair on the rest of us. That was the beginning of the end of him.'

Who would have thought that, less than ten years later, a similar problem would result in another Def Leppard guitarist losing not just his place in the band but his very life? At least Willis got out alive.

BRIAN ROBERTSON: PUB-LIC IMAGE

The former Thin Lizzy and Motörhead guitarist does his best to create a good impression after joining Statetrooper in 1987, but a drunken vocalist in Gary Barden really doesn't help his case . . .

Brian Robertson has a reputation for wild living. Well, that's what happens when you're thrown out of hell-raising bands such as Thin Lizzy and Motörhead for overdoing things a bit. So it's no surprise that when I tell people that a rendezvous has been arranged with the flame-haired Scot, they advise me that it's best to have a few drinks beforehand. Just to be on the same wavelength, so to speak.

'Robbo' has kindly offered his home address in the West End of London, but on my arrival there's a scrap of paper pinned to his front door. 'I'm in the pub,' it says, with Brian's signature underneath. What a shame he couldn't have indicated which particular one . . .

Several public houses (and inevitably pints) later, the members of Statetrooper – of which Robertson is now one – are finally located. The surprise is that the guitarist is drinking water and is completely sober. Sadly, the same cannot be said of Gary Barden, with the former Michael Schenker Group vocalist having been feverishly refreshing his throat with alcohol, presumably to help rid him of the stutter that blights his conversation. After all, it's not the best affliction for a rock singer who has to participate in interviews, is it?

The good news is that Barden has calmed his nerves to the point where his stutter has disappeared. The bad news is that he's inebriated to the point where what he's saying isn't really worth listening to. Back at Robertson's abode, the Scottish guitarist is glaring at his vocalist for potentially ruining his hopes of creating a good impression.

'My image has been a bit of a handicap and trying to live things down isn't easy,' he confides. 'I sense the pressure when I'm trying to get something together because it's like banging your head against a brick wall.' He admits that some people will only ever want to remember him for 'speeding out of my head and beating people up' – a reference to a famous fight in the Speakeasy Club that forced Lizzy to scrap a tour of America. And when I ask if he feels he's got anything left to prove, Robertson says, 'Only that I'm not a complete piss-head and dope addict.'

So it doesn't help when, as Brian talks about 'playing by feel . . . or brail', Barden quips, 'He plays by Special Brew!' The singer is oblivious to the dirty looks he's getting as he jokes about Robertson being 'offered by producer

Tony Platt on a platter – or Tony Platter' and that he is as ambitious as ever because 'I've tasted success . . . and it's a great taste – a cross between strawberry milkshake and . . . roast beef'.

'He'd better be ambitious or he's in big trouble,' says Robbo, in total seriousness, 'because I bloody am!'

'My image has been a bit of a handicap.'

– Brian Robertson

Statetrooper, whose run-of-the-mill rock never looks likely to escape Marquee Club status, achieve next to nothing in the short time they are together. And Brian Robertson, who helped originate Thin Lizzy's trademark twin-guitar sound as best heard on the classic *Live And Dangerous* album, will always be remembered as a 'wasted' talent.

BOYS ON THE BOOZE

CHEMICAL CAPERS

Heroin, cocaine, ecstasy, acid, amphetamine sulphate, marijuana ... If there's one positive thing that comes from rock stars taking drugs – at least as far as journalists who like sniffing out (if you'll excuse the term) a story are concerned – it's that some of them arrive at a place in their mind whereby they just can't stop talking about it. This, of course, makes for compelling copy because we all have a fascination with those brave substance soldiers who have explored the darkest areas of excess, which few mortals would ever have the courage to venture into – especially if they survive the journey and return home to planet Earth.

Ozzy Osbourne and former Deep Purple member Glenn Hughes are two such heavy-metal hedonists who've thankfully lived to tell their tales – well, dead men certainly won't tell us any, as the Motörhead song goes – and both were happy to discuss their battles during interviews in Los Angeles and London respectively. Ozzy was trying to write an album for the very first time while straight – if you discount prescriptive and medicinal drugs, that is – and so his coming clean on going clean, if you will, provided the opportunity to discuss how bad his habit had become and why he was trying to turn the corner. 'It's still pretty bad,' he admitted at the time, or rather slurred, clearly not in the best of shapes to be facing an interview. 'The voices are still there.'

For Hughes, it's considered part of the healing process to divulge his indulgences whenever he gets the chance. 'I feel the urge to keep rambling on about it and I don't know why,' he said, not that he got any complaints from me. The fact that his then-new album was 'totally autobiographical' in addressing substance abuse certainly helped justify my constant probing, prodding and prying. 'My obsession for coke, speed and ecstasy was *fucking mind-blowing*,' he insisted.

Whether there's as many illicit substances flying about in the world of heavy rock as some people might imagine is a matter of debate. People such as Ozzy and Hughes might reflect on their chemical capers when on the road to recovery, but musicians are rather less inclined to discuss their addictions while sticking their heads into a bag of 'blow'. Some discretion sometimes needs to be shown – if only to avoid the long arm of the law, because it's not as if stories of drug taking would damage their reputation. If anything, it enhances it – just ask Mötley Crüe.

But sometimes certain musicians are tempted to drop their guard. Such as the keyboard player who gleefully produced a bag of white powder the size of a football while backstage at the University of East Anglia in Norwich as his veteran band embarked on their latest trek around the UK. 'Hey, do you think this will last the whole tour?' he joked, knowing full well that the bag of cocaine would be more than enough. After all, they were playing a mere forty dates . . .

On another occasion, the shrieking lead singer of a legendary British group had thrown open the doors of his Buckinghamshire home for the launch party of his new solo album. There was plenty of powder by the snooker table but it certainly wasn't chalk dust, and pints of lager were disappearing quicker than red balls. Needless to say, crazed cue-holders whizzed around the table faster than Alex 'Hurricane' Higgins and Jimmy 'Whirlwind' White at their dazzling best.

And sometimes circumstances dictate that people have to hold their hands up – such as when Pete Way appeared at a backstage bar at the Reading Festival in the early nineties. The UFO bass player, nothing but a late spectator on that occasion, looked nervous and twitchy but said hello and asked if I could buy him a drink. 'Sure, Pete, no problem,' I said. Way guzzled his pint down in virtually one gulp, put the glass back on the bar and tentatively enquired, 'Er, you couldn't get us another, could you, mate?'

'Erm, yeah, okay.' And once again, a trembling Pete chucked the lager down his neck as swiftly as possible, with some of the beer dribbling down his chin in the process. He looked around the bar, spied a couple of half-empty glasses and, after checking that nobody else was looking, grabbed the dead drinks and knocked them back.

At this point, Pete felt obliged to offer some sort of explanation. 'You see, mate, I've been trying to come off the smack,' he declared. 'And I'm having a bad time of things at the moment.' It was difficult to know quite what to say. 'Right then, the same again?'

OZZY OSBOURNE: SNOWBLIND

Heavy metal's most loveable character – yes, he, Sir Ozzy of Osbourne – eventually realises it's time to confront his demons, as the former Black Sabbath vocalist reveals during an interview in Los Angeles in May 1993 when he's clearly under the influence of some mind-numbing medication . . .

It's a typically sunny day in Los Angeles and Ozzy Osbourne is taking a stroll in the park. 'Divorced!' he insists as a female in her mid-thirties passes by. 'We've got this game, you see. We have to guess if women are single, married or divorced.' At which point a blonde girl is heard screaming from an open-top car. 'OZZY . . . I LOVE YOU!'

'Single, *definitely* single,' declares the Ozz, waving to his new friend as she disappears into the distance.

Such simple games and light-hearted moments of recognition from the public make life just that little more tolerable for Ozzy Osbourne. Mentally ravaged by the legacy of decades of drug and alcohol abuse, the former Black Sabbath singer – heavy metal's most loveable character – is fighting not just for his career but possibly his life. He says he's been clean for two years now, but the grip of addiction is so strong that the self-dubbed 'Prince Of Darkness', at the time of speaking, remains in danger of being lured back into a tunnel of darkness.

'I'm an addict/alcoholic,' he states matter-of-factly. 'When you come off booze and drugs, you've got a committee in your head that's always trying to sabotage your sobriety. It's relentless, from the time you wake up in the morning to the time you go to bed at night. I wake up when somebody fires a starting gun and I spend the rest of the day running away from my fuckin' head. That's all I do, run away from myself. It's like, "Go on, Ozzy, have a drink, have a sniff, have a fuckin' sherbert dip . . ." And when I acted on these thoughts in the past and I'd drink or shoot up with something or fucking sniff something, the same voice would be there next morning, saying, "See, you can't fucking handle it." It was a fucking *nightmare*. It's still pretty bad, you know. The voices are still there. When I say "voices", it's not like I'm possessed by anything, it's like my mind is always trying to sabotage me and get me into trouble. I'm a devious little fucker, I am.'

We're seated in Ozzy's management's office now – and it's fair to say he's not in the best of shapes. In fact, it's a surprise that he's agreed to speak to me today at all, given his poor mental condition and the fact that there is no new studio album to promote. The interview had been requested partly with a view to prolonging my trip to Los Angeles, which had been organised and funded by an independent record company for a feature on one of their new American bands. A three-day visit to the hard-rock capital of the world can be extended by up to two weeks simply by contacting different labels or management companies and offering generous coverage of whatever acts they have in town on the proviso they pay for an extra couple of days' accommodation and amend the return flight ticket – a cost-effective proposition that rarely fails to turn up trumps.

And Ozzy, having a heart of gold, is the kind of bloke who doesn't like to say no too often. 'All I live for is to try and make people happy,' he admits – and it can be assumed that includes journalists looking to enjoy LA's rock playground for a little longer. But Ozzy is not having much fun himself at the moment. He's in the process of trying to write an album of new material in a sober state of mind for the very first time in his life. It was believed that his previous solo effort, *No More Tears*, was originated while clean, but Ozzy reveals that wasn't the case.

'No, the last album was the first I ever *recorded* without drinking, but I'd written it on booze,' he says. 'This album is so difficult for me because, as I got back into the studio, the old committee was going, "You can't do it without a drink, Ozzy, take a drink." So in the end I think "bollocks to it" and I just fucking go home. I haven't drunk alcohol or done any street drugs for over two fucking years now. I've been on medication because I fucked my leg up on the road, but I'm off nearly everything now.'

'*Nearly* everything?' I can't help but ask.

'I'm just taking this one pill, this fuckin' goofball,' he admits, 'that this therapy guy suggested which puts me on this super Valium kind of vibe. In five days' time I'll be cutting down. But in this town they're either lawyers or fucking doctors. If you look at somebody the wrong way in this town you get sued.'

It's no surprise to learn that Ozzy is on some form of medication. His speech is slurred, he struggles to complete his sentences and some would probably assume he is drunk. He admits he is feeling low at the moment, but is he less unhappy than he has been now that he's given drink and drugs the elbow? 'No, I'm not less unhappy; I just don't add misery to my unhappiness,' he declares. 'Add misery and unhappiness together and you've got one big fucking fall-out zone, you know. That's why I went to therapy for four weeks – it stems right back to my childhood and how I handle success. I've never really looked at myself and said, "Hey, Ozzy, you should be really proud of yourself for what you've done." I never like to say that.

'I do like myself a little bit more than I used to, but I'm still afraid. I can honestly tell you that all my troubles were directly attributed to alcohol or drugs – *definitely* alcohol. So now I don't do alcohol there's nothing out there for me. I don't fucking sit in a pizza parlour or an ice-cream parlour. What's the fucking point? I'd rather go and sit in a bar, you know. And the thing about being Ozzy Osbourne is that I'm in the public eye. Have you seen the [*National*] *Enquirer* here? If Elizabeth Taylor scratches her arse there will be somebody there with a camera and the front page will read: "MARTIAN HIDES UP ELIZABETH TAYLOR'S ARSE." So I don't go out anymore and I've become a kind of recluse. I just leave the house, come down here and then go down to the studio. I go in, do my work and go home – I'm an absolute fucking suit!'

This is not the crazed Ozzy that his fans worship – the man who has sunk his teeth into doves and bats, snorted lines of ants with members of Mötley Crüe, pissed on the Alamo and attempted to strangle his wife. The man who yells 'let's go fuckin' crazy' when he gets onstage. He's had spells in the Betty Ford Clinic but has always lost his battles with his demons and fallen off the wagon. So what convinced Ozzy, or gave him the strength, to finally get clean this time around?

'I've been trying for the last ten years,' he admits. 'I kept going back in and out [of rehab] until one day I went to Las Vegas with the producers of *No More Tears* – Duane Baron and John Purdell. I was coming to the end of this big fuckin' run. I'd been doing coke and all kinds of fucking crap. Everybody was giving me bags of the stuff like it was going out of fashion. But I couldn't get to where I used to be able. I would just go up and back down again and so I just dumped it. I said to John and Duane, "I'm getting out of here. It's ten o'clock and I want to go to the airport." When I got home, everybody was recommending that I go and see a particular doctor, but it turned out that he was more of a drug addict than I fucking was! But I got on this medication because you cannot come off dry – you have to be weaned off.

'I dunno, something changed, something clicked and I don't wanna find out what it was. If you said, "You know why, Ozzy, it's because . . ." I'd go, "Oh yes, yes, yes," and go out on the road and get fucked-up again. I don't wanna get drunk anymore. As fucked-up as my world is, I know it would make it a lot worse.'

John Michael Osbourne recorded just eight albums of brilliantly doomy, gloomy music with Black Sabbath before commencing what initially seemed an unlikely solo career under the controlling guidance of Sharon Arden, who later became his wife. While Ozzy became more successful, his old band became something of a joke as around fifteen different members – including singers Ronnie James Dio and Ian Gillan – passed through at one stage or another. But now, for the first time since 1985's short Live Aid set, a reunion of the four original Sabbath members – Ozzy, guitarist Tony Iommi, bassist Geezer Butler and drummer Bill Ward – is on the horizon. 'It's gonna happen,' he says, insisting it's more a case of giving in to public demand than anything else. 'Let me tell you something – I don't need Black Sabbath. But my biggest – and weakest – point is people pleasing. For some unknown reason, I dunno why, we've become a kind of demigod for all these young bands now. We were like the coolest thing on this fucking planet, the original early Sabbath. I was talking to James [Hetfield] from Metallica and he said, "The day you left Sabbath was the day they fucking died."'

Ozzy has been talking for some time when he suddenly decides to excuse himself and head to the toilets. He shuffles away a tired old man but returns a few minutes later almost a different person. He's alert, speaking coherently and now has a whole new zest and vigour as he reflects on the albums that make up the vast bulk of his solo career.

His transformation proves timely, as just moments earlier he'd have struggled to remember getting up today, yet alone the music he made a decade ago. But he remains as candid and unguarded as ever. *Blizzard Of Ozz* and *Diary Of A Madman* remind him of the loss of guitarist and friend Randy Rhoads in 1982, 'and that awful fucking plane crash where I was

'I was a fucking flying, fully-fledged alcoholic drug addict and I didn't give a fuck.'

– Ozzy Osbourne

watching this guy fuckin' burn to death'. Then came *Talk Of The Devil*, a hastily produced 'live' album featuring a one-off line-up to settle a contractual obligation. Ozzy gets fired up now.

'What happened was, my manager at that time was Don Arden – my wife's father – who's an arsehole, a big fat arsehole. He'd gone into CBS and done a deal for a live album, because all he wanted to do was grab the fuckin' dough and run. Randy Rhoads got killed and they wanted me to put out the *Tribute* album [live recordings featuring the guitarist that were eventually released in 1987] and I said, "Fuck you, fuck all of you, I ain't doing it, the guy ain't fucking cold yet." But I was under obligation to deliver a double live album, so I had Brad Gillis, Tommy Aldridge and – who was the bass player? – Rudy Sarzo go into the [New York] Ritz to record the fucking thing.'

Bark At The Moon has Ozzy howling about the mix of the record, although he says, 'I can't fucking complain. If anybody says it's a bad record, there are two or three million people who didn't think it was a bad record because they all bought the fucking thing.' But it's an absolute classic in Ozzy's eyes compared to its successor, *The Ultimate Sin*. 'I fucking hate *The Ultimate Sin*; it's the worst album I've ever done. Out here in California they've got no idea about getting a heavy guitar sound. It's all top-endy. They think playing it loud makes it heavy, which is bullshit.

'At that time I was a fucking flying, fully-fledged alcoholic drug addict and I didn't give a fuck. I got a new producer [Ron Nevison] in because I wasn't capable of co-producing my own thing anymore. I was too fucked up. I didn't like that album at all.

'In fact,' he says, with a devilish grin crossing his face, 'I decided to do some research a while ago, when they put all these wonderful fuckin' injections in me and I felt stoned. I was sitting at home and I thought, "I gotta see what *The Ultimate Sin* sounds like now, I wonder if it sounds any better?" And it sounded fuckin' *worse*. And I thought, "No way, man!" A dog farting sounds good when you're stoned, so it's got to be pretty bad for that!'

Ozzy admits that the negative critical reaction to the subsequent *No Rest For The Wicked* record forced him into a re-think in terms of what he should be producing. 'I liked that album a lot better than *The Ultimate Sin* but *No Rest For The Wicked* was totally fucked up by [producer] Roy Thomas Baker. The drum sound was fucking abysmal. We had to do all the drums again to patch the album up. I never read reviews of my records because they always get it wrong and I get pissed off and it fucks up my day. But one day I picked up a copy of *Rolling Stone* and the review of *No Rest For The Wicked* smacked me right between the eyes. It said, "If you're an Ozzy fan you won't be disappointed, but don't expect anything new." And it got half a fuckin' star or something. And I thought, "This is absolutely right on." I suddenly realised that all I'd been doing for years was thinking, "What will people be expecting of me?" That hit me like a fucking lightning bolt.'

By the time of the following studio album, *No More Tears*, Ozzy had decided – or rather his other half Sharon had decided on his behalf – that he was going to hang up his rock'n'roll slippers and retire from the business. 'That decision was made for me by my wife,' he confirms. 'She said, "You're gonna do your farewell tour," and I went, "Okay," because at that point I didn't really want to go out on the road that much anymore. *No Rest For The Wicked* wasn't exactly an earth-shattering hit. It went platinum or so, but it wasn't one of my greatest fucking achievements. But lo and behold, I announced my farewell tour, put *No More Tears* out and it was the biggest-selling record I've ever fuckin' had. To be honest, I thought that if it was going to be my last album, I'm gonna give it everything. I had all these commercial kinds of ideas in my head and if it's shit or bust I could afford to take a fuckin' gamble. And it paid off bigger than I ever imagined.

'My retirement never really sunk in until the final show in Costa Mesa. I thought, "Is that it?" I suppose I expected the skies to open up and say, "WE WANT YOU!" I was expecting this big explosion of emotion to come at the end of it, but nothing really happened. And the thing is, everybody's looking for that day when they can retire, but my fucking father retired at sixty when he was made redundant and he was dead in three years. So fuck off, I'm not retiring.'

The No More Tours trek produced yet another live album, *Live And Loud*, following in the wake of the belated *Tribute* in memory of Rhoads and a live mini-effort dubbed *Just Say Ozzy*. 'I don't know what the fuck that was about,' he admits, 'I haven't got a clue. I wasn't on this fuckin' planet at that point.' And he's not exactly brimming with enthusiasm about *Live And Loud*, dismissing it as nothing more than 'a good kind of stop-gap and a way of keeping the momentum going'.

'I'm not a big fan of live albums and wasn't fuckin' bothered about the thing, but I'm in a game where I have to give people what they want. It's my job; it's what I do for a living. It's nothing more than that. Some of the tracks were recorded fucking badly. I was listening to it the other day and I thought, "Fuckin' hell, man, you must be mad letting this go out like this, it's so ragged." But a lot of albums aren't fuckin' live at all – all they keep is the audience and then add a cup final crowd to it.'

Few could have blamed Ozzy for calling time on his career after having been caught up in the endless cycle of albums and tours and promotional activity for countless years. His batteries were certainly running low during a recent American tour with Motörhead, whose guitarist Würzel – during one conversation with me shortly afterwards – made little effort to disguise how badly Osbourne needed to take an extended breather. 'Ozzy is a superb man and his band are fantastic, but Sharon is a different kettle of fish,' he said. 'Ozzy needs a fucking rest, he really does. He's a beautiful fucking person and she's giving him so much shit. She's gonna get me fuckin' shot, isn't she?' he sniggered.

But it was Ozzy feeling shot – as he had admitted himself when complaining about the relentless pace of his life and the feeling that he was not fully in control. 'You've got it!' he agrees. 'I live with my manager, which is my wife who I absolutely adore. But she's turned around a bit in the last few weeks. She says, "You do it in your own time when you're ready for it." Because it was like, "I can't think of anything to fucking sing about [in the studio] and I've got this live album to promote and I've got this Sabbath thing," and my head starts screaming, you know? But things have got a lot easier over the last few weeks and I go down to the studio when I want to now.

'It was like having a choker chain on, you know? But listen, I shouldn't complain that at my age I've got so much fuckin' work. It must be a sign that I'm still quite popular. My motto is, "Keep your ear to the ground, because Ozzy's still around."

'I can't stop, you know,' he says, looking directly at me. 'I'm addicted.'

GLENN HUGHES AND DEEP PURPLE: WITH GOD ON MY SIDE

The beers are sinking but Glenn Hughes isn't drinking, as the former Deep Purple man shares lunch in January 1993 and reflects on a twenty-year booze and drugs binge that took him to the very brink of insanity. 'I was making barnyard noises,' he crows . . .

Poor old Glenn Hughes. The former Deep Purple bassist/co-vocalist and Black Sabbath frontman has spent nearly twenty years fighting against drug, alcohol and weight problems. 'I was so far gone it was almost impossible to come back,' he admits. And yet here he is, trying to get through a light lunch in a London hotel while old Trapeze colleague Mel Galley orders several Carlsbergs and makes jokes about chocolate fudge cake. As his friends at the table sink the drinks at an alarming rate, Hughes is entitled to question which of us is actually suffering from an addiction. 'You know,' says Glenn, ignoring the taunts and temptations, 'my PR guy said to me, "You can't keep talking about the drug thing, because everyone knows you're now clean." But I feel the urge to keep rambling on about it and I don't know why.'

> 'I was so far gone it was almost impossible to come back.'
>
> – Glenn Hughes

There are perhaps three reasons why Hughes is talking today about his drug-induced journey to oblivion and back. One is that he is being discreetly urged to, because the subject holds a strong fascination for those who have never been brave enough to test their physical and mental endurance and experience the danger of plunging into the abyss. 'My obsession for coke, speed and ecstasy was *fucking mind-blowing*,' he openly confesses. Another reason is that talking about his recovery is genuinely therapeutic for Glenn. And the third is that his latest record – a blues offering, entitled, er, *Blues* – just happens to be inspired by his recent visit to the world's most famous drug rehabilitation clinic. 'This isn't the comeback album, this is an album of recovery songs from all that crap I went through at the Betty Ford Centre,' he declares. 'It's *totally* autobiographical. Nine of the twelve songs are about substance abuse. It's a self-indulgent trip down memory lane to cleanse the spirit.

'I had to get clean because I was dying,' he continues. 'I'll give you an idea of my routine. I would only use drugs on a Friday and Saturday night, but I would buy an ounce of cocaine and in two days it would be gone. And when you do that much blow, it takes about four or five days to come down, because you're in such a stupor. So I was only coherent for one day of the week – and that was a shakes day. This disease drives you fucking insane. Towards the end I was making barnyard noises – I was going really doolally.'

But then God intervened, as Glenn reveals. 'It was Christmas Day and I was coked out of my brains. I couldn't breathe, couldn't walk or talk, so I drove to hospital and the doctor said the oxygen wasn't getting through to the brain. If I had stayed at home I'd have died. I'd been asking God for the last three years prior to that for a sign. I was begging for help and it eventually came in the form of an intense hospital visit. So, for Glenn Hughes, it took a very life-threatening situation.

'God has always been in my life; I just hadn't accepted him. I'm not gonna sit here and bible-thump to you, because I'm not that kind of guy. But I will tell you that God is my life. I hand my will to him. He has taken away the obsession for me to use cocaine and speed and ecstasy. It's a spooky thing, this disease. And for the first six months of getting clean, it was on my shoulder, saying, "C'mon, let's do one more line." There's only really one way out of it – and that's Jesus Christ. My acceptance of him is why I'm clean.'

'My obsession for coke, speed and ecstasy was fucking mind-blowing.'
– Glenn Hughes

Meanwhile, Galley is ordering more pints and the empty lager glasses are piling up across the table. But Hughes couldn't seem happier. 'Ozzy [Osbourne] says it's boring to be sober, but I'm really grooving on the fact that I'm sober and clean,' he smiles. 'They call it a pink cloud at Betty Ford when you feel the way I do and they normally last about six months. But it's been fourteen months for me now and I'm still racing.'

Needless to say, it was touring with Deep Purple back in the mid-1970s that saw Glenn getting seriously involved with drugs. 'It was Purple, the first tour of America,' he confirms. 'I started using coke and it started getting heavy. I never did a bad show but I was a little bit erratic to be around. I was a millionaire at twenty-one, coked out of my mind, with my own limo, Rolls Royces everywhere. I could have *shot* somebody and got away with it.'

Hughes will always be associated with the Purple legacy, for the contribution he made between 1973 and 1976, but it's not a period of his career he remembers particularly fondly. 'It was rather boring onstage,' he declares. 'It wasn't really challenging for me. I didn't enjoy the square-sounding heavy

'Lem has lost touch with this country. If it's not "Motörhead England" anymore then I don't really want to know,' declared guitarist Würzel when launching a personal attack on his frontman and the direction of the band prior to his departure. Lemmy, not surprisingly, was furious.

'I'd been doing coke and all kinds of fucking crap,' admitted Ozzy Osbourne in Los Angeles, reflecting on the moment when he finally realised the need to turn his life around. However, fans should rest assured that metal is one addiction he'll never shake. 'Fuck off, I'm not retiring!'

Forget 'Dr Rock' – it's Dr Brock (centre), the Hawkwind leader who discussed psychedelic silliness with me before a show in Liverpool. Wheelchair-bound, he was also nursing an injured ankle . . . with medication to ease the pain, it could be assumed. (Clockwise from bottom-right: Alan Davey, Huw Lloyd-Langton, Harvey Bainbridge and Dan Thompson.)

Revelling in all things lewd, crude and rude, Blaze Bayley was happy to dish the dirt on Wolfsbane's most recent trip to the United States. 'I thought I was getting my brains sucked out through my dick,' he reminisced about one particular romantic interlude.

Rick Parfitt and Francis Rossi of Status Quo enjoyed yet another 'Anniversary Waltz' inviting a bunch of liggers, giggers and extreme gigglers 'Down Down' to Butlins on the five-star Quo Express for a unique gig and party in 1990. 'Minehead, you're a rock'n'roll town!'

Lita Ford left the author boggle-eyed and tent-trousered when talking about taking her clothes off and wanting 'to get your brains fucked out'. She then did the rock'n'roll thing by swigging from a bottle of Jack Daniel's and handing it over as a parting gift. Cheers, Lita!

Former Whitesnake guitarist Steve Vai admitted it wasn't just his instrument he spent many hours playing with during his teenage years, when candidly confessing all about his sexual awakening and how he eventually learned that there's 'more to life than getting laid'. Er, really?

By royal appointment, Queen guitarist Brian May sat down for his first full-length interview following the death of vocalist Freddie Mercury, revealing his innermost thoughts on the tragedy and telling how he and his band-mates made it through the troubled times.

metal stuff they did, such as "Space Truckin'". I felt like a B act in a B-movie. It was nice singing with [lead vocalist] David Coverdale and the *Burn* record went very well. But this big live thing of five guys doing solos was the most boring shit. We got away with it but I didn't like it.'

So it's therefore no surprise to hear that Glenn intends to explore very different musical avenues, now that he has finally straightened himself out. 'At my age, I don't want to be onstage with long hair, grabbing my dick and saying I love the devil,' he insists. 'They say I've got the voice of rock but for me it's a soulful thing. I'm a soul singer in a rock genre. I've been trying to break out of the rock thing for years.'

Which explains a rather unlikely – albeit unsuccessful – rehearsal with soul legends Earth, Wind & Fire. 'It sounded like a very bad Las Vegas act,' he laughs. 'There were twelve black guys and me and when I started singing they put their fingers in their ears and said they had never heard a singer so loud. It was, "Er, can you turn it down a bit?" It was horrible!'

Hughes insists he can't get involved with musicians suffering from heavy drug problems. 'I *won't* work with people that have the disease,' he insists. 'I can't risk it. I'm not gonna be like Aerosmith or Mötley Crüe; if you're backstage with me you can have a drink, I don't care. I don't really have a problem with booze, because I only used booze to come down off the toot. But as for [others taking] coke and all the other mind-altering chemicals, I'd have a real problem working with somebody under those conditions.'

The reassurance about booze comes as a relief, as it's now time for yet another Carlsberg. 'Waiter, the same again, please.' Meanwhile, Glenn continues talking about the concept of using his experience to help others – or not, as the case may be. 'I see guys like [former Poison guitarist] CC DeVille and it's like a mini Glenn Hughes,' he says. 'This guy is either gonna end up dead or . . . I saw him at the Randy Rhoads thing and I felt like going up to him and saying, "Come on, look at *me*, for Christ's sake." But you can't do that. I'm in a very selfish programme, it's called "Let's Keep Glenn Alive And Fuck Everybody Else".'

Except Hughes is not 'fucking everybody else', if you'll pardon the expression. 'I'm sure Spike [of the Quireboys] wouldn't mind me telling you,' he confides, 'because he's been dry for almost two months now. He called me up and asked me to give him a helping hand, so I'm keeping an eye on him. And there are two other guys I sponsor – they call me every day and I give them guidelines. I live a very programmed existence. It's a twelve-step programme and I follow them all day long, so I have a somewhat boring lifestyle. But I'm around . . . and I'm gonna be around for a long time.'

Indeed he is, releasing nearly twenty albums over the next two decades and enjoying the most productive musical period of his life. Now that's worth drinking to.

MOTÖRHEAD: BUILT FOR SPEED

Meeting Motörhead in Marseille on one assignment in October 1988 is far easier said than done, but at least the boys supply 'breakfast' the next day, and the journey home simply 'speeds' by . . .

'**Y**ou're late!' croaks Lemmy as he steps out of the hotel elevator. Motörhead are in Marseille and it's the morning after the night before, the evening when the band, had their own time-keeping been in order, should have fulfilled an obligation to meet this writer at the hotel and provide transport to the gig being played miles out of town in the middle of nowhere. At Paul Ricard, to be precise.

As ever with Motörhead, particularly at this point in time when they're on the slide commercially, nothing goes quite as planned, and they're running so far behind schedule when they fly into France on Saturday evening that they decide to ditch their original plans and head straight to the festival site. And just to increase the element of chaos, and for reasons best known to themselves, they fail to advise anybody else of their change in plans.

Which means I'm left stranded, with not the faintest idea of how to get to the gig or the means – financial or otherwise – to get there even if I had. An evening in Marseille is not nearly as entertaining as might be imagined when you've next to no funds (and no cashpoint card), especially when there's the feeling that I shouldn't stray too far from the hotel just in case a message eventually does come through (which, of course, it never does).

So when Motörhead's tour manager finally makes the long-awaited call at ten o'clock the following morning and offers to meet me in the foyer, he's not exactly greeted in the most welcoming of terms – despite his apology and belated explanation as to why the band failed to show up.

Veteran frontman Lemmy, the man that is Motörhead, clearly sees the funny side of things as he arrives on the ground floor and shifts all responsibility for the previous night's fiasco onto the shoulders of others. To be fair, he offers to give an interview, but I tell him there's little point in him trying to talk about a gig I haven't seen and therefore can't write about. Journalists can say 'bollocks' too, you know.

Thankfully, the rest of the band, including guitarists Phil Campbell and Würzel, are sympathetic and invite me to return to one of their rooms for 'breakfast' – and, needless to say, cornflakes and toast are not on the menu. For normal human beings such indulgences so early in the morning would be unthinkable, but for the members of Motörhead – who all seem to have the constitutions of working farm animals – they are not just commonplace but a way of life; a daily routine no less.

Suitably revitalised, the band later leap into a minibus to head to the airport where a direct flight to London awaits. For yours truly, who has drawn the short straw, however, the itinerary requires hanging about at the hotel for another hour or so before eventually returning home – via Geneva. What appears on paper to be a monotonous journey – all the more frustrating given the fruitless nature of the trip – takes on a more promising look when a familiar face is spied at Marseille Airport; that of Phil Campbell. The wayward six-stringer has 'lost' his flight ticket and been hastily booked onto the only other plane available – which means he's also now heading to Geneva.

At this point we both realise there is good news and bad news. The latter is that there is a four-hour stopover at the Swiss airport; the former is that there is access to a first-class lounge, and the alcoholic drinks are complimentary. Inevitably, the afternoon literally speeds by; well, it always seems to be 'snowing' in Switzerland and today is no different – especially with members of Motörhead passing through. And the freezing cold weather might also account for certain travellers suffering from the sniffles . . .

KILLING JOKE: THE COLEMAN VISITS

Watching post-punk noise terrorists Killing Joke play for an audience of one early in 1994 is simply spliffing, but everyone gets even friendlier when Jaz Coleman surprisingly pops round for a cup of tea the following week . . .

Killing Joke are just beginning to crank up their menacing wall of sound when Jaz Coleman steps forward and offers the huge spliff he's just started to smoke. The post-punk noise terrorists are in a south London rehearsal studio by the name of Terminal 24, which they have made their own thanks to oriental carpets draping the walls and thin sheets hanging from the ceiling to veil various coloured lights. Large candles are perched upon huge speakers to illuminate the room and the smell of incense is in the air as the band begins to play for their rather conspicuous and self-conscious audience of one.

And it's impossible to know exactly what's in his mind when Jaz, who is dressed entirely in black, takes a long puff on his joint and then passes it over. Does he want me to simply hold – or rather *protect* – the crude cigarette for him as prepares to sing? Or is it safe to actually start smoking it – and therefore quickly erode its length? Either way, there's a genuine fear of incurring the wrath of one of rock's most intimidating frontmen if his intentions are misunderstood.

Thankfully, Jaz has more pressing issues on his mind as he attempts to orchestrate his band – which features barefooted bassist Youth and well-heeled guitarist Geordie – through golden oldie 'Wardance' and the eastern-flavoured 'Communion'. Youth has worked hard to create a relaxed ambience in the studio but there's tension in the air as Jaz struggles to find his voice amidst the chaos and cacophony being constructed behind him.

Suddenly, the singer's patience with the sound engineer snaps. 'I want somebody who fucking knows what they're fucking doing!' he spits with venom.

> # 'I want somebody who fucking knows what they're fucking doing!'
> ### – Jaz Coleman

Original members Youth and Geordie know their eccentric singer far too well to start worrying about such tantrums, but the session players on drums and keyboards clearly feel extremely uncomfortable with the anger and uncertainty as they shoot nervous looks at each other. Indeed, I sense I've witnessed something a bit too private – behaviour just not intended for the consumption of outsiders – after penetrating Killing Joke's inner sanctum.

Then, just as Coleman seems set to explode with fury, he suddenly emits a laugh that changes the atmosphere in a split-second. And no, he doesn't get his spliff back . . .

Less than a week later, the phone rings at home and it's Jaz saying he's popping round for a cup of tea. This seems no less surprising for the fact that he has indeed been invited. My girlfriend used to live with the singer many moons ago – honest – and is only too keen to catch up with him once again when she learns of our meeting the previous week. 'Give Jaz my love,' she says, 'and let him know he can always come by.'

What's not expected is that Coleman will actually take her up on the offer, and so it's something of a mild shock when, after just a few days, he rings and then turns up on our Maida Vale doorstep. Jaz is not alone, though, having dragged along a young female acquaintance who is apparently working for his record company but has more than a familiar face after recently appearing on the Soho scene.

Tea and sandwiches appear from the kitchen, but it quickly becomes apparent that our guests are not hungry; indeed, they are looking rather glassy-eyed. Pretty soon, everybody is in a very relaxed state of mind.

The television is on but nobody is taking much notice of it. That is until it's suddenly announced on the news that Nirvana singer Kurt Cobain has been found dead in Seattle after taking a shotgun to his own head. The room is filled with shock. Gee, he must have been out of his mind on *something* when committing such an outrageous and self-destructive act.

It's decided that the atmosphere needs lifting. The conversation babbles on and the sound of the TV fades into the background . . .

HAWKWIND: DOCTOR FEELGOOD

Pharmaceuticals are never far from mind when entering the orbit of space travellers Hawkwind, not least when meeting up with veteran chief pilot Dave Brock in Liverpool in October 1990, and trying to establish whether he's still partial to the odd indulgence now and again . . .

You think of Hawkwind; you think of drugs. So it's entirely natural to ask Dave Brock, the guiding light behind the band's unique brew of strangeness and charm over the past three decades, whether he still experiments with illegal substances when the opportunity arises.

'*Experiment?*' he asks, with eyebrows raised. 'I don't have to anymore. I'm a doctor now!'

Brock is seated backstage at the Royal Court Theatre in Liverpool, where Hawkwind are set to play. In fact the vocalist and guitarist remains on his backside for the rest of the evening – including the gig itself – because of a damaged ankle that is heavily bandaged. It's tempting to imagine that the entire band will end up playing in wheelchairs in the end. Not that Brock's incapacity matters tonight, as he and his fellow space bandits keep a low visual profile onstage compared to the psychedelic lightshow that dominates their performances.

Speaking of psychedelics . . . 'Well, yeah, dabbling in psychedelic drugs does influence you in your way of life really,' admits Brock when asked about the drug-infested image of the group. But he denies that the band is still 'dabbling' as much as might be imagined.

'Not the way we used to – if we'd continued to do that we'd all be wrecked,' he scoffs, looking just a little, er, wrecked. Or maybe that's because he could be about ninety-eight years of age. 'You learn all the time,' he continues. 'You take LSD and you learn from it. You don't have to be obsessively taking things all the time. Some people are addicted to these things, other people aren't. I find myself that I'm not.'

He watches me slurp at a pint of lager. 'Loads of people drink a lot,' he says with perfect timing. 'That's more serious really because a lot of people won't face the fact they're alcoholics. They have to go down the pub every day and yet they won't admit they're addicted to alcohol. Huwie [Lloyd-Langton, former Hawkwind guitarist] came to learn that.'

Another old colleague of cosmic craziness who learned a lesson or two when it came to recreational activities is Motörhead main man Lemmy, who might have considered it a bit rich for Hawkwind to eject him from the band for being caught in possession of amphetamine sulphate – otherwise known as speed – while the band were crossing the US/Canada border in the mid-1970s. 'I was the one who had to tell Lemmy,' reflects Brock ruefully. 'It was very sad. It was a bad mistake [on our part], but such is life.'

It sets Brock thinking about things he is not happy with. 'I'll tell you what you can put down,' he says, as if I'm taking notes. 'About the load of owed royalties we never get. So many stupid companies keep putting these old compilations out. But we don't get any royalties. We've tried suing people but it costs a lot of money. It's all corrupt this business, isn't it?'

> **'Experiment? I don't have to anymore – I'm a doctor now!'**
> **– Dave Brock**

Absolutely. But he's not finished yet. 'It's like a painting,' he says. 'You get an artist who can paint a picture and a band that creates music – which is basically an art form – and out of this you get huge amounts of people making money out of them. And the band are always bottom of the pile.'

And so the grumbling continues . . . 'We never actually got any gold or silver discs! That's another piss off. We sold a quarter of a million records or something and the record company were gonna give us our gold discs at some big feast they were laying on. We never went and we never got them. I wrote and so did Lemmy, but to this day we've never received any. It *really* pisses me off.'

Brock pauses to think about Hawkwind's status as non-stop road warriors who will probably continue until the planet stops spinning. 'We've become a laughable institution now,' he admits.

And everybody else in the room laughs.

SEX ON THE BRAIN

'I have thousands of people screaming at my feet, a large bank account and get laid whenever I wanna get laid.' The rock'n'roll lifestyle certainly seems to keep Lita Ford happy. And the same can be said for the likes of Gene Simmons and Rick Parfitt, among others, who down the years have enjoyed more sexual experiences than they could ever hope to remember as a direct consequence of their fame – as they happily declared to this (rather envious) writer.

There's a particular reason why the topic of female conquests was raised when I found myself talking to Kiss legend Simmons but, aside from that, there's no denying that we all have a natural curiosity when it comes to the sexploits of rock stars. They spend months on the road, are idolised by their fans and are relentlessly pursued by the opposite sex. The lifestyle presents an abundance of opportunities because rockers exude a sexual allure that mere mortals seem to find irresistible, and hence there's no shortage of willing partners (for one night, at least).

Take, for example, an early trip to Germany to join melodic rockers Shy on tour. Shy by name, not so Shy by nature it seems. The Brummies were supporting Gary Moore throughout Europe to promote their debut major-label album, *Excess All Areas*. Moore was staying in hotels; Shy were sleeping on a tour bus, such is the way things are. The band was in Hamburg, with your *Metal Hammer* representative along for the ride, when they picked up a couple of local girls after the show.

The following morning, the young females were still on the bus as it headed towards Hannover. When their presence was no longer required, the girls found themselves by the roadside in the middle of nowhere. Nobody stopped to wonder how – or *if* – they ever managed to find their way home . . .

Meanwhile, in the Soho scene around the Marquee Club and St Moritz there were plenty of girls who freely made themselves available to the bands passing through, and the theory was that if you bedded one of them, it meant you had indirectly slept with the same people they had. In moments of boredom, journalists and other regular liggers would compare unlikely Top Ten charts of distant bedfellows, with the likes of Uriah Heep rubbing shoulders with Terraplane, the Alarm, Killing Joke and, er, the Average White Band.

Musicians are rather less inclined to discuss their sexperiences for obvious reasons, but it was discovered that they would occasionally open up if talking to a high-class publication such as *Penthouse*, which I represented during a brief period, although it was very much a case of choosing one's targets carefully.

And so the boisterous boys of Wolfsbane, very much titillated by the idea of appearing in a sex magazine, were more than happy to lift the lid on a recent trek across the States, and how and where they generally accommodate their carnal cravings ('there's the dressing room, the dark alley and the back of the transit on top of all the gear'), while the supremely studious Steve Vai, a man of considerable intellect, was content to talk at length about his relationships with the opposite gender, having toured the world with the likes of Frank Zappa, Whitesnake and David Lee Roth, and developed some sense of sophistication and sagacity.

These are not words one would generally associate with Status Quo – even if they have been around for longer than some sexual diseases – and Rick Parfitt certainly didn't disappoint when we met at Wembley Arena. 'If it had long legs and high heels I'd shag it,' he quipped, although it might surprise some to learn that he was talking about his guitar. Quite how he would manage this feat was never discussed . . .

As he admitted, Rick's pulled a few birds in his time, but it's not being unkind to suggest that he lacks the sex appeal of Lita Ford or the twin sisters who fronted Gypsy Queen during their brief stab at stardom. Lita is a lady but doesn't always talk like one ('It's about wanting to get your brains fucked out,' she delightfully announced of one of her songs) while Paula and Pamela Mattioli played such games in public during our conversation that they attracted the attentions of a gynaecologist, whose number they chose not to take . . .

KISS: CALLING DR LOVE

Gene Simmons might have his 'Love Gun' permanently at the ready, but as is discovered in the early part of 1993, in rather

unfortunate circumstances, the legendary fire-breathing frontman of costumed cock-rockers Kiss might not put the X in sex in quite the way he'd like, despite his compulsion to keep talking about it . . .

Caroline the make-up artist is on top and, it is reassuring to report, writhing around in the throes of passion. She's moaning to the heavens with a succession of 'oohs' and 'aahs' (no, honest) until she suddenly announces, 'Ooh, you've got a much bigger cock than Gene Simmons of Kiss.' Talk about instant down periscope . . .

Several weeks later, Gene Simmons – of Kiss – is on the phone reminiscing about one of his sexual experiences. 'It was one of the most *magical* moments,' insists the legendary lothario, who claims to have bedded thousands of ladies in his time. 'This girl was drop-dead gorgeous,' he continues in that deep and serious voice of his. 'She had blood-red lips, turquoise pools for eyes and Technicolor hair. I remember her smell, I remember her taste, I remember the feel of her skin, but ironically . . . I don't remember her name.'

'I remember her smell, her taste, the feel of her skin, but ironically . . . I don't remember her name.'
– Gene Simmons

It becomes clear that Gene is not talking about a recent conquest in England – despite much prompting on my part, just for the hell of it – but one of his very first encounters with a member of the opposite sex back home after becoming the darkest cornerstone of Kiss, the demonic 'God Of Thunder' himself. 'She didn't have a fucking clue which band I was in, but she wanted to be with me *because* I was in a band. And I thought that was the most romantic notion I'd ever heard.'

Despite the face-paint and theatrics, New York's heaviest stack-heeled strutters were always more cock-rock than shock-rock. So it's no surprise that Simmons – whose band recorded the song 'Let's Put The X In Sex', not to mention the classic 'Love Gun' – remains quite content to continue discussing the female form. 'We have a song called "Take It Off" during the show, where we have local strippers come up onstage to, er, take it off. We have to audition each of these girls, show 'em what to do and so on . . . Well, *somebody's* got to do it,' he admits. 'One girl was so talented – she had these enormous breasts and her talent consisted of being able to crush empty beer cans between her tits. We actually have that on film, by the way.'

As if anybody would ever doubt his word. At the height of their costumed capers, Simmons and colleagues Paul Stanley, Ace Frehley and Peter Criss inspired a devoted and loyal following in the form of what was known as the 'Kiss Army'. But the band themselves lost their way and Gene admits to having become distracted by the trappings of success and fame, particularly during the 1980s when Kiss removed their comic-book faces and their music became literally faceless as co-frontman Stanley assumed greater control. 'I was seduced by [forming] record companies, [acting in] movies, [managing] Liza Minnelli and wanting to produce every act in the world,' confesses Simmons. 'In essence, I was symbolically tugging on other people's shirts and saying, "Look, I really *am* good, I *can* do other things." The reason was because I was lost in Kiss and I wasn't being fulfilled. That revelation only comes in retrospect, when you look and say, "I wasn't happy."

'I had to stop dilly-dallying with all that outside stuff, stop squiring cute models to restaurants and going to these senseless Hollywood parties where it's all about who's more famous or who's got more money. It's a lot of fun while you're doing it, but when you walk away there's a very empty feeling. The band suffered and I've got to be honest enough to admit that, for close to a decade, my contribution towards the band was pretty much nil. But the truth is that some of the crappier records sold enormous amounts, more than some of the better records.

'There's been internal turmoil, especially when certain members decided that chemicals and alcohol were more important than rock'n'roll. But when a band has been around long enough, you pick up all kinds of dirt and lice.'

Ultimately, it's reassuring to discover that Gene, master of cunning fire-breathing stunts, finds it impossible to tackle any topic in Kisstory without making some kind of sexual reference. 'When we started, we all had an innocence, a kind of open-eyed wonder at everything,' he confides. 'But once you experience something, you can never recapture that original feeling again. You can never go back to "BV" – Before Virginity.'

WOLFSBANE: THEY LIKE IT HOT

Britain's self-styled 'howling mad shitheads' have just returned from a tour of the United States in the early part of 1990 and are eager to tell their wicked tales of booze, birds and bad language as this writer – representing **Penthouse** *magazine – tries hard to squeeze the sleaze out of them . . .*

'She was such a dirty slut!' declares Blaze Bayley as he thinks back to Wolfsbane's last American tour in tandem with Overkill. 'This girl was following the band we were supporting and she even got off with the bloke who sells the T-shirts. He was terrible, absolutely disgusting, and even the other band was coming up to us and saying, "You should *see* what Paul's picked up tonight!" You'd go over to the merchandising area and there'd be this bird, who was fifty if she was a day, with eyes in the back of her head, looking like she'd been doing heroin for the last three weeks. He'd say to her, "I'd like you to meet Blaze; Blaze, this is Pauline . . ."

'Anyway, this guy then picked up this young girl; she must have been seventeen − if that − and an obvious runaway. He'd got her on the bus and she did the *entire* band, the driver, the whole bus . . . A bit later, we were in the hotel in Texas and she was still knocking around, so when the guys got bored and drunk, of course, they thought they'd have another go. There'd be four or five of them in this one room having a go at this girl . . .'

Guitarist Jase Edwards, who is keeping Blaze company today, admits he took real pity on the young woman in question. 'I asked her later if she was okay because I couldn't believe she actually wanted this to happen. I'd say, "You okay, then?" and she'd say, "Yeah." I said to her, "Look, if it gets out of hand or if they try to make you do anything you don't want to do, just let me know and we'll get you out of it." And she said, "No, I'm fine." Some of the stuff we saw, it was like, how can anybody *do* that?'

It's not quite the sympathetic view you'd expect to hear from Wolfsbane, the bunch of heavy-metal hooligans whose *Live Fast, Die Fast* debut album − produced by the soon-to-become-legendary Rick Rubin, no less − promises 'wicked tales of booze, birds and bad language'. Especially as the Tamworth quartet were hardly behaving like choirboys themselves on the road. 'The thing is, it's a very sleazy lifestyle,' admits Blaze, future singer of Iron Maiden, sitting in the lounge bar of a swanky hotel near London's Sloane Square and being egged on by yours truly for what will hopefully be a salacious feature for *Penthouse* magazine. 'On the "Birds, Booze And Bad Language" tour we were out of control really. We were absolutely outrageous, some nights it was disgusting.'

'Yeah,' confirms Jase. 'There are a few things you look back on and think, "I wouldn't do *that* again."'

Wolfsbane are rude and crude, loud and proud. There's not much room for sophistication in their world, as their stage patter with their audience would suggest. 'Hey you, you with the glasses, get your fucking hands in the air or fuck off! Let's have some fuckin' noise, you wankers!' would be a typical greeting from Bayley on the boards. But it seems that women are strangely attracted by the vocalist's unkempt appearance and uncouth ways.

'I can see that,' concurs Blaze, in his West Midlands accent, once I've put such a view to him, 'especially with some of the women I've ended up with. Most of them are after a bit of rough, d'ya know what I mean? I've usually ended up with really raunchy girls. They're sleazy, the ones who want to grab hold of your cock. On this tour, a couple of birds have unzipped my fly and tried to get my cock out, which I thought was quite amazing. I remember the time I got off with a porn-film star. I got this incredible blowjob and I thought I was getting my brains sucked out through my dick. It was absolutely the most outrageous thing I'd ever experienced.'

Not that the band would ever stoop so low as to grapple with groupies, however. 'We *never* mess with groupies,' insists Blaze. 'You've got to be very pissed or very hard up to go with a groupie.'

'I mean,' adds Jase, 'groupies are so obviously groupies.'

So, I ask, what's the difference between a groupie and any other girl that might turn up at a gig and succumb to the band's irresistible charms?

'A groupie is someone who will follow the band to more than one show, try and sleep with every single member of the band and not have very high moral standards or standards of cleanliness,' states Blaze, having clearly put a lot of thought into the subject. 'Whereas we're more into clean girls; someone who takes care of their nails and has nice underwear. The thing is, you don't know what you're gonna catch, either. [Or rather you *do* know what you're gonna catch, I'm tempted to say.] You've got to take precautions; that's a certainty. AIDS isn't the only thing around. It's a pain in the arse if you catch something, so you'd better just stick with a clean girl – someone really nice and have a great time – than go with a groupie who's just gonna be like, "Oh great, I did you a favour there."'

'And how does one find a good clean girl?' I enquire.

'It's not always easy, is it?' admits Blaze. 'You don't take the first thing that's offered to you.'

Do girls generally assume the band is staying in a nice hotel when they've actually got a battered transit van outside?

'They can't come back to the hotel anyway,' says Bayley, 'because it's generally a long drive and I'm sharing with the drummer, so it's on the dressing room floor. The last tour was a classic where it was like, "Where is he? We're supposed to be on stage now, hold the intro tape while we find the singer." Because you're in the toilet with some bird who you've been lucky enough to meet before the show.'

Not a groupie then?

'She wasn't a groupie,' insists Blaze, indicating that it was perhaps a one-off occasion rather than a regular occurrence. 'She was after a bit of rough on her night out.'

So where does 'a bit of rough' undertake his shagging after a gig?

'Well,' says Blaze, 'there's the dressing room, there's the dark alley out the back and there's the back of the transit on top of all the gear. Where else is there?'

Where indeed . . . So who pulls most frequently in the band?

'Me,' says Blaze. 'Probably.'

Is there any rivalry between the guys?

'I dunno,' says Jase. 'It depends on if somebody's got a girlfriend. If they haven't, they'll go out and have a good time. I was getting a lot of stick once about not getting off with any girls, so one night I got this girl into the tour bus. I didn't do it because I *wanted* to do it, it was almost as if I'd been put up to it.'

'The thing is,' says Blaze, 'a relationship is very hard to keep in this business, because you're in a sweetshop all the time with a fiver. You want to try everything. But I think girlfriends are important as well. It's important to have someone in your life. There's nothing like when you're in a relationship with someone, when you get on really well and you really know the person. You have great sex, don't you? It's the best, there's no two ways about it. The casual encounter is always very exciting, but it's not as good as *real* sex with someone you really know.

'I've had some great girlfriends,' he continues. 'I've really liked them and got on with them tremendously, but I've lost every one because of my commitment and obsession with the music. And being in the band. Because I've wanted that so much, it's been impossible to maintain a relationship. With the last one I just thought, "I can't go on feeling guilty any more about committing myself to my music." And it's so hard to be faithful . . .'

So what type of woman does Blaze prefer?

'Someone who has intelligence, somebody I can talk to, is brainy, been to college,' he says. 'I love brainy girls, someone you can actually sit down and have a conversation with, someone who you fancy loads but can end up talking to so much that you never actually get round to having sex with. That's my ideal woman.'

What about American girls?

'I think they're brought up to be a lot more feminine,' says Bayley, 'and brought up to have long hair a lot more. It's always been a very glamorous thing, long hair. Everybody fantasises about girls with gorgeous hair and over there it's less artistic or radical but they're brought up that way. And I love that. They're brought up to be feminine and caring, it's a lot different.'

'They look after their bodies as well,' adds Jase, before Blaze remembers a particularly enjoyable evening. 'I think it was Dallas where we were,' he says. 'They have a lot of strip bars there and it's where some of the *Playboy* bunnies work and stuff like that. And this absolutely gorgeous bird came over to the hotel one night. We were on the balcony and all these other guys were going, "Get your tits out," and all this, but she was a classic broad, even though she was a dancer. That's the thing about a lot of American bands; if a girl comes up to talk to them they instantly assume that she wants sex. Where if a girl comes up to us we think she's one of our fans. She would only talk to us and I ended up with her.'

'A lot of dancers are incredible people,' says Jase, 'because they're really wise about life and the way things are. They're not naive in any way and are really interesting. They're also very giving; know what I mean?'

'Er, yeah,' I say, pretending to be very familiar with the giving nature of American *Playboy* bunnies. 'Does booze take responsibility for some of Wolfsbane's carnal connections on the road?' I ponder.

'It's been responsible for most of my trips to the ladies' toilets,' says Blaze. 'You can find much better places than that if you're not pissed.'

And is it fair to assume that it can be blamed for an occasional dip in standards?

'Yes,' admits Blaze. 'Definitely. I'm really glad that I drink hardly at all now. I have a couple of beers after [the gig] and because you're still vibed up it goes straight down. Two bottles of [Newcastle] Brown and you're . . . But definitely, it does lower your standards.'

'Well, every woman has their pint value, don't they?' I suggest.

'Definitely!' concurs Blaze.

'There are some girls who don't look quite as good the next day,' admits Jase, 'but they've never been hideous. But after a show, you come offstage and you're full of adrenalin, so I do have a drink to calm myself down. And sometimes you have another one . . .'

'I've seen Jase have "another one" a couple of times and it's been when you've got to stay awake,' says Blaze, 'so I've had to wake him up every hour to make sure he doesn't slip into a coma. You go onto the tour bus and there's sick everywhere.'

'That only happened once,' insists Jase, 'and I wasn't with a girl.'

Inevitably, Wolfsbane are not short of anecdotes about life on the road, much to my gleeful satisfaction. 'There was the time they were looking for me before the gig,' reveals Blaze, 'because this girl was one of twins and I nearly had them both. And after the show there was another one again, another bird hanging around.'

'So does that count as two or three girls in one night?' I ask.

'I think it's got to be two,' says Blaze. 'Although I've had a snog and a fumble with three.'

'How's about that bird I fucked and nailed to the wall in Chiswick?' offers Jase.

'And there's the classic situation,' says Blaze. 'The tour manager goes round to find everybody and then he knocks on all the dressing-room doors and shouts, "Bayley, get your clothes on, we're leaving now!" When he wants to find me, that's one of the classics.

'There have been so many things that have happened. When we were doing the video for "I Like It Hot", we all went out the night before and got absolutely pissed and then, when we were filming the next day, our drummer Steve [Ellett] said to the director, "I can throw up for you." And he said, "What do you mean?" And Steve said, "Well, you tell me when you want me to throw up so that you can film it and I'll throw up for you." And the director was like, "Really?" So on the second day of the shoot, we're outside the Houses of Parliament and Steve goes, "Do you want me to throw up now?" And he goes, "Okay, Steve, let's go then." And Steve's there, puking his guts up outside the Houses of Parliament and we were laughing so much it made us all feel sick. It was totally outrageous!

'She did the entire band, the driver, the whole bus . . .'

– Blaze Bayley

'There was the tour with the Quireboys as well. We only did about six or seven dates with them, but it was totally out of hand. Get a bunch of lads like that together and it's lager for breakfast! We were at this one gig and had made a bit of money – we'd sold a few T-shirts – and I'd had sex in the bogs with some tart. I can't remember what her name was . . .'

'With a groupie or would she have been a *nice* girl?' I ask.

'She was really nice,' insists Blaze, 'although this was in the days before we made the distinction. We thought we'd get a crate of Budweiser and have a party, so Steve and Guy [Bailey from the Quireboys] start shot-gunning these cans of beer. And they were going, "I bet you a fiver I can throw up faster than you." And all you could see outside was these two people puking up the wall. It was crazy.'

If a girl tried to get into the Wolfsbane dressing room, would she always make her way in or would somebody be guarding the door in the interests of, er, quality control?

'Yeah, there *is* quality control,' affirms Blaze. 'But it's always after the show. Before the show we keep our dressing room as private as we can. The best thing is when you're supporting someone, because if you're on first you get the chance to chat up all the birds while the main band is onstage. That way you get the pick.'

'I like to go out and chat up someone when they don't know who you are, when they don't know you're in a band,' reveals Jase.

'That's one of the things I like about America,' states Blaze. 'The girls I really liked were the ones who hadn't seen the band. You see, the thing I learned from the tour in Britain – and I wasn't going to make the same mistake in America – was that I wasn't going to go with any dodgy boilers, because those were the people I'd meet again [on the next tour]. So I thought, "Right,

I'm going to really raise my standards," so the only girls I'd meet again were the ones I'd definitely want to see again. There are so many over here where you think, "Oh no, don't let that one see me." I just thought, "I'm not going to waste my time, they've got to be nice." And that's what happened, there weren't any really bad ones.'

Have Wolfsbane ever been accused of having sexist attitudes?

'All the time,' confesses Blaze. 'I think it's totally unjustified as well because, like we've said, we've never treated a girl like a groupie. We treat girls with the greatest of respect. I like feminine women.'

'I love women,' says Jase, 'so I don't see why I should be slagged off for degrading them and being sexist, because I have the utmost respect for women. I love being with women.'

'I can't see that any of our songs are degrading to women,' says Blaze. 'They're just about sharing experiences of sex. It's just my side of it.'

Doesn't the band's catchphrase of 'birds, booze and bad language' sound sexist?

'We're not sexist,' responds Jase, 'but it is a valid question to ask. We've kind of set ourselves up without thinking about it, haven't we?'

'I once had this argument with somebody,' says Blaze. 'It's like the word "birds", some people say that's such a derogatory term, but it's only like saying "the lads", isn't it? It's only a term you use and it always evokes in my mind, when you say "birds", it's like dolly birds, it's just a gorgeous, feminine woman.'

'I just feel that the more successful I become the more I'll be able to meet people like that and have a chance of making a relationship work. Just coming home to somebody is an absolute knockout, somebody who's got a brain, a body, is feminine and is there for you. So what people say about us doesn't bother me. I think you can accuse us of being sexist and good luck to the people who think that.'

'Any thoughts on the campaign against pornography?' I ask, seeing as I'm representing an adult magazine on this occasion.

'I'm not sure about it,' says Blaze, looking troubled. 'I'm not sure that it really does affect people that badly. It's the same thing as people trying to ban heavy metal. If people are unbalanced, they're unbalanced. And something will push them over, it doesn't matter what it is. No matter what kind of music they listen to or what kind of material they read. Especially hardcore porn – it's not like it's widely available, you have to go and get the stuff and smuggle it into the country. You have to do a search through really seedy shops in Soho and the magazines are all wrapped up, so you don't even know if there's a beaver shot in half of them. Let's face it, they're crap. And these places are horrible to go into. And the people that work there treat like you a cunt.'

'Not that you've been to these places,' I suggest.

'Well,' he admits, 'I have to do my research.'

'Is there anything wrong with glamour magazines such as *Penthouse*?' I ask.

'Not at all,' says Jase, 'especially if you talk to the girls in it. They find the feminist attitude towards something like *Penthouse* as offensive as the magazine is to some people. They'll shout about it, saying, "How dare these people try to take away our rights to do what we want to do? It's our right to be feminine and look like women if we want to." And I'm like, "Sorry, I was just asking, I don't mind." So you think, "Hang on a second, this woman obviously knows what she's talking about."'

'You get a superiority complex from the people who are against it,' moans Blaze. 'They're so superior it makes me sick.'

'But people put *Penthouse* in the same category as *Razzle* or *Fucking Housewife Monthly* and label it all pornography,' I offer.

'It's a terrible thing,' nods Blaze, 'although *Razzle* is a bit dodgy, isn't it? I hate it; I never buy a copy of that. I think I bought a copy once and binned it after about half an hour. Where I used to work at KP Snacks, this fella used to love anything to do with porn and he smuggled some magazines back from Amsterdam. There were some really sick ones. But even those weren't as bad as *Razzle* and some of the boilers in there. Some of these porn girls have seen the wrong side of life and they've got a drug habit they have to keep up, so that's all they can do.'

I mention that Blaze often refers to the size of his dick onstage.

'He's normally saying how *small* it is rather than how big it is,' says Jase. However, Bayley reveals that he's simply being ironic. 'When we were coming up as a young band, we were up against all the Def Leppard impersonators; the Whitesnake thing – "I am enormous and my microphone stand is totally phallic." And I just find that very amusing.'

'I always used to think how stupid they would look if you took the music away,' laughs Jase. 'All that posing about, they'd look totally hilarious. We get criticised for taking the piss out of people, but it's about not falling into that trap and being a bit more honest about it.'

'It's just a little joke I have with the audience,' confirms Blaze. 'It's just me saying, "Look, I'm the same as you."'

'You can say anything if it makes people laugh,' says Jase. 'It's about making sure people have a good time at the shows.'

'I want that big bastard laugh when I see a band,' says Blaze. 'You know, a ridiculous laugh, when you say, "Oh yes! What a bastard for doing that!" When I go to see a band, I like to see them shove themselves down your throat. There you go, you bastards!'

Are Wolfsbane generally misunderstood?

'Sometimes,' admits Blaze, before Jase picks up the baton.

'We've got a song called "Greasy" and it's about people who put you down.

It goes right back to when teachers told you that you were a waste of time because you've got long hair and a denim jacket with patches on the back. It got said to me all the time at school. "You're a waste of time, you're no good, you're rubbish, you'll never be anything." And after a while, you think, "Fuck you!" So "Greasy" is about these people who tell you that you'll never be any good.'

'What's "I Like It Hot" about then?' I ask.

'It's obvious what it's about,' replies Blaze. 'I like it hot! It's about steamy, sweaty sex – the best kind.'

'Er, thanks for clearing that up, chaps,' I say. 'Now, about the new album . . .'

STEVE VAI: 'I WAS A SLUT'

Forget the warfare, it's all about the passion as American guitarist Steve Vai relaxes in a London hotel in August 1990 and reveals his sexual journey through rock'n'roll, whereby he arrives at the conclusion that 'there's more to life than getting laid'. And no, he's not kidding . . .

'I knew I was in trouble with sex from the time when I realised how to masturbate – I would do it seven times a day.'

Steve Vai is considered a widdly guitarist. But it's obvious the G3 and former Whitesnake, David Lee Roth and Frank Zappa showman spent his formative years in New York playing with rather more than just his guitar. Not that he needed to rely on his wrist action – at least in terms of sexual matters – once he started to tour the globe.

'There was a point in my life when I pulled the feathers off every bird I could find,' he confides. 'I was very much a slut. When I went out on the road, the whole world was like a candy store. I came out of a room I'd practised [guitar] in for years and years and I had a penis. And there were a lot of other people interested in that penis. That's the way it works in this business. There are things at your disposal that aren't available to the normal man.

'I never flattered myself with the idea that I was attractive or anything,' he adds. 'But it doesn't matter, if you're in a rock band that's enough. In a situation like I'm in, you can have anything you want. And that can be pretty dangerous. Any kind of sex you can fantasise about can be made available to you. You've got to be careful with that. When I started, I was really promiscuous, I would stay up all night and meet three or four different women.'

'All at once?' I ask.

'Oh, that's happened, sure. You can get really wrapped up in that kind of thing,' he says. 'And especially when I was I out with David Lee Roth, every bird, so to speak, wanted to fly your way. And if you take advantage of that, I really think it's not the best thing.'

Vai is sitting in his London record company's offices and, because this interview is for *Penthouse* magazine, he is prepared to discuss issues rather more personal than what his favourite guitar is and who made a guest appearance on his most recent solo album. With his dark demeanour and chiselled cheekbones, it's easy to imagine women falling at the feet of Vai when he is in their company – and he smiles when I put the idea to him.

'Believe it or not,' he says, 'I never approached a woman. Once, years and years ago, I picked up a girl in a bar. Once. What I used to do was just sit there and look complacent and that was the thing that would warm up a relationship. Because if a woman thinks you're coming on to her in a very macho kind of way, it could be a turn off. And I never had the nerve to come on to them in that kind of way. But I could still put the sex vibe on them if I wanted to.'

> **'I'll be orgasming and laughing hysterically because it's so funny.'**
> — Steve Vai

Vai is considered a studious musician. Listen to *Passion And Warfare* or *Sex & Religion*. But he is equally as analytical when it comes to sex – in terms of the mental and physical experience. 'The sexual drive is extremely intense,' he says. 'It's something that's built in as the number one instinct, to carry the race on. The only reason we live is so that we can reproduce. It's something that's been in us through evolution from the very beginning.

'When you're indulging in sexual activity, you're striving for union. I mean, think of what it looks like when two people are having sex. They bang each other; they actually try to get inside each other to the point that they're hitting each other. Sometimes when I'm having sex, I find that hysterical. I'll be orgasming and laughing hysterically because it's so funny sometimes. Look at it, isn't it hysterical?

'I just love the whole feeling of orgasm and sex and that's why I behaved the way I did back then. But what I realised when I was striving for a lot of sex was that I was looking for something and basically the women were too. After the sexual gratification there was usually an emptiness and I realised I had to take a different approach.'

Vai speaks candidly as he reveals how the limitless availability of sex with virtual strangers – groupies, some would call them – began to affect not only his self-esteem but also his view of women. 'I knew I was getting in deeper and deeper,' he admits. 'It got the to the point where I would view every woman I looked at in a sexual nature. And I would think they were looking at me that way too because that's the kind of people I was surrounded by at one point. I was losing a certain respect that I had for women and I realised I didn't want to run my life that way.

'I realised I wanted to have a lasting relationship with somebody and have something I really valued. And you have to have a commitment for that. I wanted to create a real bond between me and another person because I felt that was what needed to be important in my life.

'The thing is now, when I get to different cities, I meet a lot of women and I approach them differently, with a different look in my eye. I don't set up any barriers between beautiful women and fat women – if I'm gonna sit and spend time with somebody and get to know them, I'll try to fill a certain void that goes beyond sexual desire. And as a result, I have a lot more girl *friends*. And I have a lot more respect and love for women because I'm not taking advantage of their sexual desires – because they all have them and I know how to take advantage of that.

'If I ever want one-night stands it's purely on a platonic, conversational level and we're both usually left with more than just cleaning up the mess. I don't condemn people who have sex with many women and I don't condemn people who don't – I mean, I practise celibacy at times and that's very hard. It can be dangerous too. But after a while, you realise there's more to life than just getting laid.'

LITA FORD: SHE'S GOT THE JACK

Former Runaways guitarist and solo artist Lita Ford looks so hot when being interviewed for a glamour magazine in the summer of 1990 that it's impossible to avoid asking her if she'd like to divest herself of her clothing. Look, it's a dirty job, but somebody's gotta do it . . .

'So, Lita Ford, would you consider taking your clothes off?' With her messed-up blonde hair, sexy smile and *Dangerous Curves* – as one of her album titles suggests – it's the obvious question to ask the ultimate hard-rock chick as she sits just inches away from me in a tight skirt, skimpy top and leather jacket.

'I'd love to,' she says, leaving me distinctly boggle-eyed and tent-trousered. Sadly, the former Runaways guitarist and current solo artist is responding to the idea of stripping for *Penthouse* magazine as opposed to feeling an immediate inclination to drop her knickers for the sake of it. 'It would depend on the situation and circumstances,' she adds, as she looks around the record company office she's holed up in for the next half an hour or so. 'But I don't consider myself to be a sex symbol. I think I'm more of a rock'n'roll figure.'

Lita's latest album, *Stiletto*, another mix of raunchy rockers and polished, radio-friendly tunes, didn't get the best of reviews in UK trade magazine *Music Week*, with its writer moaning, 'Surely the time has come for female rock and rollers to sing about something more interesting than, "Will you put hand on my thigh?"'

'Is *that* what I'm singing about?' she asks me, cute nose put ever so slightly out of joint.

'Well, that's what the reviewer claims you're singing about,' I tell her.

'He's a fucking arsehole,' she spits in reply. 'And he hasn't listened to my record. Fuck *you*, buddy.'

But are there songs on *Stiletto* that fall into that category?

'Of course,' admits Lita, 'but the whole album's not like that. And what's wrong with putting hands on thighs anyway? This guy's a dickhead, a *fucking* dickhead. Dickhead!

'When you're a teenager in a crazy rock'n'roll band, you learn stuff you'd never learn in school.'
– Lita Ford

'I mean, there's a song for my mother, a ballad called "Lisa", and there's nothing about hands on thighs there. Then there's "Aces & Eights" which is about the gangs in east LA and the sort of fatherly/brotherly love that sort of grows up with the dangerous, drug-infested life. No thighs in there either. Of course, "Hungry (For Your Sex)" is a song about wanting to get your brains fucked out, but it's not about putting hands on fucking thighs – and that's speaking mildly.'

There are suggestions that Lita's marriage to WASP guitarist Chris Holmes, one of rock's true wild men, is on the rocks after just a few months. But she dismisses the story as 'just a rumour' before adding, 'It's a bunch of bullshit.'

A totally pissed-up Holmes was famously seen showering himself with two bottles of vodka in a swimming pool – as his mother watched on, believe it or not – in a movie titled *The Decline Of Western Civilization Part Two: The Metal Years*, which portrayed Lita's husband as a complete alcoholic. 'A fair suggestion?' I tentatively ask.

'Yeah,' admits Lita. 'He likes to drink.'

'And is that something both of you can happily live with?' I ask.

'Yeah.'

So, does Lita also like to drink?

'Yeah,' she shrugs. 'In fact, would you like some Jack Daniel's?'

I nod. And with that, she bends down to reach into her handbag and produce a brand-new bottle of the devil's favourite whisky. There are no glasses to hand, so we take turns swigging from the bottle, which seems the rock and roll thing to do – and there are far worse experiences in the world than tasting Lita's pink lipstick on the sticky rim.

Lita's marriage to Holmes does indeed collapse the following year, going the same way as her long-term relationship with Black Sabbath guitarist Tony Iommi, to whom she was previously engaged. I suggest that all her boyfriends surely can't have been people who play in bands, but it seems that this might indeed be the case. 'Well, most of my boyfriends have been musicians,' she reveals, 'because that's who I seem to associate with most. I think musicians are exciting.'

'I've always got along better with men,' she confides. 'Ever since I was a little girl, before I knew how to play guitar, I would always hang out with girlfriends and end up going out with one of their brothers . . . well, not *sleeping* with them or anything.'

Heaven forbid such a notion. But Lita's teenage years were anything but conventional after she joined controversial Californian all-girl band the Runaways at the age of sixteen. 'When you're a teenager in a crazy rock'n'roll band that's touring the world, you learn a lot – stuff you'd never learn in school,' she says.

Do the comparisons with former Runaways colleague Joan Jett piss her off? 'I'm nothing like Joan,' she retorts. 'I don't *look* like her, I don't *sound* like her, I don't *play* like her. She's like glitter sort of pop.'

Does Lita like Jett's stuff?

'No.'

Does she keep in touch with her?

'No.'

Does she dislike her?

'No, I don't dislike her.'

Have they drifted apart?

'Yes, it's been a long time since the Runaways broke up.'

Has she not spoken to Jett since the break-up?

'No, I haven't.'

How about the other girls in the band?

'No, I don't know anything about them or where they are.'

Does she not care about that?

'I don't give a fuck.'

What *does* she give a fuck about?

'I definitely don't give a fuck about what the girls in the Runaways are doing. That was something I had when I was a teenager. I'm not a teenager anymore. I've got a new life since the Runaways – and *that's* what I give a fuck about.'

Can the woman who jokingly refers to her hit 'Close My Eyes Forever' – a duet with Ozzy Osbourne, no less – as 'Close My *Thighs* Forever' imagine the day when she might settle down and have babies? 'I'm not that kind of girl,' she states, denying she'd ever sacrifice rock'n'roll to have a family. 'I wouldn't give that up for anything,' she insists. 'It's what I do; it's my life.'

Despite her claims, Lita does indeed put her career on the backburner for several years to give birth to two sons after marrying Jim Gillette – yes, another guitarist – of the American band Nitro. But never mind, just what is it that she gets out of playing rock'n'roll for a living? 'Well,' she says, 'I get to travel all over the world and meet fantastic people in every fucking country, I get to wear great clothes and look any way I want, I get to sing, play guitar and have thousands of people screaming at my feet, I get to have a large bank account and I get laid whenever I wanna get laid.'

Sounds good, especially the bit about getting laid whenever the mood takes her. 'But surely you're faithful to your husband?' I suggest. 'Well, of course,' she insists. 'I'd never go and pick some guy up off the street. I have a husband who I call up and say, "Honey, I'm horny, fly over and meet me."'

Lita grabs the bottle of Jack Daniel's and kindly offers it to me as a parting gift. 'Here, you can have this from me,' she says, although manager Sharon Osbourne, who recently wrote a letter of complaint about me referring to her as 'Ozzy's wife' in an article about her taking charge of the Quireboys, seems even less likely to promote me into her good books when she sees me clutching a bottle that she obviously paid for. 'Where are you going with that?' she asks, implying that some kind of theft has taken place, before Lita confirms her act of generosity. Sharon frowns and the Jack begins its journey to a loving new home . . .

JIM STEINMAN: FLESH FOR FANTASY

The maestro behind Meat Loaf apparently has such a thing for the lady who is 'Brenda Bristols' – otherwise known as **Penthouse** *'editor' Linzi Drew – that in 1989 he finds himself working with famed film director Ken Russell, another man who's partial to the exposed female form when the mood takes him . . .*

Linzi Drew, depending on which magazines you read, is the editor of *Penthouse*, a glamour model or a porn star – perhaps all three. At today's photo-shoot for her magazine, she's standing just inches away, completely naked with her big boobs and purring pussy on full display, resting her hands on her hips while talking about some everyday topic as if she's waiting at a bus stop. The thought occurs to me that writing for *Penthouse* at this point in time is not without its perks.

Linzi's charms have won her several admirers in the music business – not least in WASP bassist Johnny Rod and Ultravox's Warren Cann (nudge nudge, wink wink, say no more) – and those wanting to see her bare arse only need to glimpse the cover of former Pink Floyd leader Roger Waters's *The Pros And Cons Of Hitch Hiking* album to get their reward. She also appears as Brenda Bristols in the 'porn flick' seen in the movie *An American Werewolf In London*.

Yet it's still a surprise to hear Jim Steinman, the musical magician who wrote the songs for Meat Loaf's *Bat Out Of Hell* opus and has since put out his own albums, singing the British girl's praises a few weeks later. 'I thought Linzi was *magnificent*,' he says of her performance in *Nessun Dorma*, Ken Russell's segment of the multi-part *Aria* movie. 'I'm told she's a real extrovert,' adds the American, not realising how close to the truth he really is.

Indeed, Steinman was so enthralled by the scene, in which a female victim of a motorcycle accident responds to doctors' efforts by having sexual dreams as she hovers between life and death, that he has decided to ask the flamboyant Russell to direct his latest video and reproduce the action. Ken is all white hair and flailing arms at Pinewood Studios in Buckinghamshire as Elaine Caswell, one of four female singers on Steinman's new Pandora's Box project, performs 'It's All Coming Back To Me Now'. And typically of Russell and Steinman, the themes of eroticism and romanticism are prevalent in an epic and grandiose video that has burning motorcycles, prancing horses, snakes, dancers and mountains of naked human flesh.

> ## 'It was like a beast giving birth to another beast ... or taking an enormous dump.'
> ### – Jim Steinman

Steinman stands in the wings of the studio as Russell goes about his work. 'Ken really liked the idea of doing something he'd originally done with opera and putting it in a rock'n'roll setting,' says Jim. 'He is one of my idols and the idea of working with him was just so exciting for me. It was the perfect combination, because I start over the top and so does he. And he was very honest about how expensive he was gonna be.'

Later, in his expansive/expensive suite at the Halcyon Hotel in Holland Park, Steinman reveals that Virgin's budget for the video is £128,000. 'But it is a *six*-minute song,' he says in justification, as if twice the length of a regular single equals double the cost. And he already has a visual concept in mind for the album's title track, 'Original Sin', which would see him playing a piano with Harley Davidson parts built into it. With his long, flowing silver hair, the American has the look of a mad professor about him as he describes the musical beast of his dreams. 'I've always wanted a black leather piano with studs and spikes,' he says excitedly, 'and two exhaust pipes where the pedals are, so that when you hit certain chords you get all these fumes and yellow smoke.'

And smoke is exactly what he sadly got when he attempted to sample the sounds of twenty-five roaring motorbikes for the song itself. 'I blew up the console!' he laughs. 'I just overloaded it. It was cool, we sampled the engines and changed them so that they actually had a tonal quality; it sounded like a real beast. It was like a beast giving birth to another beast . . . or taking an enormous dump, I'm not sure which.'

Steinman claims to see Pandora's Box as a 'long-term project', yet reveals he is also set to work with the reformed Electric Light Orchestra – known as ELO Part II – and his old partner-in-rhyme Meat Loaf once again. I point out that the former band is nothing without the involvement of vocalist, writer, producer and arranger Jeff Lynne, but Jim sees things differently. 'It's sort of a brand name, like Kleenex,' he says rather curiously. 'It got bigger than what Jeff Lynne [lead vocalist of ELO] was. I thought the last few albums he did with them were poor and didn't even sound like ELO. I'm not sure how people will react, it's an experiment.'

Not surprisingly, he is much more assured about what he can achieve with Meat Loaf, believing he can rescue his former colleague's ailing career. I suggest that Meat without Steinman is rather like the Beach Boys without the brains of Brian Wilson, and idea is met with some agreement. 'It's not an unfair comparison, even though I'm not sure I deserve to be in that company,' he smiles. 'But it's true that, without me, Meat is not really aware of who he is. He's kinda lost.

'I just think that when Meat Loaf does my stuff he's unique. I want to pick up from where I left off with *Bat Out Of Hell* and I consider all the records immediately after that as non-existent. They don't make sense to me, so I'd look upon this as Meat's second album. I wrote the songs for *Dead Ringer* [the follow-up to *Bat Out Of Hell*] but had nothing to do with the record. I didn't care for the album; to me it wasn't a good record.'

Jim admits that his relationship with Meat Loaf since *Dead Ringer* has been 'sort of non-existent'. 'It was terrible,' he says. 'Working with Meat is a stormy thing anyway. Making *Bat Out Of Hell* I was often pissed off, because a lot of the time I was doing all the work and others were getting the credit. Then his voice started to fall apart, there was the mess with his bankruptcy and for much of the eighties I didn't talk to him and never heard from him. The funny thing is that I never had a deeply felt animosity towards him. I always felt he was a victim of circumstances.'

Despite a number of brilliant songs, the Pandora's Box album flops in Europe and the project is disbanded, while Steinman has no further involvement with ELO Part II. However, *Bat Out Of Hell: Back Into Hell* finally emerges, going on to sell fifteen million copies . . .

STATUS QUO: FANNY PELMETS AND FLYING TACKLE

Legendary British boogie boys Quo are playing their annual pre-Christmas gig at Wembley Arena in December 1991, and founder Rick Parfitt is talking about love, sex and romance – with his guitar, partner Francis Rossi and female followers – but not necessarily in that order . . .

Rick Parfitt gets up from his seat backstage at Wembley Arena and staggers towards me to shake hands before missing contact completely. He's not drunk but he amuses himself by pretending to be.

Part of the conversation with the Status Quo co-founder is supposed to be about his trademark Telecaster for a guitar magazine. 'I'm deeply in love with that guitar,' he says, before concluding, 'If it had long legs and high heels, I'd shag it.'

Yes, quite. It would appear that sex is never too far away from Rick's mind, whatever he's supposed to be talking about. He reveals that he lost his virginity in a holiday camp at Hayling Island. 'No pun intended,' he says, 'but I completely fucked it up! I can't remember who she was but she was bloody strong because she threw me out. That's how good I was.'

> **'If it had long legs and high heels, I'd shag it.'**
>
> **– Rick Parfitt**

Thankfully, Rick's technique has improved, not least because of the amount of practice he has got since the sixties. 'I once did it on a train going across Europe, in an open carriage with other people sitting in it,' he confides. 'We just managed to do it before the ticket inspector came through the door.' Fucking all over the world indeed . . . Of course, there was no shortage of groupies during Quo's heyday and Parfitt makes no apologies for his band's behaviour.

'It was great fun,' he says, 'and they satisfied your needs at the time. We loved 'em. I mean, come on, they're standing there in these tiny fanny pelmets, with all the flying tackle, all the business . . . But we don't have groupies now, although we still have quite a lot of fans outside hotels that just want an autograph and to say hello. It was great at the time but I wouldn't look twice now.'

Having seen the average age of the crowd outside tonight's gig, that's no surprise. But Rick's looking fit and well, having recently dispensed with the beard he'd grown to disguise his flabby face. 'I had more chins than a Chinese telephone directory,' he admits. 'It wasn't really a beard, more designer stubble really, but I lost a bit of weight so consequently it came off.'

And he's never been happier with his relationship with long-time boogie brother Francis Rossi, with whom he's been treading the boards for several decades. 'Francis is one of my best friends,' he insists. 'He's certainly my best friend in this business. It's funny but, after all this time, I've only really known him for the last five years. Before that we didn't really communicate because of the drugs and booze.

'We were very good pals in the old days before the drugs and booze started. We were just starting to see the character in each other but by getting into booze and drugs we fucked ourselves up completely. Luckily we've come out of the other side of that – to the point that Francis doesn't even drink now – and we've found out, after all these years, that we really do love one another.'

GYPSY QUEEN: A LOVELY PAIR

Scotch eggs are the hot topic of conversation with Paula and Pamela Mattioli, the twins who front fledgling American outfit Gypsy Queen, when they visit London in December 1987, but it seems it's not necessarily food they're talking about . . .

Pamela Mattioli grabs her crotch and bizarrely adopts the persona of a retarded twelve-year-old girl named Jennifer, while identical twin sister Paula assumes the role of her alter ego Baby, whose gurgling noises are self-explanatory. It's a little game the Gypsy Queen singers like to play when the mood takes them – on this occasion in the bar of a London hotel – when an old gentleman approaches Pamela and says, 'Can I help you, miss? I'm a gynaecologist.'

With their big orange hair, the girls resemble twin lions – well, they are the 'mane' attraction of their Florida-based band – and it's fair to say they exude fantastic sex appeal. It's something that could serve as a big distraction to their music, I suggest, when they finally return to their normal selves.

'You're not talking about our Scotch eggs, by any chance?' asks Pamela. A look of confusion crosses my face, prompting Pamela to offer some explanation. 'Some moron kept referring to our Scotch eggs and I figured he was talking about *these*,' she says, pointing to her chest, which she is thrusting in my direction. I can't help but allow my gaze to fall on her ample breasts. 'If we really wanted to play up the sex symbol image, I'd have gone and posed for *Playboy* when they offered. If I wanted to I could make some real quick bucks that way, but we both consider that we're artists first. But look at Dave Lee Roth, he's a sex symbol.'

Adds Paula, running her fingers around the rim of her glass, 'And rock'n'roll is a very sexual thing anyway.'

'I don't want to come off as being sleazy or anything,' says Pamela, 'but rock'n'roll does have a large element of sensuality, don't you think? And with our new band, we've got some good-looking guys now and we don't expect an all-male crowd any more because we're starting to get the girls. But perhaps they think we're lesbians or something.'

'If we really wanted to play up the sex symbol image, I'd have gone and posed for *Playboy* when they offered.'

– Pamela Mattioli

Now there's a thought. 'It's really difficult for women in rock'n'roll, though,' insists Paula, reflecting on what will prove to be Gypsy Queen's one and only album. 'If you're too soft you get taken too seriously and if you're too heavy people start saying you're trashy and sleazy. That's a very fine line for a woman to walk.'

Absolutely. The two sisters are happy to sign a photograph of the pair together before disappearing upstairs. Writes Pamela: 'Dear Kirk, I'm glad you know there's more to Gypsy Queen than "Scotch eggs" . . .'

Well, of course, it goes without saying.

SEX ON THE BRAIN

CANDID CONVERSATIONS

There's nothing more rewarding for a rock journalist than to feel as if you have won the trust and confidence of an artist to the extent that they can open up emotionally and allow access to a part of their psyche that reveals far more about their personality and philosophies than you could ever have imagined. That's not often the case, of course, especially if speaking to a musician for the very first time or trying to establish a relationship and rapport in circumstances that are not necessarily conducive to candid or confessional conversation.

However, there are times – some of which can be anticipated, others certainly not so – when the interviewee is prepared to give away a part of themselves that goes way beyond the usual 'the album is hot and the fans are loving us on tour' rhetoric.

So it was a real privilege to discover the heartfelt honesty of Queen guitarist Brian May, the unexpected intimacy of Henry Rollins, the extreme emotions of Killing Joke leader Jaz Coleman, the phobias and fears of Pearl Jam vocalist Eddie Vedder, the addictive personality of former UFO axe-hero Michael Schenker, the sincerity and integrity of old David Bowie sidekick Mick Ronson, the outlaw attitude of the Black Crowes and the unique spirituality of Carlos Santana.

With May giving his first in-depth interview following the death of vocalist Freddie Mercury, there was no way the Queen man could realistically talk about his forthcoming solo project without placing it into the context of his mourning. But it was still a special moment to sit alongside the guitarist as he opened his heart and spoke so frankly about his feelings. 'I lost my dad not too long ago,' he confided, 'and you grieve because he's not there and then there's also something else going on, which is that you've lost a piece of yourself. And that's how I feel about Freddie.'

May was no less warm and engaging than expected, but it would have been impossible to predict that Henry Rollins – a man who admitted he never lets people get close ('If someone tries, I just say, "Hey man, get the fuck away from me"') – would allow me to pry so deeply into his private emotions. 'I think I *could* love somebody,' he conceded, 'although I'm not sure what that feeling is.'

Needless to say, the thrill of romance is far more up Santana's street and the Mexican claimed that 'melody and rhythm are the two lovers' when we shared a profoundly philosophical conversation. And to think I'm only supposed to ask him about his guitar. Fellow six-stringer Ronson (sadly now deceased, of course) is equally earnest about his musical motives, although it felt uncomfortable listening in as he pleaded with his woman to fly in – not least because he was sat in bed in his dressing gown.

However, this was nowhere near as disturbing as hearing Jaz Coleman talk about his 'mental breakdown' and how very close he came to 'taking somebody's life'. But while the Killing Joke singer's meandering mind has taken him on an occasionally torturous journey, arguably to the brink of insanity, the same can also be said of German guitarist Schenker, whose compulsive behaviour – be it in the form of alcohol and substance abuse or a submission to an unconventional lifestyle ideology that non-believers would ridicule as cult worship – has undermined his career and led many to question the man's stability.

And as Schenker passionately spoke in the hope of sharing his newfound wisdom, foolishly convincing himself that his former UFO bandmates might take him seriously, it was impossible to ignore the suspicion that this might just be another short-lived obsession for a man whose pursuit of self-fulfilment continues to this day . . .

BRIAN MAY AND QUEEN: A ROYAL OCCASION

It's been less than eight months since the death of Freddie Mercury signalled the demise of Queen – Britain's most elegantly stylish rock band. But now, in July 1992, following a period of silence, grieving and reflection, guitarist Brian May agrees to give his first full-length interview about the most traumatic and troubled period of his life . . .

The hair, as ever, remains a distinctive and reassuringly familiar trademark. Brian May's curly black locks caress the sides of his face as he pores over the photographs in an old book documenting the first decade of Queen's career. 'It's funny,' he muses, 'but sometimes these memories seem like yesterday while others feel as if they're a hundred years ago.' The guitarist flicks through the pages that depict the band in all its majestic glory on numerous stages across the globe. The images encourage Brian to reflect on his past and question himself about what he has become. 'All this has definitely had an effect on me,' he confides to me. 'I'm not normal.'

Queen conquered the world with magnificent melodies, hard-rock histrionics and stylish showmanship. Vocalist Freddie Mercury personified flamboyance and camp theatricality, while the band's use of elaborate, operatic harmonies on albums such as *A Night At The Opera* and *A Day At The Races* helped them produce some of the most sophisticated yet anthemic rock'n'roll of all-time. Kicking arse and then kissing it better afterwards, they perhaps should have been named Guns N' Roses for the way their musical diversity saw them shooting listeners in the chest before showering delicate petals upon their graves.

But Queen's long and distinguished reign is now over, with Mercury – born Farrokh Bulsara – having died of bronchopneumonia after losing his battle against AIDS at the age of forty-five. And May, sitting with me in his fan club's offices in London's Notting Hill and being interviewed at length for the very first time after his singer's passing, is still distressed by the way Mercury's illness and death was reported and distorted by the tabloid media.

'I think it was all very predictable,' he sighs. 'Even after Freddie's death, there were some people who still wanted to have their little digs. And, of course, now they do could what they liked because they were free of the laws of libel. So some of them really laid into him with complete lies. I was appalled and it made me so angry. Not just because they were slating Freddie, which was bad enough, but also because it was dangerous for other people. They were saying that Fred got AIDS because he was promiscuous, but the rest of us needn't worry. And to print that stuff is going to make a few kids think they're okay and the next day they'll be HIV positive. I think the people who put out that kind of stuff are guilty of something very serious.'

Mercury's homosexuality may have been common knowledge but his HIV status – although strongly hinted at by elements of the media – was publicly confirmed only twenty-four hours before his death. Queen had therefore been forced to record albums such as *The Miracle* and *Innuendo* in unnaturally difficult circumstances, as Mercury deteriorated in front of the eyes of his close colleagues – including bassist John Deacon and drummer Roger Taylor – who had pledged to keep the truth of the situation confidential.

'I think we all thought *The Miracle* was going to be the last one because there were no guarantees about how long Fred was going to last at that time,' reveals May. 'He'd been told by his doctor that he probably wouldn't last the duration of that album. So we just knew we had to press on and do what we could. In Freddie's mind, it was totally clear to him. He just said, "I want to go on working, business as usual, until I fucking drop. That's what I want and I'd like you to support me in being able to do this and that's why I don't want any discussion about this."

'I think we were all going through miserable, difficult times and the studio becomes the only place where you have some sort of refuge. And I know for Freddie it helped keep him alive. He was already having problems doing *The Miracle*, but by the time of *Innuendo* he could barely stand. And by the end of that album he could sing just one or two days a week. It was tough psychologically having to keep it from everybody else – I never told my family or anything.'

May is unspecific about the time when all the members of Queen learned about their singer's plight. 'Well, there were various private moments, but I suppose it was a gradual thing,' he says. 'There was a lot of unspoken stuff for a long time and then, yeah, there was a point where we sat down and talked about it.

'You'll find things on *The Miracle* [released in 1989] where we've already started to address things. For that album we actually managed to write stuff together, which is a miracle in itself because we all used to be very pig-headed and possessive about our songs. But we wrote together and there's certainly stuff on *The Miracle* where we're talking about what it's all going to mean as we wind things up. You can see that now and it got very direct on *Innuendo*. It's painful when you hear some of those songs, especially on the radio when you're unprepared. Sometimes you just hear a snatch of Freddie's voice and you think, "Christ, he's not around doing that anymore." You think you're prepared for it but we were totally destroyed. He was exceptional.'

Mercury was a man of contrasts. His charisma as Queen's frontman saw him dominate the world's concert stages but his character as a private individual was much more fragile than his adoring fans would ever have believed. 'I think he was a very unusual person – quite complex but yet inside, like the rest of us, quite small,' reveals May. 'The feelings of insecurity and smallness that we all have propel us to do all sorts of things, don't they? You build up your compensation screen and develop all these ways of dealing with life. And even if you lose touch with it, which some people do and I did at a certain point, it's always in there somewhere – this little person that's still basically a child and very vulnerable. And Fred was no different. Sometimes his methods were very blunt and crude, but he had that ability to

Guns N' Roses
guitarist Slash might
be the coolest dude
ever to hail from
Stoke-on-Trent, but
no amount of begging
could persuade him to
speak on Axl Rose's
behalf. 'Bad back?'
Slash repeated
quizzically when
asked about the
mystery injury
that forced the
frontman to cancel
our interview.
'Oh yeah . . .'

'I'm the product of a typical American dysfunctional family.' Henry Rollins, a man who admits he doesn't 'do holidays, think about Christmas or have relatives I visit', managed to get it all off his chest when speaking intimately about his life of relative isolation.

Above: 'You wouldn't know what it feels like unless you've been shot out of a fuckin' cannon,' insisted bassist Johnny Colt (left, beside guitarist Rich Robinson), backstage in Brixton, in an attempt to explain what life on the road with the Black Crowes was really like. 'Unless you've lived in a tornado,' he added.

Right: Former UFO guitarist Michael Schenker spoke passionately about the powers of 'positive energy' and how the 'tools of transformation' gave him strength, but suggestions that the band reform to fund the building of a spiritual retreat left his former colleagues unimpressed.

Grunge rockers Pearl Jam were exploding big time with the release of their debut album, but vocalist Eddie Vedder insisted he was desperate to 'slow it down a bit'. 'I can almost feel sorry for Kurt from Nirvana,' he admitted as he stared into his crystal ball and feared the price of fame.

Former David Bowie, Mott The Hoople and Ian Hunter guitarist Mick Ronson was perhaps caught off-guard when he opened his hotel room door in his dressing gown with a cigarette in his mouth, but the relaxed surroundings made for one of the most candid interviews he ever gave in the years before his untimely death.

'Helping out' backstage at London's 100 Club on the evening of Metallica's secret gig proved to be a unique experience . . . in fact the author found himself cuddling James Hetfield's stage monitor for the duration of the show. My hearing has only recently returned . . .

Iron Maiden bassist Steve Harris – described as 'Roy of the Rovers' by vocalist Bruce Dickinson, in not entirely complimentary terms – isn't shy when it comes to inviting people to parties, as I discovered when the band played at the Brixton Academy on FA Cup Final day in 1998.

Sharing dinner with the mighty Meat Loaf was an interesting experience, not least when he started drinking. Meanwhile, his former partner-in-rhyme Jim Steinman (who wrote Bat Out Of Hell*) claimed that 'without me, Meat is not really aware of who he is. He's kinda lost . . .'*

make contact with people, to stir up things. Sometimes he stirred up hatred in people, but he got a reaction from everyone.

'It's almost a selfish thing to say, but you lose a part of yourself [when somebody dies]. I lost my dad not too long ago and you grieve because he's not there and then there's also something else going on, which is that you've lost a piece of yourself. And that's how I feel. I've been close to Freddie for twenty-five years and so there is a gaping hole. And it will be a long time before it doesn't feel like that.'

May pauses for a few moments as he reflects on how the rest of the band handled Mercury's death. 'I think we all got completely messed up in our different ways,' he reluctantly confesses. 'It was a continuous process, of which the actual death was one part. I think we all got seriously messed up in the time leading up to it, because you're part of it and you feel so helpless. None of us could believe it was happening right in front of us. I think the last two or three years actually brought us together, as there was this feeling that the world outside could crumble but there was something here that was worth doing. So we did get pretty close and I think we still are.'

> **'Sometimes Freddie stirred up hatred in people, but he got a reaction from everyone.'**
> **– Brian May**

Some of the world's top rock artists were provided with a unique opportunity to join the remaining members of Queen and pay tribute to their former vocalist at the Freddie Mercury Tribute Concert for AIDS Awareness, which took place at London's Wembley Stadium on 20 April 1992 and was televised live across the globe to an estimated audience of around one billion viewers. May admits the decision to stage the event was not a particularly easy one to take.

'We had a lot of doubts,' he reveals. 'On the night that Freddie died we announced that, when the time was right, we'd send him off in the right manner and style to which he was accustomed. So it was in our minds from the beginning. But we went through quite a time where we actually didn't want to do it. When we looked at it and realised we were going to be on stage with somebody else singing Freddie's lines, we weren't sure whether we did want to do it or not. I think Deaky, in particular, said that he didn't.

'Then we got to the point where we said, "Okay, let's contact some people and see how *they* feel about it." These were key people who we thought it would be nice to work with and who we knew had special feelings about Freddie. And they were so enthusiastic that we sort of gained momentum from that point. I'm talking about George Michael, Elton John and Guns N' Roses, for example.

'There were times in rehearsals when it would all get too much. The first time we met all these people and went through the songs, there were some incredibly emotional moments. And I think the three of us got through a lot of that before we got to the actual gig – not all of it but a lot of it. I think we were aware that if we were in tears the whole time [during the event], it would be a joke and just wouldn't work. It had to be an up thing. Fred would have hated people mooning around and being maudlin over him. So we wanted the event to be rejoicing about his life.

'I think most of it worked. We made some mistakes but I think, for what we took on, most of it came off as an event. As far as playing, it was a case of getting through because there was so much to worry about in terms of the show. But there were some great things, you know, such as seeing [Guns N' Roses vocalist] Axl Rose and Elton [sing "Bohemian Rhapsody"] together. And I was personally very proud of Liza Minnelli being there because I think Freddie would have wanted that. I think she's quite close to him in spirit. Almost everybody disagreed with me, but I don't think anybody else could have stepped into that spot at the end of the show for "We Are The Champions". I could have sung it but I don't think it would have meant quite the same as it did that way.'

> 'Part of me is beginning to feel sort of comfortable about it, especially the fact that Freddie's not suffering anymore.'
>
> – Brian May

May has been working on his first full solo record, nearly a full decade after the *Star Fleet Project* mini-album credited to Brian May and Friends. *Back To The Light* was constructed over a number of years and features hard-rock stalwarts Cozy Powell on drums and Neil Murray on bass. Says May, 'I've written a little explanation on the album and what it says is that I've been working on this for five years and during that time my life and feelings have changed. So the music is a cross-section of all that. I was in a pretty low state five years ago; I was very un-together and in much pain.'

The genesis of the material coincided with the guitarist's first marriage, to Chrissie, ending in divorce, while the album's recording was completed in even more tragic circumstances following the demise of Mercury. And May believes the creative process played a part in helping him grieve. 'I made a conscious decision that I would work my way through it and I think it's helped,' he says. 'I just plunged myself into recording almost every day. I still don't know if we're actually through it yet. There's a part of us that doesn't believe Freddie is not there. It takes a long time to really adjust and re-draw your map, you know. I still expect him to come through the door, particularly when I'm in the studio. But some of it's quite nice. I'm not a heavily spiritual person but I could feel what Fred would have said. I can hear him saying, "No, c'mon, you can do better than that." Part of me is beginning to feel sort of comfortable about it, especially the fact that he's not suffering anymore.'

Mercury's death inevitably permeates some of *Back To The Light* but, as May says, in discreet ways. 'There's quite a bit, I suppose, but you'd have to fish it out quite carefully. Some of it is quite ambiguous. When I used to listen to Bob Dylan and John Lennon I'd get a piece of life from them that meant something to me. "Nothing But Blue" happened because Cozy came in with a backing track and told me to play something on it. It was the night before Freddie went, but for the first time I had this complete conviction that his death was imminent, that he was going at that point. I used that track and wrote the song about how I felt at that point.'

In stark contrast, 'Driven By You' rolled off the conveyor belt in rather less emotive circumstances after being commissioned for a Ford television commercial. But May insists the track was not purely a corporate cop-out, as some have suggested. 'I approached the song on *two* fronts; one was for the advert – which obviously had different words – and the other was for *me*. And it was only because I could do it for me that I did it at all.

'This album is a sort of divide, a crossroads. I wanted to make this record on my own, with nobody else to argue with, just to see what happened. My major driving force really is to do something worthwhile so that when I die I can say I'm proud of that. The worst thing you can do is stick out more wallpaper for the world. I would hate to put out anything that I thought was just repetition or superfluous. The only reason I've put this album out is because I think I actually do have something to say – and it's worth saying. I could have chucked out all sorts of stuff; I'm quite good at being a craftsman and know I can create pop songs. But I wanted this album to be *special* to some people.'

As yet, there has still been no formal notification of Queen's split. But May insists such a thing isn't particularly necessary. 'I don't know what splitting up means really,' he says. 'I mean, we're not doing anything together at the moment except making sure that all the old stuff is properly handled [with the back catalogue being re-mastered for CD]. And if you don't keep an eye on all that stuff it doesn't get done right. For example, half the original master of the first album is missing – it's quite shocking. But we talk and, when we feel a bit more ready for it, we'll go back into the studio and look at the material which Fred has sung on and that we haven't released yet, because there is a bit left – about half an album's worth [which eventually appears as *Made In Heaven*].

'We always said that if any of us disappeared that would be the end of it and I think that's right really. I don't have any inclination to try and be Queen without Freddie. That doesn't mean I don't ever want to work with the other two guys again because I like working with them and I think we do have the ability to play together, which the [Freddie Mercury Tribute] gig showed. But how we do that in the future, I've no idea. All I know is that I don't feel comfortable about doing something like that at the moment. I don't want to do another thing like Wembley. It's been suggested we could do other things like that, but I don't want to make a career of it. That was for a purpose.

'I think a lot of people thought that Queen was very calculating, that we had this plan for world domination, but in fact we didn't. The major thing for us was to keep ourselves in areas that we thought were worthwhile. And even though we didn't have a master plan, we always fought for control and so I think any mistakes we made were our own. I think I'm still trying to get my perspectives on what this all was. And I feel very proud of what we were. I consider that I was very fortunate to be a part of it all and we found a combination that was magical and worked.'

Band or no band, Brian May will always be the guitarist of Queen – and forever recognised by the public as such. 'You know, there have been times when I physically haven't been able to relate to what people say,' he admits. 'It makes you feel almost sick because somebody might come up to you and tell you how wonderful you are, but inside you feel that you honestly can't relate to that and that they're almost talking about someone else.

'It's funny, but I went to a book launch the other day and this guy came up to me and said, "Hullo, pleased to meet you, I'm a socialist." Or something like that. And he said, "I just want to tell you that I really like some of your work. That was the first album and after that everything was crap and commercial and everybody knows that." And I said, "I guess so, I suppose that includes 'Bohemian Rhapsody' and 'We Will Rock You' and all that stuff." And he said, "I still wanted to say, you know, you did do some good stuff."

'That was the conversation really – and it just confirmed that everybody has their own point of view. That's his opinion and it wasn't worth arguing with him because that's the way he sees it. There are some people who hated everything we did, you know. But that's life.'

The interview is over, one that has been a privilege to conduct, yet Brian is in no hurry for me to leave. Once again he picks up the book of *Queen's Greatest Pix* – which has been brought along for him to sign – and we continue to chat for another fifteen minutes or so as he ponders the passing years.

Eventually he signs a photograph of himself in typical axe-hero pose with 'cheers' as the message. Cheers indeed, Brian.

HENRY ROLLINS: THE END OF SILENCE

He's the hero of hardcore, but that's not to suggest that Henry Rollins – an intimidating vision of resentment and rage onstage – cannot open up to reveal his more intimate feelings, as is discovered in September 1992 when he agrees to talk despite having cancelled all interviews . . .

'**D**o you ever wonder about your capacity to love another human being?' It's 8:00am in London and my colleagues raise their eyebrows as they drag their hangovers into the office and overhear a snippet of what would evidently appear to be an intimate and deeply personal telephone conversation. They naturally assume it's a private call, to a close friend or former partner even, but the reality is that the intrusive question is being asked of Henry Rollins – furious fist-clenching front man of the Rollins Band and former singer of US hardcore heroes Black Flag.

Onstage, Henry personifies rage and resentment. Yet somehow, today's conversation is addressing much gentler emotions, such as matters of the heart. They say it's difficult to show love if you've never been *shown* love and Henry's unhappy childhood and upbringing have clearly damaged his ability – or willingness – to establish close personal relationships with other members of the human race.

'I'm the product of a typical American dysfunctional family,' he declares. 'There's *nothing* unique there at all. But I was raised in an environment of constant violence and humiliation. I don't have any brothers or sisters, nor was there ever a feeling of community. I never loved my father, I only feared him. And I never loved my mother; I just kind of stayed out of the way. I have no idea how many brothers or sisters my father has. I met my mother's mother a few times and the only memory I have of her is as a drunk woman with her make-up on all crooked. The thing I remember about my mother's sister was getting stuck out at her place with her kids and getting yelled at and smacked around by my uncle. And so, at this point, I *don't* love anybody and I don't really like people getting close to me. If someone tries, I just say, "Hey man, get the fuck away from me."'

The candid conversation is even more remarkable for the fact that Henry wasn't even planning on talking today. He is on tour in Australia and, for reasons best known to himself, had scrapped all the press interviews arranged on his behalf, except his record company are surprisingly keen for this particular feature to appear in the inaugural edition of *Metal CD*. So they decide to keep Henry's wishes to themselves and tell me that he'll be ready to take my call at 8:00pm local time. Given that Rollins is one of one of the most physically intimidating characters in rock, with his muscular, tattooed body ('Search & Destroy' is emblazoned across his back above a huge tribal sun image) giving the impression that he could rip your spine out with a flick of his wrist, it's just as well that I'm not aware of his press officer's cunning plan.

The receptionist of the Crown Lodge Motel is happy to put the call through to Henry's room.

'Hello.'

'Hi. Is that Henry?' I ask.

'Yo!'

'It's Kirk from London.'

'Yeah?'

'How are you?'

He pauses, 'All right.'

'Er, were you not expecting this call?'

'No.'

A silence opens up which allows me to ponder where we go from here. Then Henry makes the first move.

'But it's okay. What's up?' he says.

'Well, we're supposed to be doing an interview for *Metal CD* magazine.'

'They told me I had some interviews but I told them I didn't wanna do them. But, hey . . . let's do it.'

The brutal and bruising music of the Rollins Band, never bettered than on his breakthrough album, *The End Of Silence*, revolves around the central theme of alienation. So it's fitting that, once he feels comfortable with talking, Henry admits that getting intimate with people is pretty low down his list of priorities in life. 'I'm just not interested,' he says. 'I'm a pretty cold person in lots of ways. Not to say that if your leg was cut off in a car accident I wouldn't care – I just don't get involved with people much. I don't do holidays, think about Christmas or have relatives I ever visit.'

Which brings Henry back to his parents, who divorced when he was very young, resulting in Rollins living in a variety of homes with his mother in Washington DC before getting involved in the punk scene and eventually relocating to California to join Black Flag. 'I don't talk to her very much,' he admits. 'She's a good person and did the best she could as a single mother to raise her kid. I don't *hate* her or anything; I just don't know her and I really don't want to know her. My father, I've seen him twice since I was eighteen. He came to a show about five years ago and I talked to him for about a minute. And then he showed up at one of my talking gigs and he said "hello" and I said "hello" and he turned around and walked away. And that was the last time I ever saw him.'

So, given his (potentially) painful experiences, it's perhaps a surprise that he responds in a positive manner when I ask about his capacity to love another human being. 'Yeah, sure, I think I *could* love somebody,' he says. 'I loved my friend Joe [Cole], who got killed [murdered, in fact]. I've loved two girls in my time; at least I *think* I did. I'm not sure what that feeling is, though. It's an emotion I'm really not that attuned to. I'm sure there are a lot of people who feel that way. And love is such a strange feeling that it's *got* to be different for every single person on the planet. Me, I just never felt very close to people, you know?'

But with Rollins enjoying major success – with his band and as a spoken-word performer, author and occasional actor – in various territories across the globe, it's inevitable that people try to get close to *him*. 'I'm really not interested in being a celebrity or rock star,' he states when asked about his increasing public profile. 'I kind of figure it would be cool just to be able to play a gig and walk into a restaurant across the road and not get bothered. People have been kind of *on* me, like asking for an autograph or whatever, since I joined Black Flag. It's not that I don't like these people; it's just that I'm not really a social person. I don't have any answers for anybody and I don't have interesting things to say. People come up and kind of put an invisible coin in me and expect me to spout for them – and I'm not [built] that way. They'll start talking to me and I'll just stare at them. Hey, if I don't have anything to say, I'm not gonna *make up* conversation. So I just try to be cool and, if they have a direct question, I'll try to answer it. But what they don't understand is that this happens all the time – the same questions, month-in month-out, year-in year-out – and it kinda gets to you after a while.'

> '**I was raised in an environment of constant violence and humiliation.**'
> **– Henry Rollins**

Henry is equally disillusioned with the violence seen at his shows, particularly on the current Australian tour. 'I've been kind of disgusted with some of the incidents and the last few shows have been really aggravating,' he complains. 'We played in Perth the other night and the bouncers were just beating the hell out of people – and at the end of the night they wanted to beat *me* up too. Some of these [security] guys are just assholes and into beating people up.'

So what's his motivation for continuing with the group? 'I don't know, it's what I do,' he says. 'The tiger is underneath the tree and gets up and runs across the field and comes back and lies down. And one guy says to the other, "Why did the tiger do that?" And the other guy says, "Because he's a tiger." I honestly don't know. I get a real rush out of playing. I seem to have a lot of difficulty coping with the real world and so writing and playing music seems to really keep me regular.'

It's not as if Henry longs for the comforts of [his Los Angeles] home while he's on the road. 'If you saw how I live, it's not much to miss,' he admits. 'It's like, do you miss your office? I don't live in a dump anymore but my room is nothing but a computer, a stereo and some CDs, while another is just nothing but weights and the other room is my book company [named 2.13.61 after his date of birth]. I don't know many people outside of the ones I work with. For instance, on a Saturday night, no one calls me. I don't have a girlfriend. Sometimes I go to the local record store with my pal Gary who works at the book company and we'll check out the jazz records. Other than that, people don't call me and say, "Hey, wanna go to a party?"'

But if there is solitude at home, there can also be great solitude when living out of a suitcase. 'You can get really way out after three or four months on tour, you can get very lonely and isolated,' he states. 'Playing live is a very isolating experience. For me it is because all these people *kind* of know me, but I don't know them at all. And how do they know me? They know me from things that strangers are saying about me in newspapers. And that's always weird.

'It's a very strange, abstract loneliness [on the road], because I can't visualise anyone I'm lonely for. And when I do have the opportunity to be with someone, all I do is clam up anyway. So it's something that doesn't really resolve itself. The only thing that occurs to me is just to get on to the next town.'

And with that, the tiger returns to its natural habitat.

MICHAEL SCHENKER: CULT INFLUENCE

He's the impulsive axe-hero who made UFO special in the late seventies. However, by November 1992 it's not the drink and drugs that are controlling Michael Schenker, but a cult new philosophy by the name of positive energy. He wants to reform the classic line-up of the band to fund the building of a special retreat centre – much to the consternation of former colleague Pete Way, who thinks it's 'like the fucking Moonies'...

'Everybody wants to build their garden, their beautiful garden with flowers where they experience all this happiness. And I was the one who wouldn't accept any tools. So I was digging with my hands and started to bleed. And when people would say, "Michael, are you okay?" I would hide my hands and say, "Yes, I'm fine, I'm great." And there are so many people doing this, while their neighbour who accepted the tools is whistling while they work. We can either bleed or we can enjoy – that's the difference.'

Michael Schenker is in confessional mood. The innovative German guitarist, whose blistering and fluid white-lightning solos propelled him to stardom while a member of the classic UFO line-up of the late 1970s – as captured perfectly on the double live album, *Strangers In The Night* – has never been able to shake off his reputation for mental instability.

After quitting UFO at their peak of their powers amid a storm of smashed Gibson Flying Vs, shorn blond locks and unexplained disappearances, the eccentric six-stringer's subsequent career under the MSG moniker can kindly be described as erratic at best as he struggled with one chemical dependence or another.

And having spent years discovering that those electric blue eyes of his weren't quite enough to help him escape from the darkness, the man nicknamed 'Metal Mickey', as he nudges into his forties, believes he has finally seen the light.

'I was chasing something – happiness – but looking in the wrong directions,' he admits. 'I was confused and waking up every morning, thinking, "Is this all there is to life?" I would drink and the alcohol was always the thing that gave me the answer, so you have another drink. Until one day you decide that this is enough, it's just a lie. When you think that is what life is all about – drinking – you don't grow.'

Schenker has just released a new solo album, entitled *Thank You*, which appears on his own Positive Energy label. An acoustic, instrumental offering, it's a huge departure from his trademark electric sound that inspired legions of air guitarists across the globe. But Michael is really excited by his latest project, especially as it reflects his newfound philosophy in life, as he explains down the phone from his home. 'It's just great acoustic music and it's really full of positive energy, because that's what I'm doing – promoting positivity,' he says enthusiastically. 'It's definitely going to help bring people together on a universal scale. I'm well known for being able to speak through my music and you're really going to be able to feel it.'

The answer, you see, is positive energy, as Schenker explains. 'For the past three years, I have been surrounded by positive energy. I chose to be open to it. People think that I have had a great time – Michael Schenker, one of the world's most famous guitarists, who played with all these great bands, must have had a great life. And all I can say is that I didn't really. And only in these last three years, when I started to accept certain tools, did I realise that there is more to life than I had experienced before. For so many years all these doors were closed because I wasn't able to accept or open up – and then everything changed.

'There are many people who have secrets they want to take to the grave because they're too embarrassed to let them out – and it's these secrets that control your life and keep you so busy. We're living in a world where everybody pretends that everything is fine but, within, everybody hurts. People very often end up killing themselves – or they can simply surrender and accept that it is okay to release. And when they start releasing they realise it was something that was imprisoning them.

'Different people experience it at different times – some when they're five, some when they're thirty, some when they're seventy and some never do, in *this* lifetime. The whole point is that when you're ready you make the change. As long as you have a certain thinking pattern, then nothing will change in your life. And if you're desperate for change, if you keep experiencing the same old roundabouts, then something happens.

'For me, I had an experience. I was just sitting in my place and all of a sudden I experienced that joy. I wasn't totally happy because I knew I was on Valium, but I realised that if I could get rid of this Valium I could feel it again properly. And when I realised that, I made an effort to change my life, that I wanted to get rid of drinking and all these things.

'It's to do with trust. There are so many tools in this world, yet everybody still thinks they can do it by themselves. The ego is in the way; it blinds all these spots. It's only when people suffer disasters – if like in one family the parents die, for instance – that all of a sudden people wake up and have a different perception, because it's like a slap in the face. That's how it usually happens, so that's why people should understand that problems are actually a blessing. Problems are a positive thing because they keep you moving forward.'

I listen attentively as Michael speaks, respecting the fact that he seems to have found something that has wrestled his demons into submission – for the time being at least. The man deserves some peace. But as with anything we don't really understand, there's always a little cynicism nagging at the back of your mind. Nevertheless, I ask Michael how one discovers more about positive energy.

'First of all, you know everything,' he declares. 'You are perfect the way you are. You are made in the image of God and you have the right to experience everything you want. It's just that your personality is in the way. All you need to do is open up and be willing and thirsty. You have to change your way of thinking.

'It depends on how motivated you are. All you need to know is that there's a way to go forward in a positive way and a way to go in a negative way. And you know within yourself what's positive and negative. With a positive outlook, you automatically attract the tools of transformation that you need.

'What I did, I started listening to subliminal tapes and doing visualisation exercises – they are very powerful and they boost your concentration. And I learned to meditate. In meditation you learn to find yourself. I started with positive affirmations, because my thinking was in such a negative state that I needed to renew myself with positive thoughts – all the time, you know. So I did it day after day, week after week, month after month, up to the point where I was just having headphones on twenty-four hours a day. I slept with it and maybe had one ear free for conversation. I was convinced it sounded as logical as putting petrol in a car.

'Life is about progress. It's based on your own experiences and where you're at in life. And you can only go as deep into your heart as you allow yourself. Everything I have experienced in my life, up until today, is just fine the way it was, because I'm very happy with where I'm at today.'

Listening to Schenker speak about positive energy, it dawns on me that an intrinsic part of the philosophy is to preach to others in a bid to convert them. So is this what he is trying to do? 'What happens is,' he begins to explain, 'the closer you get to finding yourself, the more you want to help other people. It's something a lot of people can't picture. But I can tell you, the more you are positive, the more you move forward, the more you do the best you can every day and not let people drag you down with their negativity, you automatically have the desire to help people. When you make a transformation, you see very clearly how stupid you've been in the past. It makes you suddenly realise because you see things other people don't see.

> **'Everybody pretends that everything is fine but, within, everybody hurts.'**
> **– Michael Schenker**

'I don't have an answer for everybody,' he admits, 'because there are people who are happy with what they are doing and that's fine. It's just that I know where I've been and I've been stuck. And at that time I'd have appreciated it if somebody could have let me out of it – which finally did happen because I opened up. I have the choice to be happy or miserable, it's all a choice. Nobody forces you to be happy or miserable, it's all in your head. Your life is in your head and your heart.'

Schenker's post-UFO career in the early eighties started brightly, but with the Michael Schenker Group mutating into the McAuley Schenker Group and the onset of an increasingly bland, Americanised sound, his original fans have longed for the German to reunite with vocalist Phil Mogg and bass player Pete Way to get his old band off the ground again. And he admits, when asked, that he is keen on a reformation – on the strict basis that the other members of UFO adopt his personal beliefs and change their naughty ways.

'Yeah, there's a possibility,' he says, 'but only if it's done in a positive way – meaning to leave the negative stuff out and move forward positively. That's what I'm promoting and if I do a UFO reunion it would only be under those circumstances. I want to encourage them [Mogg, Way, second guitarist/ keyboard player Paul Raymond and drummer Andy Parker] to understand how much it could encourage other people to have a different outlook on life. First of all, life is not about making music or any of these other things that we think it is – like money, houses or any of that stuff. Life is about being happy. But we're all running in the wrong directions. So I want to make UFO realise that I'm not changing my direction just to have a reunion.

'UFO has a great chemistry and it's a powerful band, but if I do have a reunion it will only be if it's done in a positive way. If it were done in a negative way it would last maybe half a record. If it was done in a positive way it could last as long as twenty or thirty years. If it's done in a positive way, it means there's a totally different understanding between each individual member of the band and, with this approach, things can last – if you're there with your heart.

'People would love to see UFO back together, although there are some in Japan – for some reason they're more concerned about me – who are really frightened. They say it's going to be really dangerous for me, because of the way UFO are and with their negativity. But if the other members of UFO, just for their own sakes, change to the positive, then it's going to be much more worthwhile.'

UFO's reputation for embracing hedonistic habits is legendary in the world of hard rock. So it seems totally implausible that any kind of common ground could be found between Schenker and his former bandmates to facilitate a reunion under the conditions that have been set. Nevertheless, I then ring Pete Way – who I've got to know since a new line-up of the band was formed for a one-off album (*High Stakes & Dangerous Men*) – to provide an update on what's going on in Schenker's head.

He is intrigued about what Michael has been saying, especially as he has just received a letter from the guitarist's manager, Bella Piper, inviting the key original members of UFO to reform the band – on very specific terms. Indeed, it's even suggested that the proceeds from UFO's tours and albums be used to fund the building of a special centre for believers of positive energy. Way laughs as he struggles to get his head around the concept of the band giving away their money, to support what he views as nothing more than a crazy cult. And he insists on reading out the letter, while interjecting his own thoughts at regular intervals.

'There's such good stuff about the retreat they want to buy,' he says. 'I'll read this to you . . .

'"*For three years now, Michael has been without drink or drugs. He has been free and clean of those old habits; he has developed healthy habits and surrounded himself with people to keep him in the positive programme. Michael, as you all know from the past, is an extreme person and has taken his new direction to the extreme.*"

'Now that's another thing that pisses me off,' says Pete, 'but anyway . . .

'"*Michael is a very sensitive man, which also shows itself in his guitar playing. He has always played from the heart. And being clean and clear as a person, he operates from the heart. Michael sees the value in sharing and giving encouragement to others to spark and inspire others to live a happy life, to help them realise they're not a hopeless case, which at one point he thought he was. The name of Michael Schenker has a lot of power to influence*

— for kids who have heard his interviews and read about what's happening, Michael has changed their lives on the spot. Michael, after seeing the difference he's made in others' lives, has made a commitment to promoting positive energy as his life's work, to maintain a balance in his own life as a living example."

'Now, to me, Kirk, that's like the Moonies. You know what I mean? It's like, "Michael, you're doing well, my son."

"Michael wishes to use his privileged position to promote positive energy and well-being."

'Now, the only reason he's got any kind of privileged position is because of UFO. Everyone has just about given up with his solo albums, so his guitar playing is the only thing he's got going for him. The only time he plays any guitar now is on an old UFO song, so they're obviously going, "Michael, let's go back to that."

"For Michael to move positively forward, he has to be selective and careful as to who he spends his time and energy with. For the first time in twenty-three years, Michael is free to make his own choices without being signed to contracts."

'Well,' laughs Pete, 'that means he's been dropped by everybody!

"His commitments are his own and having this freedom gives him such a great feeling that his creative level has reached a new height and pureness."

'What the fuck does that mean?' he asks.

"Michael also has a plan to build a retreat centre . . ."

'This is the bit I like . . .

". . . that people like yourselves can come and stay at and get all the tools of transformation."

'Now, what the fuck are the "tools of transformation"?

"Everything can grow musically and spiritually."

'Well,' says Pete. 'I don't think I need to grow musically and spiritually myself . . .

"And as far as working with all of you in the return of UFO, we need a full commitment from all of you that you would like to participate in this way of living."

'What, you mean participate in the "tools of transformation"?

"And being that you're all willing to grow and develop . . ."

'See, this sounds like the fucking Moonies . . .

". . . healthy habits . . ."

'You see, the thing is, Kirk, I don't need the money from doing this. You know what I mean? I'm quite happy with like, living in a house, paying the rent, having a beer, going for a meal . . . I'm not unhappy doing that.

". . . and transform the old habits and do whatever it takes."

'Old habits? You don't see me do drugs, do you? And drinking? I haven't drunk for a couple of months. Well, I drank a bit too much the other day, but . . .

"In fact, Michael and I feel it's important for everybody to go into the twelve-step programme. We feel it would be most effective to do it in Arizona and it can be part of the pre-production programme. UFO has the power as a group to help people all over the world. The return of UFO can really be a lot of fun."

'Fun? I like that bit!' he laughs.

"As well as to get positive messages out to help others."

'Now, what are we, playing in a rock band and making records? Or are we out to change people's lives?

"We have a private investor willing to finance the entire project from beginning to end."

'Bearing in mind that you've got two big record companies interested and [Metallica/Def Leppard manager] Peter Mensch wants to manage it. Michael said to me, "I think Peter Mensch is being negative." Well, all he did was tell Michael that his career is totally fucked. Michael asked him for something like $200,000, which is something I certainly wouldn't do. So anyway . . .

"However, I feel UFO can start its own label, fan club and merchandising company and that the band should maintain total control over the creative process. But for everyone involved to put everything they've got into it, we need to ensure that everyone is of like mind and willing to sign a contract stating that there will be no drugs or drinking during the project."

'Yeah, that's all right, no problem,' says Way, a little surprisingly.

"And anyone who breaks the agreement will be held responsible financially to the project and the investors."

'I can understand that,' concedes Pete, 'because I can imagine being pretty pissed off myself if Phil suddenly decided to go on a bender.

"We also have a major world promotion plot to tie in with a huge corporation to launch and fuel the return of UFO. I would like to speak to each one of you to talk about where you are in your lives and how each of you would feel about this proposal. And what your personal goals are and if we can all come together to make this ship fly. So please call so that we can be more positive forward."

'See,' adds Pete. 'That's Michael's writing there, "more positive forward".

"Right now, we are on the road promoting the Thank You *record."*

'Did you know it was called *Thank You?*' he asks, without waiting for a reply.

"We are going to keep moving forward until we receive all agreements and then we can start pre-production and rehearsals in AZ. If we can't agree it's okay, we'll just keep moving positive [sic] forward. We feel this will be good for all of you, a great time for change and growth and a positive move for everyone. All I want is the best for everyone involved. And as Michael's best friend and manager, it is my intention to help him maintain his new fountain to peace and make a difference. Love, Bella."'

Way reveals he had no idea that Michael had been listening to subliminal messages on cassette tapes, but admits, 'Nothing surprises me.' However, he finds it difficult to know how to respond to Schenker's requests. 'It's a really odd situation for me,' he confides. 'Phil is very mellow about the whole thing. I mean, Phil will go without drinking, the same as me. But to be honest, you start to feel very let down. You can have respect for somebody, but after a while you start to say, "Hang on, I don't know if this will work for any of us." It's a bit odd, isn't it?'

Of course, there is to be no immediate reformation of UFO. Several years later, however, Schenker does indeed eventually reunite with his old colleagues to tour and make a handful of albums. None of the guys are required to become believers in positive energy. There is no retreat centre built in Arizona from UFO funds. And Schenker later succumbs to further alcohol problems and embarrasses himself with a dreadful stage performance that becomes something of a YouTube favourite among hard-rock fans with a penchant for watching their musical heroes commit professional suicide.

The 'tools of transformation', it would appear, have stopped working.

KILLING JOKE: THE JAZ SINGER

Jaz Coleman is known as the Black Jester but there's little to laugh about as the Killing Joke frontman delves into the darkest depths of his psyche in the early nineties to discuss mental disorders, murder and music. Which is heavy going when you're trying to eat your dinner . . .

Jaz Coleman, it is fair to say, has not been having the best of times. 'During a period a few years ago, which represented the lowest ebb in my entire existence,' he confides, 'there were a lot of terrible emotions, prompted by people who knew of my situation and really tried to finish me off, who made a conscious effort to drive the last nail into my coffin. And yes, I was very, very close to taking somebody's life.'

Killing Joke's erratic frontman has never been applauded for his sanity. This is, after all, the man who is said to have once secretly fled to Iceland with just one pound in his pocket after blowing all his cash; who apparently slashed his own arm and dripped blood over a bootlegger dealing in unauthorised Killing Joke tapes; who deposited a pile of maggots and raw liver at the front desk of *Melody Maker* after a bad review; and who allegedly threatened a record company executive for his lack of honesty after first daubing himself in war paint.

But recent experiences did indeed send Coleman over the edge, resulting in a two-month stay at an asylum. 'A lot of personal things, such as looking at myself over the past ten years and seeing that I was somebody that had absolutely zero morality, all got to me,' he reveals. 'The stress levels put me in the bin and I had a complete nervous breakdown. I wanted to die.'

Of course, this is not the kind of conversation you would usually expect to have with a member of a band celebrating their reformation. They generally tell you how the latest record is the greatest thing they have ever made and how the new live show knocks spots off their old one. Not that the vocalist actually attempted to end his life . . . or thankfully anybody else's, for that matter. But Jaz Coleman is no ordinary artist or human being. 'I had to radically change my life in terms of attitudes to people and respecting myself a little bit more,' he admits. 'I've always had an innate problem with people because I'm a very intense person and I say what I think. This [rock music] business makes you very suspicious of people in terms of their intentions and motives. Of course I like people, but I find that if you spend too much time with them you can become very drained. Generally speaking, I like isolation, which is why I live nearly 14,000 miles away [in New Zealand].'

Today, however, Jaz is mingling with other members of the human race in London. He has agreed to meet me in a small diner just off Ladbroke Grove and talk about the philosophy of the band that, after its initial heyday in the 1980s, continues to regroup whenever the mood takes them. 'Killing Joke is a lifestyle,' he declares. 'We've been hanging out together – myself, Youth and Geordie – for some time, a lot of it in New Zealand, some of it in London,

> 'I was very, very close to taking somebody's life.'
>
> – Jaz Coleman

all over the place really. The way we play our lives is as important as the way we play our instruments. We know each other so well; we know everything about each other's personal lives. We have a lot of personal freedoms as individuals. We make our lives as colourful as possible and then we get onto our instruments and we just let go. We become mindless; it's utterly spontaneous.'

Killing Joke's sonically harsh and abrasive music is confrontational and uncompromising in its attitude. So it's perhaps fitting that the same can be said of the relationships between the three members when they reunite for each new project. 'There are character associations going down,' admits Jaz, 'and it's trying on every level, in terms of morality and what you suppose you believe. The whole thing is a very stressful time. We launch into each other and you have to stand your ground if you believe in something. They are intelligent, articulate people, with a very black sense of humour. It's a constant challenge and we channel that into the music.'

It almost feels a little dangerous for me to ask Coleman if Killing Joke is a democracy – actually one of their album titles – given that he is very much considered their leader. Typically, he laughs at the suggestion when I put it to him. 'We're all a bunch of fascists,' he says. 'Basically, we just clash and that's what the sound of the music is. It's the sound of fury, absolute fury. Killing Joke represents an exorcism for me. I've gone through years of guilt and pain and I view Killing Joke as my release. The band has been an excellent experiment in manifesting dreams. And dreams always come true – always.'

'Do they *really*?' I ask, somewhat sceptically.

'Oh yes,' he insists. 'That's if they are true dreams and are based on the right foundations. That is your birthright, your karmic birthright. And I know that *anything* is possible. You can't have beauty without pain. I don't think you can have excitement without fear. I don't see life as black and white. My life is colourful, extraordinary and beautiful – and I feel a great sense of personal destiny. I want to master what I do. I want to perfect Killing Joke, to tap the spirit of it further, to make it even more explosive. I want to use our music as a political weapon and a spiritual medium.'

When we've finished talking, Jaz proudly produces a big red book of squiggles and musical notes that he insists represents a symphonic score of Rolling Stones songs, of all things. I think he's pulling my leg but the expression on his face suggests he is deadly serious. 'Wow!' I say, still not totally convinced. The album duly appears as promised . . .

PEARL JAM: EDDIE NOT READY

Grunge rockers Pearl Jam are set to represent the sound of Seattle for the next two decades, but during a January 1992 conversation singer Eddie Vedder insists that he wants to 'keep it small'. Oops!

Eddie Vedder is a worried man. Pearl Jam, you see, are becoming really quite popular. And it's something the vocalist of the Seattle grunge outfit is feeling extremely uneasy about. 'The band will probably really hate me for saying this,' he warns, in that laidback drawl of his, 'but I just feel like it's getting a little too big too quickly. And believe me, I'm trying to hold it within. I'm really trying to keep it small. These are intimate songs and I think that, if nothing else, we're robbing the music of getting a chance to live in an intimate stage.

'Some people hear this music, like Anthony Kiedis [of the Red Hot Chili Peppers, with whom Pearl Jam have been touring] told me that he hears "Alive" as some sort of anthem or something. And as nice as it is to hear that, I just have to shake my head and say no, it's a small thing that should be listened to where everybody can connect and bond with the band and with each other. There are just too many other things happening when it's bigger. Some people are saying, "Let's ride the wave to see how big it can get." But I want to slow it down a bit.'

Eddie is holed up in a Seattle studio, where he is supposed to be laying down vocals for some new songs. Instead, he's on the phone expressing his concerns about increasing fame and fortune. It seems only right for me to point out to Eddie that Epic Records, part of the huge Sony conglomerate that the band are signed to, are unlikely to take into account the group's personal feelings when structuring their mass marketing campaign.

'Especially *mine*,' he concurs. 'Believe me, it's a struggle I'm going through and I'm tormented by that right now. Have you heard of a band called Fugazi? [Yes, I say, eager to protect my punk-rock credibility.] They came from Washington DC, out of that hardcore movement that produced Black Flag and Bad Brains. They won't play a show unless it's [open to] all ages and five dollars [a ticket], while they go out of their way to make it under 500 people. And these shows are fucking *religious*. It's just such an amazing thing that goes down.

'And when you get bigger you start losing control; you've got people in seats, they can't move around the way they like, they can't express themselves, they've got security people standing in front of them, they maybe can't even see or perhaps hear. At a certain point, it's very hard to go back and play intimate shows.'

This is not the philosophy of many rock stars, most of whom are eager to shift as many units – in terms of records and concert tickets – as quickly as possible. 'The thing is,' says Eddie, 'you can only go so high before you start sounding silly. In a way, I can almost feel sorry for Kurt from Nirvana. I don't know what he's going to write about for the next record. How frustrating can it be having as much money to do whatever you want to do, you know? Like how is he going to sing to the punk-rock kids?'

The idea that Mr Cobain might one day commit suicide is not remotely considered, of course. Not that death is far away from the origins of Pearl Jam, with the band emerging from the ashes of Mother Love Bone – or 'Lover Moth Bone' as Vedder jokes – following the heroin overdose of singer Andrew Wood. 'Andy and I are on different avenues, our trips are just totally different,' he insists, before adding, 'Our lives have been led very differently.'

That shouldn't suggest that Eddie enjoyed the happiest of childhoods, although music did represent some form of salvation. 'I think I had a kind of difficult . . .' he begins, before the sentence trails off. 'There were things that weren't pleasant about growing up. And while it seemed that I couldn't depend on anything and everything else could let me down quite easily, with music I could always go and put on certain records and they were always there. Pete Townshend saved my life a few times, whether he knows it or not.'

Years after this conversation, Eddie would get the opportunity to inform Townshend of his emotional influence when he befriended The Who's guitarist and musical originator to the point that he would be invited to appear live onstage with the legendary British band. Indeed, Townshend would even claim that he dissuaded a disillusioned Vedder from quitting the rock business at one point in the 1990s.

Because *Ten*, the band's first album, would indeed catapult Pearl Jam into places they – or at least their vocalist – didn't want to go. If Nirvana's *Nevermind* was the first major grunge album to be sold to the masses, *Ten* followed effortlessly in its slipstream to eventually rack up multi-platinum sales. 'It definitely marks the time that we did it,' says Eddie, who acknowledges the subconscious ideas behind the album. 'It's weird because there was nothing specific that we were thinking about at the time. And then after the record was done and we were getting mail from people who had listened to it, all of a sudden we realised there was a running theme about the appreciation of life. Songs like "Porch" talk about how this could be the day, how randomly our lives could be taken. And "Alive" and "Deep" are about substance abuse; of people not appreciating life and being quite decadent in the way they live it.

'I think we were all feeling that way for different reasons,' he offers as explanation for the album's subject matter. 'Obviously, you had what [guitarist] Stone [Gossard] and [bassist] Jeff [Ament] had been through [with Mother Love Bone]. And I'd been through some loss in the past that I had never really dealt with. And just in the honesty in the record, all of a sudden looking back, we kind of realise that's what we were feeling. We still kind of feel that way now, like we're living it by being onstage and going out of our way to just appreciate what's around us. It's been a good bible to live by.'

> 'I keep on giving and I end up walking home naked.'
> – Eddie Vedder

Eddie describes listening to *Ten* as 'looking at the animal in the zoo' while experiencing the material live is 'like seeing the animal in the wilds'. But what the audience chooses to take from Pearl Jam's work is entirely up to them. 'People use it for different things,' admits Vedder, 'whether it's background music or something that helps them keep strength in their lives. And I think our music, if you want more out of it and listen to it deeper, there's definitely more there for you.

'Even right from the beginning, that's what was different with this band for me, because you kind of lose yourself in it. The music has hypnotic qualities to it. You can hold your breath and get down a little deeper, into this meditative state, and all of a sudden you're dealing with deeper issues or feelings.'

All of which makes it difficult for Eddie to connect with his audience on occasions before taking the stage. 'It's weird because I really like meeting people when we travel,' he says. 'But the thing is, before [playing] I'm really a basket case, like you really shouldn't try to talk to me because I'm just trying to get myself in the right state to connect with these emotions. I get a little crazy just trying to get focused. And then, after being through it all, I'm pretty much a wreck.'

Eddie has seen how the public's perception of him has changed since the band became successful. 'People think you're some kind of big star. You know, you're not like this person; you're more like this *thing*, this kind of *commodity*, because they've seen your face on MTV and in magazines,' he says.

'I don't mind [giving] autographs or any of that stuff, it's just when people start asking for your shoes. They want so much more, it's so funny. And the thing is, the trap is that I will give them anything. So they just keep on asking and I keep on giving and I end up walking home naked, feeling like, "Why did I do that?"'

It's still early days in the band's career, but there's further conflict in Eddie's head regarding the financial disparity between what Pearl Jam are spending as a group and what the members are actually earning. 'My refrigerator is completely empty,' he declares. 'I want it to be the cover of the next record. The fact is that I'm having a hard time keeping ends together, like everybody does. So why spend $40,000 on a video? That just seems totally insane. We're in the studio right now, we're spending a thousand dollars a day and I hate spending money.

'When there's so many people hurting in the world,' he adds, 'it's hard to justify.'

I thank Eddie for his honesty and valuable time, but he seems in the mood to continue talking, especially when I casually mention that few bands – let alone high-profile American ones – bother visiting Southend-on-Sea, as is the case when Pearl Jam arrives in the UK next month.

'Really?' he responds.

I try to say goodbye but there's no getting Eddie off the phone.

'Now, tell me just a little more about Southend,' he says. 'Nobody plays there; why is that?'

I explain to Vedder that the town in question is on the Essex coast, at least an hour's drive from London, and that the most notable group to emerge from the area is Dr Feelgood, an old R&B band from Canvey Island.

'And you say that's near the coast?' he asks.

'It's actually *on* the coast,' I tell him.

'Wow, so maybe I'll get to see some ocean then,' he says.

I joke that the resort is rarely referred to as Southend-on-Sea but Southend-on-Mud, such is the state of the beach.

'Really?' says Eddie. 'Well, I'm still looking forward to it. I'd love to meet you there. By the way, I'm sorry I was a bit fuzzy this morning, my throat's really hurting.'

He explains that Pearl Jam have been recording songs for the *Singles* soundtrack, which also includes contributions from other key Seattle grunge outfits such as Soundgarden and Alice In Chains. 'We're in the movie actually,' he reveals. 'I'm in Matt Dillon's band. We form a band called Citizen Dick and I'm the drummer.'

'So there's no proper acting on your part then?' I ask.

'Well, I'm not really a drummer,' he says, stating the obvious. 'So I think it's some pretty *amazing* acting . . .'

Perhaps inevitably, Pearl Jam goes on to sell an estimated sixty million records worldwide over the next twenty years.

MICK RONSON: HULL OF A GUY

As he climbs back into bed in a dressing gown, a fag hanging from his lips, you wouldn't think Mick Ronson was one of rock's most respected guitar-slingers but, as our meeting in February 1989 proves, the former David Bowie and Ian Hunter sidekick was always far more down to earth than his legendary status suggests . . .

The foyer of the Plaza on Hyde Park is mysteriously empty. Ian Hunter and Mick Ronson are supposed to be meeting members of the London press to discuss their latest reunion, which saw them play a successful gig at the Dominion Theatre last night. But there's no sign of any PR people or record company personnel – or rock'n'roll stars, for that matter – until the doors of the elevator suddenly open and a certain Mr Hunter, eyes hidden behind his trademark dark glasses, strides into view.

I naturally approach the former Mott The Hoople frontman and ask him what's happened to the interviews that he and Ronson had been scheduled to undertake. 'We've cancelled them,' he says, with no further explanation. 'But Mick's up in room 302 if you wanna try him.'

Feeling as if permission has been granted from the highest authority, I duly make the call from the reception desk and a sleepy-sounding Ronson eventually responds. 'You're downstairs in the foyer? Well, you might as well come up then,' he says, rather generously when you consider the circumstances. I make my way up to his room and, when the door opens, one of Ziggy Stardust's most visually striking old Spiders From Mars is standing there in his stripy dressing gown with a cigarette hanging from his lips. 'In you come,' he says in his East Yorkshire accent, before shuffling off to make his first cup of tea of the day.

The bed seems the obvious place for me to sit, despite Mick then getting back in it as if it's nearing midnight rather than midday. The obvious question to first ask is what the guitarist has been up to in recent times having seemingly disappeared off the map for a lengthy period. His stints with David Bowie and Mott The Hoople, as well as the *Slaughter On 10th Avenue* and *Play Don't Worry* solo albums, are distant memories from the seventies as he subsequently became a hired gun embroiling himself in session and production work. Rather than leaving the planet, however, it becomes apparent that this journeyman has actually been exploring it.

'I've been doing quite a bit of production and travelling a lot, spending time first in Italy, then France and over here in the UK for a while,' he explains, ruffling his blond hair. 'But when I was here I wasn't having a very good time. There were a lot of things going on in my life that weren't right, so I decided to take myself off to Nashville, where I stayed for most of last year. People were suggesting I stick around in Nashville. I could get a lot of work down there but it would have felt as if I was retiring, like it was pipe 'n' slippers time or something. I'd given up playing guitar for a long while but then I started wanting to play again.

'So I rang up Ian, who I always talk to whether we're working together or not, and said, "Look, I gotta do *something*. I want to play the guitar again and get out there." I didn't want to be in the studio all the time, because that just seemed like I was doing a regular nine-to-five job or something. And the reason I wanted to get into the music business in the first place was that I valued my freedom. I needed to be able to do what I wanted, when I wanted, but then I ended up in a situation where it was almost like doing a normal job – and that I *refuse* to do. That's not what music is all about.

'The business has changed a lot in that respect,' he continues. 'When I started, people used to play because they wanted to. It never really entered their heads about making money. But these days it's just about making money, that's really the extent of it. Half the people you see think they're in the fashion business or something – they're in it for the money and that's their priority. It's all bullshit!'

Ronson pronounces 'money' as if it's a dirty word. He speaks fervently of how the rock'n'roll business has been exploited by those whose motives are very different from his own.

'We've never really been typical pop stars, on the front pages of magazines and all that business,' he says of his pairing with Hunter. 'That's for celebrities, people who *need* to be stars. There's no such thing as a star really – you just do what you do. If you strive to be in the gossip magazines and look like a model, then that's your trip.

'We're not after that at all; appearing on the covers of magazines and trying to look like Greek gods. We're here to play our new material and to play what we *want* to play, *whenever* we want to play it. I don't care about the other side of the business.

'Last night we played nine new songs and only six old ones – and that's the idea. We're not here to pat ourselves on the back, to tell ourselves how wonderful we are and say, "Don't these people love us?" That's for those who choose to reform for a quick cash-in. If it comes across like that, I don't want any part of it. The whole idea is to play new material and that's what we should be doing. You should always go forward in life; you should never go back.'

Yet Ronson has frequently revived his working relationship with Ian Hunter. The guitarist co-produced and played on the singer's *Ian Hunter*, *You're Never Alone With A Schizophrenic* and *Short Back N' Sides* albums and made a guest appearance on *All Of The Good Ones Are Taken*, as well as touring as part of the Ian Hunter and Hunter-Ronson bands in the past. He suggests that the magnetism exists because of the productive chemistry between them.

'We don't really know what it is but we do work very well together. We always have done and there's some kind of reaction when we do. It does happen with people. You get two personalities together and for some unknown reason it's like a magical kind of thing,' he says.

'And two heads are better than one anyway. Ian is very opinionated about certain things but, then again, so am I. We see things very differently in a lot of ways. But we can work things out and that's good for both of us. I don't get things all my own way and neither does he.

'I can say to Ian, "Look, that stinks, that's rubbish!" He's done things with other people and I don't think they're being honest with him half the time. It's like, "Yes boss, no boss." They generally agree with him on everything, but you don't want that. You want somebody you can talk to and be honest with. And that's why I think it works.'

As Ronson speaks, the phone next to the bed starts to ring. He excuses himself and takes the call. It quickly becomes apparent he's talking to his missus – well, I assume it's his wife – who was due to fly over from the States for the remaining few dates of the UK tour, but has seemingly had a change of heart. 'C'mon, baby, just jump on a plane and come over,' he says. 'I want to see you.'

Needless to say, I feel slightly embarrassed to be listening to Mick's personal conversation, so I make some motions to suggest he might prefer some privacy. But he's having none of it.

'No, you're okay,' he says before turning back to the phone.

'I *need* you, baby,' he pleads. 'Come on, baby, what's the problem? Just come over. Look, I'll sort the flight out, just try and get here as quickly as you can. I *need* you.'

But Mick fails to convince his partner to make the trip and, with some sadness, he eventually puts the receiver down.

'Where were we?' he asks, after taking a few seconds to refocus his thoughts. I remind him that he was talking about Ian Hunter and take the liberty of suggesting that Ronson might enjoy something of a love-hate relationship with the singer given the pair only seem to work with each for limited periods of time.

'It's not that,' he says. 'I remember we went on a couple of tours after the *Schizophrenic* album and they were good. But shortly afterwards, I felt that I wanted to do something else. I didn't feel right; I didn't feel as if I was being honest with myself. I didn't want to play the guitar that badly and I didn't want to play "All The Young Dudes" again.'

He reveals how he headed to Canada and produced the likes of the Payolas and Lisa Dal Bello before considering retirement from the music business all together. 'I thought about going to college and becoming a chef,' he reveals. 'I didn't want to be known just as a guitar player for the rest of my life. For a while there I lost myself. People do, they lose themselves and, when that happens, it can last for years.'

Ronson starts to make himself another cuppa. He insists he 'doesn't care' if the public remembers him for being Bowie's sidekick more than Hunter's. 'People can think what they like,' he shrugs. Last night's performance was his first with Hunter in London since the 1970s, when he started to spread his wings in terms of who he worked with.

'I got involved with Bob Dylan and Van Morrison and Dr John,' he explains. 'I just wanted to explore. I wanted to get involved in different kinds of music and work with different people. It's something I had to do; otherwise I'd have kicked myself in the teeth when I got older. People have these regrets and wish they'd done different things when they had the chance. I don't want to turn round and say that to myself.'

But as he readily concedes, when people take risks they can also get things wrong. 'They make mistakes, I've made *lots* of mistakes,' he admits. 'But you've got to make mistakes to learn. The mistakes make you stronger. You should never be frightened of making mistakes because if you are that makes you super-careful. And when you're super-careful there's no soul anymore.

'Yes, my career has meandered but that's an advantage, because you have to keep your ears and eyes open, d'you know what I mean?'

He pauses for moment. 'I don't have any regrets,' he confides, 'but there have been a few times where I haven't felt very good about myself. And I haven't felt very good about anybody else either.'

Hunter resides in New York while Ronson has a home in Woodstock, although he says, 'I'm not sure *where* I'm living right now. I don't know where I *want* to live right now. I've had a house in Woodstock for about ten years but I haven't spent that much time there. It's just a base; somewhere I keep my belongings. It's a lovely place and I really want to keep it. But I don't want to be tied down to that place – or any one place. Sometimes I think maybe I'll go to Amsterdam for a couple of months and then maybe Brussels or Paris . . .

'Maybe I'll come back to London for a few months. Once we've done our next record I'll just leave for wherever I feel like going. I like moving about and living where I feel like living at the time – and why not? Why do you want to tie yourself down?'

I say that Ronson is fortunate in as much that he has a freedom that many people don't. 'Yeah, but that's because they choose *not* to,' he responds. 'People can have a lot more freedom if they want; they just decide not to. And it's the same musically. Musicians can get into a routine and then it ends up just like a normal job.'

I ask if Ian shares Mick's feelings about being a rock musician.

'Yes, he does,' he says emphatically. 'We talk a lot; we always talk. We talk for hours, we always have done. I know I can talk to Ian about *anything*.'

He insists he has absolutely no intention of producing the next album with Hunter – which eventually appears under the title *YUI Orta* – because he doesn't want to be 'babysitting the project'. He adds, 'I just want to go in, play the guitar and when I get tired, I want to be able to leave. I'm looking past the album, but this thing will last as long as it lasts. If there comes a point where I don't feel it's progressing and it's becoming a stalemate or something, then I'll know it's time to move on.'

> **'There have been a few times where I haven't felt very good about myself.'**
> **– Mick Ronson**

But there is no denying that Ronson is hungry to play the guitar again when I suggest that's the case. 'You bet I am, more so than ever,' he insists. 'You have to remember that I only recently started again. And it wasn't difficult because I *felt* like playing. It's down to instinct, you know. It's as simple as that. You follow your heart and you follow your conscience.

'There was a time when I didn't want to play my old stuff; I didn't feel the need to. And that's why I stopped. But now I don't mind playing that material again because we're approaching things in a different way. Those songs are part of something I was involved in and they are a part of me.

'I'm enjoying playing again,' he adds, drawing on another cigarette. 'I'm not very good at conversation, especially onstage, so I'd rather talk through the guitar. I think I can say a lot through that.'

Just a few years later, at the age of forty-six, Mick Ronson dies of liver cancer. A memorial concert featuring Ian Hunter and members of Queen, the Who, the Rolling Stones, the Clash, the Sex Pistols and Def Leppard, among others, eventually takes place in London, while a third solo album titled *Heaven And Hull* – acknowledging the final and first places on his life's journey – is released posthumously. Yet there's no denying the suspicion that his maverick spirit might still be wandering . . .

CARLOS SANTANA: SPIRITS ARE UP

It feels strange ringing guitar legend Carlos Santana at his home in May 1992, but that's nothing compared to being invited into his garden of spirituality while he's trying to 'chop flowers for a bouquet'...

Carlos Santana has recorded more than twenty-five albums of latin-laced string strumming 'n' strangling (*Abraxas*, *Moonflower* and *Inner Secrets* among them) in a long and distinguished career spanning several decades. Today the Mexican legend is being interviewed for *The Guitar Magazine* and so I need to ask questions of a vaguely technical nature when he picks up the phone at home in Los Angeles. 'Well then, Carlos,' I begin, as I prepare my opening gambit, 'when you pick up your guitar, how is that you never run out of new places to stick your fingers?'

It might sound like a silly question, indeed it is really, but Carlos is taking the answer very seriously. 'Music is like a river,' he states, 'and every time you dive in you touch a new part of the water. The best music is like clean water that you would trust your baby to drink . . . but, sadly, sometimes the river is polluted and people shit in it.'

Er, quite. 'The message,' he continues, 'has always been, like Bob Marley says, "We heal the people with music, we free the people with music." It reminds us all that we're eagles, not turkeys. It lifts up the spirit and tames the beast. A lot of people say, "Well, if it tames your spirit you'll become a wimp." Wrong! You get more energy from the spiritual than the physical.'

So how does Carlos continue to come up with new ideas and inspiration? 'I love a lot of music,' he says, 'from Marley to John Lee Hooker to John Coltrane to Marvin Gaye to Jimi Hendrix, so that's a big garden. And what I try to do with my guitar is chop certain flowers for specific places to make a bouquet. It's just a better presentation of a huge garden.'

The analogies continue, however. 'Basically, melody is female and rhythm is masculine,' he explains. 'The bed doesn't matter – it can be reggae or Afro-Cuban or heavy metal or country and western – but the melody and rhythm are the two lovers. I'm always trying to combine different colours and textures. I listen a lot to Wayne Shorter and Jimmy Page, so I'm a student. I'll never be a master, for I believe that when you're a master you're dead, because there is nothing left to learn.'

But after decades as a musician, surely Carlos has mastered the guitar by now? 'No, no, every time I play it, man, I feel like I've just picked it up for the first time.'

Thankfully, for all our sakes, Santana's records don't sound as if his guitar has been placed in the hands of a complete novice. He spent more than twenty years recording for CBS, which later became Sony, but he's happy to have escaped the commercial influence of that particular corporate entity.

'CBS brought in dumb songs, dumb producers,' he complains. 'To me, their approach to music is like the American way of building McDonald's. What I'm trying to tell you is that in my heart I feel that quality and quantity can go together. The majority of stuff they play on the radio is microwaved, plastic music. I know that Bob Marley and Jimi Hendrix are gonna sell more records eventually in life than Madonna or Michael Bolton. A cage can be made out of gold but it's still a cage.'

I ask Carlos what he thinks of modern-day hard-rock heroes such as Metallica, for instance. 'Yeah, them and Guns N' Roses have taken the place of the AC/DCs and that sort of stuff,' he says. 'But to me, I heard most of it through Jeff Beck, Jimmy Page, Eric Clapton and Jimi Hendrix. They were the four corners of the ring – everybody else has to dance in the middle of it.'

'Can real music change things in society?' I ask.

'Music is like a river . . . but, sadly, sometimes it's polluted and people shit in it.'
– Carlos Santana

'Of course,' he insists. 'The Berlin Wall isn't there any more. That wasn't brought down by politics or religion. That was brought down by music, the social changes that music brings.' And is he playing his role in that? 'Absolutely. Music is like a ministry without selling religion. Because I don't believe in religion, or politics, but I do believe in the spiritual side of music that makes Clapton or Marley or Page touch somebody in a hospital. They're ready to go and the doctor says, "Man, we've done everything for you medicine-wise, it's up to you." The person might not wanna live but if he hears one of those musicians he bounces back.'

'But aren't the problems in society getting worse?' I dare to suggest. 'That's absolutely right from the point of view of one eye,' he concedes. 'But you have two eyes. With one eye you can say that life is crap, there's nothing but war and violence and brutality. But you've got another eye, so why don't you look through the one where you see flowers and children being born and rainbows and a world that is dominated by angels and not by governments or presidents of companies? You've got a choice.

'You know, I've never seen a shrink, a psychiatrist, a psychologist or a therapist because when I let go I let go. I never go to bed saying, "I should have done, I should have been, I should have said . . ."

'The fact is, I actually snore at night . . .'

THE BLACK CROWES: IN CONSTANT FLIGHT

Georgia's finest (no, not REM) prove themselves to be an accommodating bunch backstage in Brixton during their early-nineties peak, when they insist they're 'never going home' and reveal that one of their former members is now a 'dead man' . . .

There's a bowl of M&Ms – with the brown ones *not* removed, as Van Halen used to famously demand – in the corner of the Black Crowes' dressing room at the Brixton Academy. Vocalist Chris Robinson is holding court with members of the Verve and the editor of the *NME*, while in the opposite corner Radio One DJ Annie Nightingale is chatting to Quireboys guitar-slinger Guy Bailey, who appears to have gotten bored of clutching his girlfriend's backside and posing for shaven-headed photographer Butch every time the camera is pointed his way.

The other members of the Atlanta, Georgia band – Johnny Colt, Steve Gorman, Rich Robinson and Marc Ford – make frequent appearances while the southern-rock sounds of the Allman Brothers and Lynyrd Skynyrd fill the room, the CDs plucked from a flightcase that also contains music by the likes of Neil Young, Bob Dylan and Leon Russell – all of whom provide an appropriate soundtrack to backstage life with the Crowes.

Colt spots my crumpled white jacket on a chair and picks it up to inspect its many creases before requesting a coat hanger from his ever-helpful tour manager. Next he's flicking through the pages of a magazine in which Rolling Stones legend Keith Richards claims the Crowes used to send him cassettes of their demos before finally winning a record deal. 'He's getting us confused with the Quireboys,' insists Colt. 'We never sent him any tapes.'

There's something of the outlaw Richards' spirit in Colt. The Black Crowes are relentless road warriors – and their bass player wouldn't have it any other way. Their previous tour spanned twenty epic months and, even though Chris Robinson had complained in a separate conversation with me that 'everyone was frazzled and wanted to go home', Colt takes a rather different view.

'You don't *go* home,' he states, sipping at a beer. 'There's no home to go to. It's all in your head. You may sleep in a bed that you go to once a year, but you don't *ever* go home. This isn't *about* going home.'

The band's first two albums, *Shake Your Money Maker* and *The Southern Harmony And Musical Companion*, established the Crowes' irresistible template for southern-fried, blues and soul-drenched rock. There's a strong feeling of comradeship among the quintet, which is just as well given the amount of time they spend in each other's pockets.

'The relationships between us are probably as good or better than they've ever been,' says a colourfully dressed Gorman – the one with the short hair – as the drummer pulls up a chair. 'I think everyone looks around right now and says, "This is the only band I want to be in and these are the only people I want to play with." And when you're in that situation, you're gonna get on with people pretty well.'

'Plus,' interjects Colt, 'if you're being that close on the road for so long, you can't hide anything from people. Even if you don't want to be honest, everyone will figure you out. There are days when you want to strangle each other. But the only people who know what we're going through are the other guys in the band. What may be a hard day for me is gonna escape someone else, who might have what you call a normal job. And their [idea of a] hard day would escape me. I don't understand their problems and they're not gonna understand mine. The only people I can go to – and nobody in other bands because no other band is like this one – are the ones around me. They're the only people I can speak to.'

'There are days when you want to strangle each other.'
– Johnny Colt

As the frontman of the group, Chris Robinson has attracted most of the public spotlight – and the troubles that brings. 'I've watched him have some problems,' confides Colt. 'Sometimes you get the weird people, that's the only thing that worries me. I've been scared for him before, just that something could happen or get out of hand. I guess that's a little paranoid of me.'

Chris had previously admitted 'it's not easy being in this band because it's full tilt all the time'. And Colt at least concurs with that. 'It's twenty-four hours,' he says. 'Like I said, you don't go home. This is it. As much as me and Steve can want to fucking kill each other one day, if you put us on two separate desert islands in the sun – which we've done before – after just a day we get in touch with one another.'

Gorman adds, 'None of us knows how to function without everyone else around. It's just like a family.'

Except the 'family' lost original guitarist Jeff Cease, for reasons they are reluctant to be too specific about, before he was succeeded by Ford. Do they consider Cease a lost friend?

'I consider him a dead man,' says Colt. 'He's just gone, simple.'

Gorman: 'And that's not because he's out of the band, he was gone before he left. He just sort of drifted off . . .'

In mind before body, it would appear. 'You wouldn't waste everyone's time by deteriorating and belittling what we do, you would get out,' says Colt. 'The deterioration factor belittled everything that the band was and took it down. You're only as strong as your weakest link.'

'But surely the band could see what was going on?' I ask.

'Well,' says Colt, beginning to get a little uptight, 'you wouldn't really know what it feels like unless you were shot out of a fuckin' cannon with five other guys. It's that radical. Unless you've lived in a tornado . . . You're trying to hold your own shit down and then you just lose one. But it wasn't like attempts weren't made.'

Gorman: 'He didn't go through anything none of us ever did. It's just a matter of . . . I dunno, I'm not a sociologist.'

There's a sense of improvisation in the two shows the Black Crowes play in London. The set-list changes from night to night, new songs are aired according to the band's (ever-changing) mood and it could be argued that their live values evoke the spirit of the 1970s. Not that Gorman is in agreement when I throw the idea at him the following evening, having been invited back for the second gig. 'I don't think it's got anything to do with the seventies,' he retorts. 'I didn't like the seventies, I grew up in the seventies and I wasn't the happiest person in the world. I wouldn't want to go back.'

Yet the drummer is happy to make comparisons with far earlier times. 'It's just music,' he states. 'From the first music that's ever been made, music for many hundreds of years has been played to a small group of people in an intimate setting – people actually hitting, strumming, singing, whatever they're doing. When rock'n'roll came along it was another form of music but it was the same way. You can say it's a seventies vibe, you can also say it's a vibe from madrigal times.'

'Exactly,' agrees Colt. 'You can connect us with fifteenth-century lute players; there's no difference. Just because technology has moved along, it doesn't mean that everything it's produced is a worthy thing. You should spit back the crap. The five of us can make music with our hands with the shit in this room. It's *in* you. You don't have to have Marshall amps or Fender Telecasters.'

Right, wandering minstrels – the musical type as opposed to the chocolate variety – they are then. So, for how much longer are they going to be staying on the road this time?

'As long as it takes,' says Colt.

'Er, as long as *what* takes?' I ask.

'The whole thing,' he says.

Johnny Colt leaves the Black Crowes in 1997; Steve Gorman follows him through the exit door five years later before rejoining in 2005 after the band have taken a break from business. Sometimes, it would seem, they *do* need to go home after all . . .

METALLICA: INVASION OF PRIVACY

It's the summer of 2009 and, after more than twenty-five years as a member of the mighty Metallica, guitarist Kirk Hammett finally tells his millions of fans that, when it comes down to it, he's actually 'a private person who's a bit of loner'. Funny job he chooses to do, then . . .

'Hi Kirk, it's the *other* Kirk here.' It's impossible to respond to Kirk Hammett's welcome down the telephone line from Copenhagen without informing the guitarist that I'd used a similar introduction myself when we'd met in a London nightclub many years earlier. 'Oh *really?* I don't remember that,' he admits. Well, as if he would . . .

Hammett is ringing *The London Paper* to promote Metallica's forthcoming appearance as headliners of the 2009 Sonisphere Festival at Knebworth, following the success of the new *Death Magnetic* album. You'd think he'd be pleased when I tell him that the Rick Rubin-produced record appears to be a real return to form for the band, but Kirk, as nice as he is, reacts a little indignantly at the implication that the previous album, *St Anger*, was a disappointment. 'People can pretty much think whatever the hell they want to think about it,' he says of the latest release. 'The main thing is that people like it, understand it and are entertained by it. I would say it's a return to form but it's *not* a re-hash. It's not something we're doing to try to recapture past glories.'

Yet the fact remains that the band played not one single song from the *St Anger* album at their recent show at the London 02 Arena, which surely tells you everything you need to know about Metallica's view of that material – recorded during difficult times when the group was on the verge of disintegration. In truth, many people think it's a dog of a record, with a primitive production making Lars Ulrich's drums sound like hollow biscuit tins as the band tries in vain to return to their frenetic thrash roots. Yet Hammett jumps to the record's defence.

'I think it's a great album with some great songs,' he insists. 'We had to make that album to get to the point where we could make *Death Magnetic*. I see that album as the best we could have possibly made under those circumstances, which were very unusual for us.'

Indeed they were. As documented in great detail in the riveting *Some Kind Of Monster* movie, the band invited a therapist to help them resolve their internal conflicts, which saw singer/guitarist James Hetfield walk out of Metallica and into rehab before returning to inflict sobriety instead of alcoholism on his colleagues. Robert Trujillo, previously a member of Ozzy Osbourne's band, had little say after eventually being recruited as the replacement for former bass player Jason Newsted, so it was partly down to Kirk – along with the hired help – to act as the pacifier in the war of words that continued between Hetfield and Ulrich, the two dominant forces in the group. Such turmoil with bands is usually kept under lock and key, but *Some Kind Of Monster* threw open the doors and windows of Metallica's house to expose the band's inner psyche to the whole world.

It's natural to ask Kirk, who seems happy to adopt the role of the 'quiet one', if he has any regrets about the band revealing so much about themselves in such a candid manner. 'Well, I'm a very, very private person who is a bit of a loner and thrives on his own solitude,' he confides. 'So everything you've touched upon there resonated quite heavily with me when I found out that the movie was being made.

'People can pretty much think whatever the hell they want to think about it.'
– Kirk Hammett

'But my whole take, at the end of the day, was that there was a healing process being filmed and one that a lot of other people go through in their lives. You don't have to be in a band to experience some kind of break-up or shake-up. So if it's something that could help other people, then I just have to swallow my own idiosyncrasies towards my privacy – and feelings on what people should or shouldn't see – and kind of embrace the greater good.'

The film has a happy ending, of course. But five years on, is it fair to assume everything has been hunky-dory – particularly between James and Lars – since then? 'The thing is,' says Kirk, 'we now know how to deal with issues of contention and different points of view because of what we experienced through working it all out. We're just better equipped to deal with each other these days.

'In those five years we recorded, went away on tour and learned how to be a band again. In being a new member, Rob brought a lot of great energy, positivity and enthusiasm to the band that wasn't there before. He has established himself as a creative part of the band and we all discovered how much fun it was being in Metallica again. Being away from the therapist and cameras and being left to figure things out for ourselves, you can say we've been learning how to fly again.'

The current tour is set to continue into 2010 as *Death Magnetic* – the band's fifth successive Number One album in the United States – continues to sell in huge quantities across the globe. Once upon a time, the band dubbed 'Alcoholica' could survive the boredom of the road by partying its way from territory to territory. But Metallica are now family men and their new lifestyles dictate that they can no longer spend intense periods away from home – as they did when slogging their guts out to promote the self-titled, multi-platinum 'Black Album' in the early 1990s.

'We have children now but we also have to go out on tour,' says Hammett, 'so we've devised a schedule where when we visit Europe it's two weeks on, two weeks off. And when we're on tour in the States it's one week on, one week off. That allows us to spend quality time with our families and re-energise both sides of the two separate worlds that we live in – one of being a professional musician and the other of being a father and a parent. The fact that we're going to be on tour for at least another year doesn't weigh so heavily on us knowing that the schedule is not that demanding and the separation from our families is not too great.'

Like fellow pioneers Motörhead, who helped take heavy metal to new extremes before them, Metallica have been forced to come to terms with the dilemma of either trying to be the hardest and fastest or simply consolidating their established, recognisable sound. In other words, let others pick up the baton and set new speed records while Metallica concentrate on being what they genuinely are. Put in this context, it's little wonder that Hammett opts for the second option.

'I would definitely say the latter,' he says. 'We're definitely aware of a lot of new bands and the state of heavy metal today, but, you know, our whole thing whenever we've gone into making a new album is just to do the best we can. We just try to make the best record we can with the resources we have available and where it falls within the overall picture [of hard rock] is where it's gonna fall.'

Of course, Metallica are not getting any younger. At the time of speaking, Hammett is forty-six years of age and it's wondered how much longer the guitarist wants to keep playing the likes of 'Blackened' and 'For Whom The Bell Tolls', having done so for around a quarter of a century. Kirk points to the reunion shows of Mott The Hoople to suggest you're never too old to rock'n'roll. 'Ian Hunter is in his seventies,' he says, 'so the bar keeps on getting raised. And the [Rolling] Stones are still playing in their sixties. I'll keep doing this for as long as it's still fun and creatively rewarding.'

COMEDY OCCASIONS

Sheer unpredictability is one of the many things that makes the rock scene irresistible to many, with unsuspecting victims (rock journalists included) often finding themselves in farcical situations they could never have quite anticipated. That's especially the case in the world of heavy metal, the very nature of which ensures that unexpected and comedic moments are never too far away.

The fact that metal is a live beast certainly helps, with the concert or club arena providing an exciting environment in which unforeseen events can occur. And so a 'secret' Metallica gig at London's 100 Club turned out to be a uniquely memorable experience; as did a visit to the Monsters Of Rock Festival at Castle Donington when Ozzy Osbourne and his band found themselves presented with gold discs.

A press junket to Minehead to see Status Quo perform at Butlins was always going to be a comical affair; as, perhaps, was the Macc Lads at the Marquee Club – not that the London Poll Tax Riots that day seemed much like a laughing matter. Yet both gigs took place against unfamiliar backdrops that ensured they'd never be easily forgotten (however much drinking was done).

When it comes to riotous affairs, Iron Maiden have enjoyed some legendary parties in their time – but it's safe to say their Dogstar bash after one performance at the Brixton Academy wasn't exactly one of them, being a relatively straight-laced affair for members of their inner circle. But you can never legislate for who you might bump into at these things . . . or what might happen next.

It would be rude not to mention a Joan Jett party after a show at the

Hammersmith Odeon, where attendees included a motley assortment of fading glam-pop stars who no doubt inspired the former Runaway to declare 'I Love Rock 'n' Roll' during her teenage years. Slade's Noddy Holder could be seen in one corner while Gary Glitter was in another. The complimentary bar had closed and the drinks had sadly run dry when Glitter, the self-styled 'Leader Of The Gang' who would later be jailed for collecting child porn, decided to head to the toilets. Or what those using Cockney rhyming slang would indeed refer to as the 'Gary Glitter'. He rather stupidly left behind a full bottle of champagne in a bucket of ice on his table, and the temptation to take advantage of his negligence was far too much for us to resist. Needless to say, when Glitter returned to find his table empty he produced a look of wide-eyed shock that equalled any of those preposterous facial expressions that were part of his act on *Top Of The Pops* all those years ago. Cheers, Gary . . .

Of course, working for *Metal Hammer* was always going to provide the opportunity to enjoy some unlikely adventures, but two specific days will always stand out as being especially absurd. The English edition of the magazine was initially produced in Dortmund and my role involved visiting their head offices on a fortnightly basis to ensure that each issue went to press with the minimum of mistakes (and to prevent German acts such as Warlock and Running Wild from ending up on the UK cover – although the Scorpions were allowed, of course).

The way two particular journeys back to London unfolded could never have been foreseen – one coinciding with a 'takeover' by *Kerrang!* staff and culminating in a drunken visit to a Paddington restaurant by a certain 'David Coverdale'; another involving a missed flight, a potentially lethal combination of Schnapps and a Bavarian antique (of a sort). Tales of the unexpected indeed . . .

METALLICA: DON'T TREAD ON ME

Sneaking into London's 100 Club as 'Damage Inc' warm up for their 1987 Monsters of Rock appearance turns out to be a more thrilling experience than expected when this writer spends the entire gig onstage . . .

It feels as if I'm the secret fifth member of Metallica. The other, more recognisable four, who, it must be said, contribute rather more musically, are noisily thrashing the hell out of their instruments at London's tiny 100 Club, just two days before their performance in front of 100,000 fans at the Monsters Of Rock Festival at Castle Donington. Meanwhile, temporary, mysterious, unidentified member number five is sharing the small stage by hugging a sound monitor and staring up at James Hetfield's bulging crotch, which is just inches away as the band stampede their way through 'Master Of Puppets'. All around, there is complete bedlam, as stage-divers invade Metallica's professional territory and hurl themselves back into the crowd like lemmings off a cliff. But at least the band's equipment – or one small piece, it is hoped – is going nowhere.

The demand to see Metallica – or 'Damage Inc', as they have been billed, after one of their classic song titles – is intense despite the supposedly secret nature of the gig. And that desire applies not just to fans but also journalists such as this one, who had not been included on the minimal and highly exclusive guest list. But Chuck, one of the Marquee's regular security staff, comes to the rescue when revealing that he is in fact moonlighting at the 100 Club this particular evening and can discreetly squeeze one more person in – on the basis they flex their muscles and get their hands dirty. It seems like a fair deal, until Chuck decides he needs an extra man on the back door, from where absolutely nothing of the show can be seen as it's around a corner.

There is complete bedlam as stage-divers invade Metallica's professional territory and hurl themselves back into the crowd like lemmings off a cliff.

'Okay,' he says, turning and pointing towards a shiny white piano, which looks as if it should be positioned under Barry Manilow's fingers at the Royal Albert Hall rather than on the 100 Club stage. 'Look after that instead. In fact, guard it with your life!' he orders.

But first there's the small matter of helping to hold back the excitable crowd and forming a corridor through which the members of Metallica – or rather 'Damage Inc' – can reach the stage from their dressing room as the introductory music, 'The Ecstasy Of Gold', emerges through the speakers. It's far easier said than done, however, but, after much pushing and shoving, Hetfield and his colleagues eventually reach their destination.

A position is quickly taken up by the gleaming piano, as instructed, but all hell breaks loose as the band tears into 'Creeping Death', sparking an explosion of energy from the audience, many of whom decide they want to share a piece of the action under the hot spotlights.

Chuck, a man who takes no shit, jumps onto the stage and starts kicking people back into the crowd but quickly realises he's fighting a losing battle. And it seems the piano is not quite the priority it once was as he beckons for my assistance before the stage becomes completely over-run. Suddenly there's a seven-foot mutant warrior, complete with mohawk, tattoos, ripped combat gear and rippling muscles, hogging the limelight and waving his arms about in a threatening manner. Chuck takes the initiative by grabbing hold of the brute but then suddenly elects to delegate his responsibilities. 'Get rid of him!' he barks before shoving the alien intruder in my direction.

Gee, thanks. Staring up at the huge creature's face, I feebly decide that a diplomatic, rather than purely physical approach should be taken and it's hoped he has excellent lip-reading skills as it's obvious he can't hear a single word said given the racket that Metallica are rudely making. 'Er, would you, er, possibly mind, er, leaving the stage . . . *please*?' It's unlikely he considers that he has met his match but clearly feels there's no point in hanging around for the sake of it – and hence he complies with the polite request and hurls himself into the swaying mass of bodies below. That's just *got* to hurt for the poor souls flattened by the huge lump of flesh and bone as he crashes on top of them.

The stage is eventually cleared of trespassers but the monitors are strewn around like wreckage from a plane crash, and so Chuck issues his latest order. 'Get that monitor back in front of Hetfield and *keep* it there,' he shouts. 'Lay on it if you have to.' Er, well, whatever the man says . . .

And so the rest of this very special Metallica performance is witnessed from the unique vantage point of clinging on to a vital piece of the band's PA on the front of the stage, with Hetfield crashing out the rock-hard riffs and growling into his microphone immediately above. It's just as well that I don't need to make notes for a review of the show.

Of course, embracing a sound monitor with Metallica bashing out the likes of 'Leper Messiah' and 'Seek And Destroy' at an alarming number of decibels is not recommended for those looking to preserve their hearing, but orders are orders. And there is no denying that there is a certain novelty attached to sharing the band's stage in such circumstances, although when 'Crash Course In Brain Surgery' is delivered, it does occur to me that such a thing might soon be required.

Bodies occasionally go flying over the top of me but the rest of the gig passes off in successful fashion, much to the delight of the 350 or so lucky punters squashed into the hot and sweaty confines of the club. 'It's been a memorable night,' says Hetfield after the show. That, it can safely be emphasised, is something of an understatement . . .

STATUS QUO: ANNIVERSARY WALTZ

It's all aboard the Quo Express in October 1990 as Messrs Rossi and Parfitt celebrate yet another anniversary by rockin' all over the world . . . in Minehead, of all places . . .

'Crikey, that coke must have been good!' A key member of Status Quo's songwriting team is shocked by how quickly the Quo Express, carrying around 200 giggers, liggers and – after several bottles of Chateau

Meaume – extreme gigglers, seems to arrive at Taunton Station ahead of the band's special show at Butlins Somerwest World in Minehead.

It's twenty-five years since Francis Rossi and Rick Parfitt first met at the famous old holiday camp and – in typical Quo fashion – if there's an anniversary to celebrate, they can always be relied upon to take full (commercial) advantage of the opportunity.

And celebrate they do, by rushing any journalist with a vague interest in the band's trusty three chords towards the West Country and feeding them with mushrooms à la grecque, rack of lamb with apple and nut stuffing and apple crumble as the train, emblazoned with the Quo logo down its two sides, greedily gobbles up the miles from Paddington Station.

On the final leg of the journey by coach, guests enter the spirit of the occasion by singing along to 'Rockin' All Over The World' before Chris Tarrant, the radio and television presenter, is asked if he is a big fan of the Quo. 'Of course I am,' he insists to the TV crew, looking a little insulted. 'I've seen them on all fifteen of their farewell tours . . .'

'Crikey, that coke must have been good!'

Everybody feels like happy campers when they're shown to their chalets, where a bag of goodies awaits them, complete with blow-up plastic guitar, the latest – but certainly not greatest – Status Quo compilation and a packet of condoms. It's hoped the final item might prove somewhat more useful than the others . . .

Tonight's show takes place in the Prince's Ballroom and hits all the right notes, in a *Carry On . . . Rocking* kind of way. 'Caroline', 'Roll Over Lay Down' and 'Hold You Back' are reminders of the days when Quo's dirty denim boogie machine belched out genuinely oily exhaust fumes, but the likes of 'Marguerita Time' and the closing 'Burning Bridges' – the latter infuriating with its bouncing, nursery-rhyme keyboard sound – confirms Rossi & Parfitt's transformation into the new Chas & Dave. Gertcha indeed.

'My wife can't see,' complains one of the many Butlins holidaymakers making a rare excursion into rock'n'roll territory behind me, while pointing to his partner, around whom he has wrapped both arms. It appears that Shakin' Stevens would be more up his street.

Afterwards, it's the main event as far as most of the invited guests are concerned – the post-gig party. Broadcaster Annie Nightingale is clearly having a good time but her mood mysteriously changes when I accidentally catch her gaze, and suddenly a terrified expression crosses her face as she shakily points an accusing finger in my direction. 'YOU! It's YOU, it's . . . YOU!' she shrieks as if she's seen the devil, before turning and disappearing into the crowd.

Later, she emerges from the toilets shortly before tonight's stars Rossi and Parfitt also return into view from the same direction. Were they discussing the possibility of performing a session on her radio show? Er, probably not.

THE MACC LADS: ANARCHY IN THE UK

It's 31 March 1990, the day that will always be remembered for the London Poll Tax Riots, but there's little refuge inside the Marquee Club as the Macc Lads deliver another tasteless set of bogie-flavoured boogie . . .

A mighty lump of phlegm – the greenest of grollies – flies through the air from audience to stage before hitting the microphone stand and spending the next few minutes dangling down and slowly drooping further towards the floor. Muttley McLad, lead singer and bass player of the Macc Lads, steps forward and catches the string of saliva and mucky mucus in his hand, then sticks it on his tongue, prompting half the Marquee crowd to retch and turn away in disgust and disbelief at the vomit-inducing act.

Fans of the Macc Lads should not be too surprised – after all, the band's *Macclesfield Recipe Book* features a dubious dish known as Uncle Knobby's Special Treat, the ingredients of which include 'solidified phlegm, vomit and snot' (as well as 'stale beer, sweat and urine'). It all makes the terrible trio's *Beer &*

> **'We sing about three things – beer, sex and sheep-shagging.'**
> — Muttley McLad

Sex & Chips 'n' Gravy album – featuring the likes of 'Sweaty Betty', 'Now He's A Poof' and 'Twenty Pints' – seem positively tasteful by comparison.

But not everyone inside the small club is a die-hard Macc Lads fan, for outside on Charing Cross Road the scene resembles a war zone and the chaos and carnage is such that ordinary members of the public have been escaping into the Marquee for refuge and salvation – without having the foggiest idea of what they're letting themselves in for.

For this is the day of the London Poll Tax Riots – true anarchy in the UK – and police vehicles are screaming up the debris-strewn road and sirens are wailing as crowds of agitators, protesters and spectators are dispersed in all directions. The unlucky ones find themselves inside the Marquee Club and, although they've dodged the various dangerous missiles that are still occasionally being thrown outside, there are projectiles of a different kind now flying through the air – and it's not the sort of stuff anybody wants to get hit with.

Backstage, Muttley admits that dealing with such activity is 'an occupational hazard' for the Macc Lads, as they swear, burp and fart their way through their set for the uncouth youth that make up their fan-base, but one they are slowly beginning to master. 'Maybe we should rehearse with people spitting at us and throwing bottles of piss,' he suggests in all seriousness. 'It's difficult when you have to move your finger up to that next fret and it's stuck by a big bogie; it doesn't sound that good. But Dire Straits wouldn't come across as good as we do if they were getting gobbed over.'

The industry insiders who read trade magazine *Music Week* will no doubt make note. As for the gooey gunge that was hanging from his microphone, Muttley believes he has identified its source, at least in terms of geographic origin. 'I think it was somebody from Macclesfield who did that,' he claims. 'There's no way a gay southerner would manage to throw a lump of gob of such humungous size – and so accurately as well.' He defends the band's lewd and crude material ('You can use her piss for perfume and her pubes for dental floss/ And her shit would make good toothpaste because she's so fooking posh' – 'Lady Muck'). 'Most people sing about love, unless they're a heavy-metal band and it's all about devil worship,' he states. 'At least we sing about *three* things – beer, sex and sheep-shagging.'

An hour later, Muttley admits he's been puking up on the dressing-room floor. 'I think it's some kind of bug that's been going round,' he moans. Nothing to do with sampling other people's saliva, of course . . .

OZZY OSBOURNE: HELLO DONINGTON

Being roped into presenting a gold disc to a member of Ozzy Osbourne's group at the Monsters Of Rock Festival proves a little more testing than imagined . . .

Ozzy Osbourne is playing the 1984 Monsters Of Rock Festival and his most recent album, *Bark At The Moon*, has sold so well that his record company owes the good man a gold disc. So it's decided that the presentation will be made not in some boring, corporate office but onstage, at Castle Donington, in front of 80,000 frenzied fans.

Frank, the marketing manager of Epic Records, is looking for familiar faces to assist him in handing out the goodies, as every member of Ozzy's band is also entitled to a disc. He recognises me in the backstage area and promises a drink or two if I agree to hand one of the glass-framed items over to drummer Tommy Aldridge. Talk about drawing the short straw . . .

'Right,' says Frank, once he has completed his recruitment drive and everybody is assembled stage left at the end of Ozzy's regular set. 'We wait for the band to return for their encore and we then rush the stage to dish out the discs as allocated.' At which point a half-naked Ozzy appears from nowhere, picks up a bucket of water, pours it over his head – as he is wont to do – and heads back out to greet the heavy-metal hordes.

Frank dashes to Ozzy's microphone to announce that a very special presentation is to be made, while Aldridge returns to his stool by the only obvious means – climbing up onto the drum-riser and clambering over the front of his mountainous kit. Needless to say, trying to follow him is a lot more difficult – almost impossible, in fact – when you've got a gold disc under your arm and, by the time I eventually reach the summit, after what seems an eternity, the band are ready to kick back into gear. 'Thanks,' says Tommy as he grabs his prize, and promptly chucks it over his right shoulder.

The sound of an expensive gold disc shattering into splinters and shards in the pit below him might have been painful to hear, if only the noise of its crashing and smashing had not been drowned out by the sudden roar of guitars and Ozzy's shriek of 'Let's go fuckin' crazy!!!'

At this point, the manic masses are wondering why there's a strange bloke clinging onto Aldridge's drum kit while gingerly trying to negotiate a safe route back down to the stage. The sea of rabid revellers is a sight to behold, but this is no time to be admiring the view, so I decide that a big leap to the ground is probably the best – if not necessarily the safest – solution.

A half-naked Ozzy appears from nowhere, picks up a bucket of water, pours it over his head and heads back out to greet the heavy-metal hordes.

There's just time to raise a fist and yell, 'Thank you, Donington!' before disappearing into the waiting wings and bidding an emotional farewell to an adoring audience baying for more – of Ozzy, that is.

OZZY OSBOURNE: SLURP OF THE DAY

Sharing dinner with Ozzy at a record company convention in Bournemouth in 1983 is never going to be an entirely sober affair . . .

Ozzy Osbourne stares down at his bowl of soup and a deep frown spreads across his face. It's green – the soup that is – and so it's assumed that the substance staring up at him might be pea-flavoured. And this would not appear to be to Ozzy's liking. 'I can't eat this,' he moans in his unmistakeable Brummie brogue.

'Oh, of course not,' agrees wife and manager Sharon, sitting alongside him. 'Waiter! A bottle of sherry, please.' The bottle swiftly appears and is immediately handed over to Ozzy, who proceeds to pour as much of the sherry into his soup as is physically possible. He uses his spoon to stir in the alcohol and then takes a sip. 'Mmm, that's better,' he says with a look of satisfaction. At which point, Ozzy drops the spoon, picks up the bowl with both hands and begins to noisily slurp down the soup, seemingly oblivious to the fellow diners who are silently watching with incredulous wonder.

Suddenly, the legend that is Ozzy becomes aware of the people sitting with

Ozzy proceeds to pour as much of the sherry into his soup as is physically possible. him – not least this journalist sitting opposite. He puts down the half-empty dish, picks up the bottle of sherry and passes it across the table to me. 'Do it!' he demands. And without question, I follow his orders . . .

DEATHWISH: BRIGHTON ROCKS

In February 1989, a PR's attempt to curry favour with a bunch of journalists by keeping them well lubricated on their way to see a thrash band in Brighton is in danger of backfiring when nobody can remember a bloody thing . . .

Joe the press officer, being the crazed face that appears on the cover of UFO's seminal live album, *Strangers In The Night* (you didn't really think it was a genuine crowd shot, did you?), really should know better. He's managed to persuade a small group of rock writers to watch little-rated thrash band Deathwish (with one album under their belts) in their hometown of Brighton – and has brought along a few drinks to keep us entertained on the hour-long train journey down from London. Within seconds, Joe produces a bottle of Jack Daniel's, a bottle of Thunderbird, a bottle of vodka, followed by several cans of Special Brew and numerous other lagers and bitters.

Instead of individuals being allowed to select their preferred tipple, however, the various bottles and cans are passed around in circular fashion – meaning that everybody has forgotten who they are, where they are and the reasons for their existence by the time the train arrives on the south coast.

It transpires that Joe was never entirely certain where the Escape Club – the venue where tonight's gig is taking place – is located. And he is even less sure after having drunk enough to kill a rhinoceros. Hence it takes an hour of staggering up and down Brighton seafront, stopping off at a couple of pubs (just to ask for directions, of course), before the club is eventually found and entrance is finally gained. There's already a band onstage and, in a desperate attempt to appear vaguely professional, I spend the next thirty minutes paying strict attention and making copious notes about the pros and cons of Deathwish – the first list being considerably shorter than the second – only to discover that I've been watching another group entirely (the supporting act).

By the time Deathwish finally build up a head of steam, my drunken scribbles resemble some kind of ancient Arabic scripture, meaning they are completely indecipherable when I eventually attempt to remember everything I've forgotten (which is everything). It almost goes without saying that the rail journey home is not without its problems, with one Scottish journalist deciding to amuse himself by setting fire to a seat while another attempts some 'performance art' by trying to squeeze various bits of furniture out of the train window – not with much success, it must be said.

Joe produces a bottle of Jack Daniel's, a bottle of Thunderbird, a bottle of vodka, followed by several cans of Special Brew and numerous other lagers and bitters.

The next day, every one of the five writers – who somehow make it home without being arrested or dying of alcohol poisoning – put in calls to most of the others to request help with their reviews. When the pieces finally get published, they all say very nice things about Deathwish and bear a remarkable similarity to each other, with – it should be added – a little help from Joe the press officer.

IRON MAIDEN: RUN TO THE HILLS

Maiden bassist Steve Harris offers a personal invitation to a party in May 1998, but one of the guests turns out to be a bit too friendly . . .

The office phone rings. 'It's Steve,' says the voice at the other end of the line, as if it's a friendly call he makes every day of the week when the truth is that he has never rung me before in his life. 'Er . . . Steve *who?*' I enquire. 'Steve Harris – you know, from Iron Maiden,' he responds. 'We're playing a gig on Saturday; do you wanna come along? There's a party afterwards.'

It's amazing what some people will do if you send them a free copy of *Hammers News*, West Ham United's official magazine – worth a whole £2.50 – every month. But in reality the kind gesture says a lot about the appreciative kind of guy Steve Harris is. And, after all, we Hammers do have to stick together.

The last time I'd seen Steve was in the Horse & Cart. You could say it's his local, given that he doesn't have to go very far to get there. That's because the pub is actually *inside* his house – and fully stocked it is, too. 'There's a nearby pub that provides us with stuff,' he reveals as he sits on a barstool. 'But, to be honest, we don't have that many parties now, not like we did during the first two or three years here.'

The Maiden bassist shares his Essex home – a fifteenth-century structure – with his wife Lorraine and four children, who obviously represent his greatest love. But the evidence of what comes second and third in the list of things he adores – his band and West Ham United – is everywhere to be seen. A case of 'come on you Irons' indeed.

The first thing that unsuspecting visitors to the house come across is a giant fibreglass head of Maiden's famous mascot Eddie, which illuminates as vehicles enter the grounds. The electronic gates were installed after trespassers repeatedly set off Eddie's lights and were once scared into driving into a gatepost.

'When I've been away a long time, I come home and I feel like kissing the ground.'
– Steve Harris

Inside the house, other Maiden memorabilia from their lengthy past, as well as a multitude of gold and silver discs, includes an upright Egyptian mummy from the *Powerslave* era. 'It's all part of my life,' beams Steve. 'I love it and am proud of what we've achieved. The Eddie thing, obviously that's a novelty, yeah, but I thought, well, it's only gathering dust in the warehouse otherwise.'

Steve proudly holds a West Ham shirt – given to him by one of his playing pals – while a signed ball from the 1980s, an 'I'm Forever Blowing Bubbles' poster and a Hammers team photo from the early 1900s suggest that he is no fair-weather fan. Indeed, he even has a full-sized football pitch in his grounds. 'I'll tell you what,' he says, 'I'd much rather watch West Ham in the bottom division than a club like Crystal Palace in the top flight. In fact there's a rumour going round that I'm buying into the club, but of course I'm not,' he adds. 'Some people think you're worth millions . . .'

Yet Steve had no problem funding the construction of a thirty-two-track recording studio in his home, where Maiden have recorded several albums. 'I thought it would cost millions, but it actually cost less to have the studio installed than it did to record our most expensive album, *Somewhere In Time*. It also means we can spend more time in this country. I really miss England. Sometimes, when I've been away a long time, I come home and I feel like kissing the ground.'

I tell Steve to save the turf kissing for Wembley – if West Ham ever get there. And it just so happens that the Maiden gig that Harris kindly invites me to a few years later – at the Brixton Academy – does indeed coincide with FA Cup final day (Arsenal are playing Newcastle, just in case you're interested). Maybe, given his work commitments, it's just as well that Steve's beloved Hammers are not playing at Wembley on this occasion (although, it should be stressed, they *did* reach the quarter-finals).

On the big day itself, Brixton is suitably rocked, with Steve supplying the galloping bass lines that have been a fundamental part of the Maiden sound since the band's inception in the late seventies. Bruce Dickinson screams to the heavens, Janick Gers and Dave Murray's duelling guitars intertwine like loving snakes and Nicko McBrain pounds away on his drums like a very angry old man.

At the after-show knees-up, at a club called Dogstar on nearby Coldharbour Lane, it's a very select gathering of Maiden members, their road crew, management personnel and close friends, so there's a distinct lack of boring record company executives and pissed-up journalists (well, apart from this one). And chatting with Steve in the middle of the room is a footballer whose love of hard rock makes him something of a rare species. The fact that he has two bottles of beer in each hand suggests he is very pleased that the league campaign with his new club up in the north is now over and he can finally let his hair down.

Indeed, the player is so keen to make the most of the evening that he suggests moving on somewhere else when the Maiden party starts to wind down. 'C'mon, let's go out,' he says. 'Er, aren't we *already* out?' I ask. 'The night is still young,' he insists, ignoring that it's way past midnight, before deciding that our destination should be the Stringfellows club in London's West End. 'I'll get us in, no worries,' he says, despite the heavy-metal denim on display, and with that he's soon attempting to hail a cab outside, although the fact that he is pogo-dancing in the middle of Brixton Road and waving a bottle of booze in the air does little to enhance his chances.

Finally, after several rejections, a taxi driver gives him the benefit of the doubt and pulls over. Fifteen minutes later, the doors of Stringfellows are being thrown wide open and, if there hadn't already have been a red carpet on the floor, they would probably have rolled a special one out for the football celebrity and his new mate, such is the warm welcome offered. Twenty quid disappears into a whip for cocktails – which goes absolutely nowhere – and suddenly the player is getting just a bit *too* friendly. 'It's okay,' he says. 'You don't have to resist.'

Needless to say, I offer my excuses and make the hastiest of departures. Maybe the player's recent transfer away from London was quite a timely one after all . . .

THE DYNAMO FESTIVAL: GARDEN PARTY

Put various members of Skyclad, the manager and drummer of Venom, plus former Thin Lizzy and Motörhead guitarist Brian Robertson around a table and the drinks are gonna keep flowing – all night – as is discovered on a trip to Holland for the 1992 Dynamo Festival . . .

Backstage at the Dynamo Festival at the Kunstijsbaan Stadium in Eindhoven, Holland, you'd expect the musicians to be warming up for their performance with a bottle of brandy or a few swift halves. So eyebrows are naturally raised when Henry Rollins is seen physically *working out* – appearing to be in some kind of highly meditative state – on a carpet in front of his tour bus in the car park. 'It doesn't matter where you put us on the bill or who you put us on the bill with, the result is always the same,' he later insists. 'When we do work, you get destroyed.'

Fittingly, 'destroyed' is a perfect description of how certain parties are feeling after the previous night's indulgences – not least Skyclad and Venom manager Eric Cook who, in a moment of madness, decides to try and out-drink former Thin Lizzy, Wild Horses and Motörhead guitarist Brian Robertson. He's a silly man. And the Geordie has got the hangover to prove it as he watches Pagan thrash-metallers Skyclad gigging and jigging later in the day.

Female fiddler Fritha Jenkins pivots and gyrates in manic fashion as demented and diminutive frontman Martin Walkyier barks out the lyrics and the guitars of Steve Ramsey and Dave Pugh jostle and joust with each other. Robertson – who earlier introduced himself with some Scot-speak that was indecipherable, apart from the words 'coffee', 'cunt' and 'are there any beers around?' – duly appears during the encore to play with the band on a rendition of Lizzy's classic 'Emerald', reminding everybody what a distinctive guitarist he is when relatively sober.

But Cook has another reason for a headache after the set when learning of an altercation between Walkyier and an inebriated Ramsey – who apparently throws a punch – that results in the guitarist's sacking, if only for a few days. By the time fellow Brits Paradise Lost are onstage, parts of the arena – which houses 25,000 fans today – resemble an apocalyptic scene, with a mass of tangled bodies lying strewn in the mud, covered in squashed chips and stale lager.

Undeterred, messrs Cook and Robertson are still in a thirsty mood when returning to their hotel after the festival and the drinks are duly lined up on a table in the front garden. Venom drummer Abaddon – real name Tony and moonlighting as Skyclad's tour manager – has decided to enter into the spirit of things, although tonight he looks less like a worshipper of Satan and more like he's ready for the disco, with his white wing-tip collar shirt and black shades. He certainly takes more than a passing interest in any ladies that come into view as the hours gradually tick by.

'Robbo' duly reveals that he is working hard on some new material with the unlikely figure of former Pogues singer Shane MacGowan, prompting the rest of us to think that there's as much chance of an album ever seeing the light of day as there is of the latter giving up the Guinness. And how many acid tabs a day for the Irishman was that?

Our party expands to about six or seven bodies, with various members of Skyclad showing their faces, while the rounds of drinks keep on coming . . . and coming . . . and coming . . . Night slowly turns into day and all the residents seen disappearing into the hotel the previous evening are eventually seen coming back out again in the morning. These normal, well-balanced people have gone to their rooms, had their allotted eight hours' sleep, showered and bathed, eaten breakfast and packed their cases to return home. Outside, meanwhile, reality has disappeared in a blur of alcohol and it's almost been forgotten that flights back to London are scheduled in just a few hours' time.

One middle-aged woman emerges from the hotel with a look of complete horror as she takes in the shambolic, alcoholic sight in front of her. 'Outrageous!' she exclaims, before disappearing with haste.

'Yeah, she's got a point,' says Robbo. 'It's about time I got another round in.'

'DAVID COVERDALE': WOULD I LIE TO YOU?

A **Kerrang!** *invasion, a hastily consumed bottle of vodka, a surprise appearance by UFO's Pete Way, a smelly pile of vomit on the carpet, some bad David Coverdale impersonations and an unpaid restaurant bill make for an usual day in the* **Metal Hammer** *office in late 1987 . . .*

It has the makings of an extraordinary day when a phone call comes into the *Metal Hammer* offices in Dortmund to warn about rumours that the existing editorial team in London is about to be replaced by the members of rival magazine *Kerrang!* 'We're being taken over,' claims the worried source, 'and we're all going to be sacked.' It seems too ridiculous – not to mention horrific – to be true.

If there is any consolation in being in Germany on this very day, it's that the alarming allegations can directly be put to Jürgen, the magazine's owner and publisher. 'These stories are not true,' he insists when confronted. 'You have nothing to worry about.'

My colleague Dave is unconvinced and suggests that a bottle of vodka is purchased for that afternoon's journey back to London, after putting the latest edition of the magazine to bed. 'But it's only a fifty-five-minute flight,' I insist – a warning he clearly chooses to ignore as he emerges from the duty-free shop at Düsseldorf Airport with large bottle in hand.

Standing on the moving walkway at Heathrow, one dizzying plane ride later, there's still a third of the vodka remaining. 'Come on,' says Dave. 'We can finish this off before we get to passport control.' And the last drops of the forty percent-proof alcohol are duly swallowed before smiles for the airport officials come rather more naturally than would usually be the case.

It makes sense for us to head straight to the pub or even go home. But Dave strangely suggests a return to the *Metal Hammer* office, for reasons best known to himself. The Tube is negotiated, stairs are climbed and the office door is pushed open . . . to reveal the sight of the entire *Kerrang!* editorial team sitting in chairs at desks that do

It's too much for Dave to absorb, and he duly vomits in the middle of the office floor.

not belong to them. It can only be compared to the manager of Manchester City walking into his office to discover Manchester United boss Sir Alex Ferguson occupying his private space. These people, from the enemy camp, are on the phone. 'Yeah, we're running the show now,' they all seem to be saying in unison. Bizarrely, UFO bass player Pete Way is sitting in the corner, complete with trademark stripy trousers. It's too much for Dave to absorb, and he duly vomits in the middle of the office floor, spoiling the brand-new carpet that has been put down during his week-long absence.

Nobody seems to be impressed by Dave's involuntary parking of a custard, although Pete Way has surely seen far worse behaviour in his many years of rock'n'roll partying (not least from himself). Suddenly, dethroned *Metal Hammer* editor Harry – as of this moment, it seems – appears from out of nowhere and rounds up the members of his old team for a consolation dinner he kindly wants to pay for. It seems that Jürgen's masterplan was to recruit staff from the competition to improve *Hammer*'s credibility and destroy *Kerrang!* in the process (a ploy that ultimately fails to work, but that's another story). Our party of six duly arrives at a nearby restaurant in Paddington and spends the next few hours drowning our sorrows, during which time Dave does his best to convince one of the young waitresses that he is not a rock journalist who might have just lost his job but David Coverdale, the singer of Whitesnake – as you do.

Given that Dave wears glasses and has wild ginger hair, it's hard to believe that anybody could be fooled by such a ridiculous claim, but the waitress does a great job of playing along with the idea. 'Ooh, I love your stuff. What's that slow one you do?' she gushingly asks. 'That'll be "Is This Love",' says Dave, who remembers he's got a twelve-inch single of the song under (what used to be) his desk. 'I'll bring one in for you if you like,' he offers, and everybody laughs at the absurd scenario that's unfolding.

Eventually, it's time for Harry to settle the rather substantial bill for the boozy bash, and it seems he has conveniently mislaid his wallet. Never mind, the restaurant owner trusts Harry implicitly and generously allows the party to leave on the basis that he returns the following day to pay what is owed. We assume the matter has been resolved when Dave suggests a return to the same eatery for lunch later in the week, by which time it appears that our jobs are safe . . . for the time being.

The same waitress is again on duty and she looks delighted when Dave hands over the Whitesnake record. 'Oh, that's fantastic,' she says. 'Is there any chance you could sign the sleeve for me?'

At this point it becomes clear that she is not merely playing along with Dave's pretence but has been gullibly taken in by it. Our laughter continues for what seems an eternity. Then the manager of the restaurant appears. 'Hi chaps,' he says. 'You couldn't happen to have a word with your friend Harry and ask him to pop in and settle the bill from the other night, could you?'

We pass the message on as requested but Harry fails to cough up – in the short term, at least. And the restaurant boss is none too pleased with being owed nearly two hundred quid. He starts to wonder how he can claim his cash and suddenly remembers that a certain 'David Coverdale' was a member of the defaulting party – and advises the police accordingly. The next thing we hear is that the cops have been ringing up EMI – Whitesnake's record company – to try and track down the real Mr Coverdale, only to be told that the former Deep Purple vocalist has been on tour in the United States for the past six months and has not even set foot in England, let alone done an unlikely runner from a Paddington restaurant.

Harry eventually pays his bill to the establishment. And a certain 'David Coverdale' never eats there again.

MEAT LOAF: MEAT AND GREET

Meat Loaf attends a record-company dinner in the early eighties but decides to resort to the menu he is more familiar with . . .

The table place-card to my immediate right reveals that a certain 'Mrs Loaf' will be attending dinner tonight. This is unlikely to be her real name, of course, but it does appear to be the unfortunate moniker one would find themselves burdened with should they decide to get matrimonially manacled to the mighty Meat, who has also deigned to dine in the company of various record company executives at an Eastbourne hotel.

'Mrs Loaf', when she does eventually arrive, proves to be a bright, bubbly blonde and it transpires that she does, contrary to first impressions, have a first name, which is Leslie. For the rest of the evening then, she will be known to the guests of the table as Leslie Loaf – which has a certain alliterative ring to it, although hardly does her diminutive body justice.

The man-mountain known as Meat, meanwhile, has a personality as powerful as his most successful music, although he is in a relatively mellow mood tonight. It could be that he realises that his latest album, *Midnight At The Lost And Found*, is a real stinker that suggests that, without the lyrical and musical inspiration of classically-trained co-conspirator Jim Steinman, he has no real vision of his own, while his voice – used to such dramatic effect on pseudo-operatic offerings such as *Bat Out Of Hell* – has been reduced to a cringe-worthy croak. Or it could simply be because Meat is being forced to endure a sober evening, having revealed he is currently off the booze.

> **Meat Loaf staggers into view, clutching a bottle of spirits and lumbering his way down the corridor.**

Several hours later, as some of us head to bed, a tremor is felt on the third floor of the hotel. Suddenly, from around the corner, Meat Loaf staggers into view, clutching a bottle of spirits and lumbering his way down the corridor. His eyes have a demonic look – sort of like Jack Nicholson's character in *The Shining* – and thin strands of hair are stuck to his fat, sweat-covered face as he passes by and disappears into the distance. Any wagon might struggle to accommodate Meat's substantial weight, but it's clear that he's already fallen off this one.

HAMMER HORROR: ONE NIGHT IN DÜSSELDORF

An issue of Metal Hammer *magazine is not the only thing that gets put to bed in the late eighties as a journey from Dortmund to London goes horribly wrong . . .*

As we head into the Crest Hotel close to Düsseldorf Airport, we encounter a picture of sultry sophistication in the form of a mature, blonde-haired woman wrapped in an expensive fur coat and diamond earrings. Just behind, fellow *Metal Hammer* scribe Dave is wearing his scruffy Slayer T-shirt and baggy Iron Maiden tracksuit bottoms. These two people from two very different walks of life should not be occupying the same space, but it's fair to say that today's events have not gone according to plan.

The first indication that our journey back to London from *Hammer*'s offices in Dortmund (where another edition of the magazine has been signed off) was not going to be entirely straightforward came when, earlier that afternoon, business manager Henry revealed that the company's driver was unavailable, and so he would provide the funds for us to travel back to the airport by rail.

This idea seems fine until we belatedly learn mid-journey that our standard-class tickets are not valid for the high-speed train heading towards Düsseldorf unless a surcharge is paid. After several pleas of poverty are made to the ticket inspector, he shrugs his shoulders, mumbles something in German (probably about paupers and peasants) and walks off down the carriage.

Everything looks to be on course until the airport comes into view – and the train speeds on past our destination into the city centre. It transpires that we're on a service for Düsseldorf Central and passengers for Flughafen Düsseldorf needed to switch trains at the previous stop. Needless to say, by the time we pull in and talk our way onto a service that does indeed head to the airport, any hopes of catching our plane back to London are dashed as, upon our arrival, it's announced the gate has closed. And, of course, it's the final flight of the day.

Sadly, this means there's no chance of us getting to see Bonfire – ironically a German band – performing in London this evening. But the real problem is establishing where the night is going to be spent, with a trip back to Dortmund the last thing anybody wants to consider. Thankfully, Henry comes to the rescue when he issues the order to head to the Crest, where two single rooms will be booked under his name and paid for on *Metal Hammer*'s account.

By the look of some of the residents, it's an expensive place to stay, but that's Henry's problem. Dave initially suggests he might just go upstairs and have an early night, which is somewhat out of character, but he's quickly persuaded that it's worth visiting the bar – especially as our good friend Henry is footing the bill. He soon gets into the spirit of things as the barmaid offers either a light Weizen beer in a pint glass or a much stronger dark beer in a smaller measure. 'No,' says Dave. 'We want the dark beer . . . in the BIG glass!'

The barmaid puts up some mild resistance before reluctantly giving in and serving up two large pints of the evil brew. A couple of drinks later, Dave decides it's time to move onto the range of multi-coloured schnapps displayed on a shelf behind the bar, intending to try them all if possible. The barmaid explains in broken English that it's 'not possible' to mix one particular flavour with another but, just when the argument is in danger of being lost, a middle-aged woman at the end of the long bar – another resident – decides to intervene. She speaks in German for a few seconds and suddenly Dave's wish is the young barmaid's command, with the worst possible combination of schnapps appearing as if by magic.

The female introduces herself as Ferdi and reveals that she is an antique dealer from Bavaria. 'She's a bit of an antique herself,' quips Dave when she's out of earshot.

Ferdi wants to know what two long-haired guys from London are doing in an expensive Düsseldorf hotel bar (apart from drinking, of course), and Dave explains that our trip to Germany was to 'visit' the offices of *Metal Hammer* magazine. This is, of course, absolutely true but fiction begins to erode fact when Dave claims that we are both heavy-metal musicians – members of Fastway, apparently – and that there's a new album for us to promote. 'We've been doing some interviews,' he says, which isn't entirely untrue. The drinks continue to flow and soon Ferdi is running her fingers through Dave's highlighted hair – which wouldn't look quite so unusual if it wasn't for the fact that it was ginger in the first place. 'How did your hair get to be so streaked?' she asks. 'Oh, that will be the Californian sun,' says Dave, pretending that a recent trip to LA to interview Megadeth or somebody was actually to play some support dates with the band.

She opens the cardboard lid only to discover that the first condom is missing. 'My husband!' she gasps. 'He must be cheating on me!'

Ferdi is clearly impressed by the idea of getting to know two globetrotting guitarists and is soon talking about 'the three of us' heading upstairs to her room. The idea of shagging the Bavarian beauty – well, after a blizzard of booze that might be a fair description – seems highly appealing until the sickly thought of seeing Dave without his pants on suddenly springs into mind. Thankfully, Dave decides he needs to visit the gents and so I suggest to Ferdi that it's best for us not to wait – because he can always catch us up if he wants to. She leads the way to her room on whatever floor it is and, by the time her door is thrown open, Dave is so far down the other end of the corridor as he emerges from the lift that it's impossible for him to establish exactly where his two friends have disappeared to. He can hardly go and bang on everybody's door if he wants to join in, so he has little choice but to return to his own room – and wait for a call that is never going to come.

In her room, Ferdi quickly produces a bottle of fine champagne – and believes it's best consumed by pouring it all over my fully erect penis and licking it off. This is indeed an arousing experience – although the same can't be said when the champagne eventually runs out and she tries the very same tactic with a bottle of German pale ale she discovers in the darkest corner of her mini-bar.

Finally, she decides it's time for some traditional sex and digs into her handbag, where she finds a packet of condoms. She opens the cardboard lid only to discover that the top perforation has been ripped and the first condom is missing. 'My husband!' she gasps, jumping to the only logical conclusion she can draw when knowing she has not used any herself. 'He must be cheating on me!' It's not easy for me to feel any sympathy for her partner's apparent infidelity, given that she was intending to commit the very same crime herself (a fact that appears to have passed her by).

When I wake up next morning, Ferdi has packed her bags and checked out, no doubt on that 6:45am flight to Israel she was talking about. Dave can't ring through because he has no idea what room I'm in and so yet another flight to London looks like it's going to be missed, until a late dash rescues the situation. 'I can't believe you went off with that old trollop,' says Dave as he jokes about Zimmer frames and false teeth.

Clearly, he has forgotten about the threesome that had been on offer the previous evening, one that he is quickly reminded about . . .

MOTT THE HOOPLE: A 'PLAICE' TO STAY

Former Mott bass player Pete 'Overend' Watts is happy to offer accommodation to his ex-girlfriend and her new boyfriend for the night in the mid-eighties . . . as long as he can talk about his favourite subject . . .

Pete 'Overend' Watts, the bassist of Mott The Hoople in what must feel like a former life, is talking about fish. Perhaps this shouldn't be too surprising, as he has been using his rod and reeling them in – in one sense or another – for more years than he would care to admit.

But angling would undoubtedly seem to be Pete's favourite subject – or indeed his *obsession* – right now, given that he has the uncanny knack of bringing every conversation round to the subject of fish, irrespective of what he has initially started talking about.

It's my new girlfriend Monique's idea to visit Pete when her flat in Shepherd's Bush suffers a power cut. 'He runs an antique shop in Chiswick; he'll be happy to let us stay the night,' she says, failing to mention that 'Pete' just happened to be the man more commonly known as 'Overend' – the former bass player of early-seventies legends Mott – who she had slept with back in the mists of time (and, yes, she would have been much younger than him).

Monique, an American with a suspect past that includes 'turning tricks' – as she calls it – in New York and a spell in a London clinic for those suffering from addiction problems, cherishes her distant memories of the Hoople, but Pete would appear to have rather less affection for the old days. He's cheerful and chummy as he sits in his favourite armchair in the flat above his shop, but the bald patch in the middle of his head is a daily reminder that, although glam rock was fun while it lasted, it wasn't the best of ideas to repeatedly spray his hair with silver car paint to attain the required glittery image.

> ## The bald patch in the middle of his head is a daily reminder that it wasn't the best idea to repeatedly spray his hair with silver car paint.

Hit singles such as 'All The Young Dudes', 'All The Way To Memphis', 'Honaloochie Boogie' and 'Roll Away The Stone' were classic examples of Mott's stardust-sprinkled good-time rock'n'roll, with Cockney-sounding crooner Ian Hunter – actually from Shropshire – hidden behind his trademark black shades.

But Pete found it difficult reconciling the hero worship of the fans with the music that Mott took to the world's stages during their heyday. 'I used to look down on some of those people going crazy in the crowd and think how stupid they were,' he said. 'Anybody could play what we did.'

Hearing Pete dismiss something she loves so much is hurtful for Monique. 'Oh Pete,' she says mournfully. 'How can you say that?'

But Pete is not really listening. Moments later, he's talking about fish again.

SAMSON: HELLO MANCHESTER

Joining British rockers Samson on tour for a date up north at the end of the eighties isn't quite as glamorous as it might have seemed . . .

Paul Samson rolls a fag as the tour bus – well, it's a *minibus* really – takes his band up to Manchester. The group, which played a part in the movement known as the New Wave Of British Heavy Metal at the start of the eighties (otherwise known as NWOBHM) and presented future Iron Maiden vocalist Bruce Dickinson to the world without ever really becoming a major force, are nowadays scraping by with a new line-up and a strictly independent record deal. And so a big-budget tour of the UK this most certainly isn't. 'You know what?' says the curly-haired guitarist, after meditating on a thought for some considerable period of time. 'I just love cunt.'

Seconds later, the drummer sets fire to the newspaper the bass player is reading. Whoosh! The whole thing goes up in flames and causes something of minor panic. Oh well, anything to relieve the tedium of the long journey north from London. When the vehicle eventually arrives in Manchester city centre, Paul announces that tonight's venue – the impressively sounding International 2 – should be just around the corner. The bus makes the final turn and all eyes fall on . . . a single doorway next to a Chinese takeaway. It appears that Samson, the band that still seemingly harbours dreams of cracking the big time, are set to play in what amounts to a telephone box.

Thankfully, the club is reminiscent of the Tardis in *Doctor Who*, which means the inside is much bigger than ever seemed possible from the outside. The support band, Rhode Island Red, has already arrived, but they seem to be under the impression that they are headlining the gig. Samson, inevitably, insist that it is they who are topping the bill and that the other band must take to the stage first.

A childish row ensues, with both parties refusing to set up their gear unless they get their own way. Meanwhile, and perhaps not surprisingly, the promoter of tonight's event is nowhere to be seen. The members of Samson decide that the best way to sort things out is to head to the local pub and not come back until very late, by which time the rival group will have had no option but to play their set.

The devious ploy works as Samson ultimately win the argument – and hit the boards so late (and not entirely sober) that they find themselves playing to one of the smallest crowds of their career (and that really *is* saying something).

GUNS N' ROSES: AXL'S BACK

Hollywood hell-raisers Guns N' Roses live up to expectations . . . by failing to live up to expectations despite agreeing to talk to Penthouse *magazine the day after their Wembley Stadium show in August 1991 . . .*

The call comes through to my home early on Sunday morning. Last night, Guns N' Roses headlined at Wembley Stadium on their *Use Your Illusion* tour, with Skid Row and Nine Inch Nails in support. And today it seems they have agreed to talk to *Penthouse* magazine, so I'm duly summoned to meet and greet top Gunners W. Axl Rose and Slash at their hotel in Chelsea Harbour. There are no prizes for guessing the key topics being lined up for discussion – sex, drugs and rock'n'roll. After all, what else would LA's notorious hell-raisers – whose multi-million selling *Appetite For Destruction* album represents a lifestyle manifesto – have to talk about?

Of course, any particular Guns N' Roses day only begins in the early evening, so a 6:00pm time is set to meet Arlette, the band's American press agent, who travels the world with them and does her damnedest to make sure her boys do what they're told in maintaining media relations. When I arrive at the hotel, she tells me to wait in the bar – a considerable hardship, as you might imagine – before eventually leading the way upstairs to her room.

Slash soon arrives and the guitarist is exactly as a caricaturist would depict him, with his top hat, shades, cigarette and bottle of Jack Daniel's all in place, just as you would expect to see them. 'Hey, man,' he says, in the most American accent you'll ever hear from somebody born in Stoke-on-Trent. He's warm and friendly as he shakes hands but reveals that today's interview responsibilities have been passed over to Axl, who will be around later. Arlette suggests waiting in the bar – oh no, not again – but before I leave her room I notice that she has scrawled Slash's room number on the notepad beside her bed.

Slash is exactly as a caricaturist would depict him, with his top hat, shades, cigarette and bottle of Jack Daniel's all in place.

Several drinks are consumed before Arlette phones down to say something about poor old Axl having a problem with his back, hence the delay in getting to talk with the volatile vocalist. She'll call back as soon as there's more news. This stalling continues for some while – a good couple of hours, in fact – before she eventually breaks the news that Axl is in such pain that he has apparently been forced to go to hospital. The interview is off. 'Sorry,' she says.

It seems as if I have no choice but to head off home when suddenly I remember that Slash's room number has been mentally stored for possible use in emergency circumstances. Surely the guitarist will be only too happy to speak in the absence of his sadly injured colleague in order to rescue the interview and preserve valuable media coverage in such a prestigious publication as *Penthouse*?

The number is dialled and a phone rings. 'Hi,' says the voice. It does indeed belong to Slash. It's not difficult to imagine what he might be getting up to in his room. There's bound to be booze and drugs involved. And he's probably getting a blowjob from some floozy as he speaks, the lucky bastard. But it's still worth asking him if he's prepared to talk. 'Er, Slash, it's Kirk from *Penthouse* here. I've just heard about Axl's back problem; I guess you know all about it . . .'

'Back problem?' he says lazily, suggesting that he knows little about it. 'Er, yeah, yeah,' he suddenly adds, somewhat belatedly and rather unconvincingly.

'Well, I was wondering if, given the circumstances, you'd be available do the interview instead. After all, Axl can't do it if he's gone to hospital.' There's a short silence before Slash responds. 'Oh no, Axl wouldn't be happy if I stole his interview. Axl would get *very* upset if I were to do anything like that,' he says.

Given all the trials and tribulations of the band's controversial career, which has involved riots, drug and alcohol problems, changes in personnel, cancelled gigs and fines for late appearances, among other things, it's impossible to believe that Axl would even *notice* if Slash was interviewed in his absence, let alone get upset about it. Or that Slash would really care even if Axl did.

I make some further pleas – 'It'll only take fifteen minutes,' for example – but it's futile trying to persuade anybody to talk when they don't really want to, especially if they're probably getting noshed off at the same time.

'Well, thanks then, Slash, take it easy. Oh, and tell Axl I hope his bad back gets better.'

'Bad back?' he says. 'Oh yeah, of course . . .'

COMEDY OCCASIONS

THE SOHO SCENE

Few involved in the London hard-rock scene in the mid-to-late eighties will have managed to avoid being irresistibly drawn to the centre of Soho. The magnetic presence of the Marquee Club, which existed at 90 Wardour Street from 1964 through to July 1988 before relocating to the Charing Cross Road, represented the fulcrum of activity in a musical sense. Meanwhile, The Ship public house and the St Moritz Club, less than a minute's walk away on the same road, were equally busy, accommodating the needs of a thirsty crowd made up of musicians, journalists, PRs, record company executives, producers, music publishers, Marquee staff and DJs, hairy hangers-on, good-time girls and various other boozers, cruisers and losers enthralled by the vibrancy of the social scene and the charismatic characters that helped shape it. It couldn't last forever but, at the peak of its popularity, the Wardour Street scene was compulsive to the point that it became something of a personal and professional playground . . .

Sid and Lila have been running The Ship for donkey's years. The Wardour Street pub, with its dark wooden décor, fading wallpaper and well-worn carpet, has long been a magnet for the rock fraternity because of its proximity to the Marquee Club. And its veteran landlords have pretty much seen it all since the early 1960s. Indeed, Lila enjoys recounting tales about her friendship with rockers on the razz such as Keith Moon and Harry Nilsson during the early seventies to any punters willing to listen. 'They were so good to me,' she smiles. 'Keith even came to visit me in hospital, you know.'

Sid is equally entertaining – in his own miserable way. His idea of providing fine cuisine for his starving customers is to crudely make a cheese sandwich on the bar. He slaps the bread down on a plate, applies a thin layer of butter and presses a hard lump of cheese on top, while a cigarette hangs from his lips and drops ash in front of him. 'D'you want pickle with that?' he wheezes, before coughing and spluttering all over the cheese, which is instantly coated with piccalilli – or something that resembles it. Sid grabs the top slice of bread, flattens the sandwich with his palm and hands it over. 'There you go, that will be fifty pence, please.' Well, this is the late eighties . . .

The Ship is the established meeting place for people heading to the Marquee and there are always recognisable faces among the regular crowd of drinkers. On one particular day, the pub has barely opened when Buster Bloodvessel is found sitting at the bar and in the mood to get plastered. The bald and bulging Bad Manners singer – a real Mr Blobby lookalike – has already had a pint or two when he decides it's time to take things to a different level. 'Right, let's do some slammers!'

Being a strict lager drinker (generally), I feign ignorance, yet Buster responds by detailing specific instructions. 'Okay, lick your left hand, then pour on the salt,' he orders. 'Right, cover the glass, bang it on the bar, knock the tequila back in one and then suck on the lemon.'

This procedure is followed to the letter, although Buster has an unconventional way of doing things. 'Right, now let me do this,' he says, leaning forward to grab two fistfuls of hair and commencing a violent shaking action that sends my vibrating brain into outer orbit. 'Isn't it great?' says a highly amused Buster. 'Okay, now you do the same to me,' he insists, before whizzing through the routine with the salt, lemon and tequila. 'C'mon, now you've got to shake my head!'

The opportunity to inflict some immediate revenge seems highly appealing until it quickly becomes apparent that getting to grips with Buster's greasy bonce is no easy task. Indeed, it feels like trying to keep hold of soap in the bath. 'C'mon, get on with it,' says Buster, eager to experience the feeling of exhilaration. The only solution is to grab his ears – as if they were the handles of the FA Cup – and start shaking the living daylights out of him. 'Yeah, that's it, more!' he demands.

At which point a dozen or so rugby fans spill through the doors of the pub to be confronted with the bizarre sight of Buster Bloodvessel of Bad Manners – a figure they're more than familiar with thanks to hits such as 'Lip Up Fatty', 'Special Brew' and 'Can Can' for the ska band – appearing to be physically assaulted . . . and loving every second of it.

Buster comes down to earth with an almighty splash as he instantly finds himself swimming in an ocean of lager, with the egg-chasing fans battling with each other to buy their heavyweight hero – and his new mate, of course – a pint (or six). Needless to say, by the time my girlfriend enters the pub ahead of the John Waite gig at the Marquee that evening, I can be found happily snoozing at the bar . . .

Inevitably, the crowd in The Ship – for those still conscious, that is – generally moves on to the Marquee, the bar of which often appears to be a more popular attraction than the headlining band. The security is often a bit on the relaxed side, so familiar faces exploit the freedom to push their way through the backstage door and into the tiny dressing room, which is notable for the graffiti (indicating decades of decadence) that adorns the walls and ceiling of the club's most private area.

On one memorable evening, Fast Eddie Clarke is at the bar. The guitarist left Motörhead years ago, but whatever he's now up to, it appears to be thirsty work. 'What do you fancy?' he asks me after being introduced by a mutual friend. I decline his kind offer because I already have a drink, but Eddie is insistent. 'Don't be silly, what are you having?' He orders a pint of lager and hands it over. 'Now, what else d'ya want?'

I raise my two glasses to suggest that immediate replenishment of refreshment is hardly necessary. But Eddie is having none of it. 'Right, another lager it is.' And so another pint duly arrives. 'Time for another?' he swiftly asks, less than a minute later. Suddenly, the penny drops with Eddie that, with three pints forming an orderly queue, the offer of yet another is somewhat ridiculous. 'Sorry, mate, you're obviously struggling there,' he says, 'I'll get you a short.'

Meanwhile, Jessie, an American girl in her mid-twenties, has recently become one of the regulars at the club. She claims to be responsible for the scar on guitarist Gary Moore's chin. Of course, nobody believes her. She also says that she once lived with Iggy Pop. Nobody believes that, either. What's more plausible, however, is her admission that she works at the Nude Bed Show in Wardour Street.

She first appears at the club one evening, immaculately dressed in a black suit and hat, with her blonde hair perfectly groomed. It's a very different image the next day, however, when she arrives for lunch looking like a punked-up porno princess. Underneath her beaten-up leather jacket is a ripped T-shirt, which goes rather well with the short leather mini-skirt and fishnet stockings. Her shiny black, high-heeled shoes have little silver padlocks on them. With her fluffed up hair and pouting red lips, she looks like she's well up for it.

Sadly, she isn't – at least not with me – as is evident after returning to my place one night, obviously far more reluctant to take her clothes off at night than she is by day. She curls up under the blankets with her leather jacket firmly zipped up, although perhaps that's no bad thing given she's spent half the journey being sick out of the taxi window and splashing vomit over the windscreen of the car behind us.

By this time my flatmate is beginning to tire of having his sleep interrupted by late-night disturbances – not least when he gets up at 5:00am on one particular morning to discover a drunken, half-naked girl sitting on her backside in the cat litter tray. The bang seems to have done something to her head as well. She rings my office later in the morning and breaks the news. 'I've done it, I've left him,' she says.

'Er . . . not on my account, I hope.'

'Oh no, I was going to do it anyway,' she insists. 'So . . . I was thinking, could we get together again some time?'

'Er, I'm not sure that's such a good idea,' I say, especially as the young lady in question just happens to be married to a rival journalist. A few years later, I'm in Hammersmith with a friend who stops to talk to a girl whose face looks vaguely familiar. 'So who was that?' I ask. 'Oh, she used to be married to a friend of mine,' he says. 'He's much better off without her. Yeah, she was terrible. I mean, she'd go with *anyone* . . .'

She claims to be responsible for the scar on guitarist Gary Moore's chin. Of course, nobody believes her.

There's something sentimentally special about the sticky floors of the Marquee in Wardour Street, but it's not quite the same when the club moves to Charing Cross Road. The venue is bigger and has seats upstairs, but it lacks the intimate character of the old place. Predictably, the bar is still the main area to hang out in and bump into people.

On one occasion, former Quireboys guitarist and new Wildhearts frontman Ginger is less than impressed by a review of his latest band in which I question his vocal capabilities. He spots an opportunity to gain revenge – and swings a punch in my direction. Thankfully Ginger is extremely pissed and is hopelessly off target. He disappears into the crowd and seems to forget everything about the incident, because he couldn't be friendlier the next time we meet. From a Wildheart to a mildheart, it seems.

Post-gig, it's time to head to the St Moritz. The dark basement bar, underneath a restaurant of the same name, is run by a legendary figure known as Sweety. Indeed, former Clash singer Joe Strummer's 101'ers even recorded a track called 'Sweety Of The St Moritz' in his honour.

At this point it should be stated that Sweety – who is Swiss, in his fifties and mostly bald – is something of an erratic character. 'I want your cock!' he frequently offers as a greeting on the door. When he's in a less friendly mood, he refuses to provide the free entry that is generally taken for granted. 'No, you pay this time!' he grumpily insists. On one such occasion tempers flare and I somehow end up pinning him against the wall. The result, inevitably, is a six-week ban from his club, but everything is quickly forgiven and normal service is soon resumed. 'I want your cock!'

Downstairs, Motörhead main-man Lemmy, as always when in London, is feeding the fruit machine, with which he has developed an intimate relationship. 'This is Lemmy . . .' I say to those looking to be introduced to the great man, '. . . and this is his wife.' Of course, I'm talking about the fruit machine rather than one of the Japanese girls who generally trail in his wake.

One evening, a journalist passes Lemmy while carrying a tray with around half-a-dozen drinks. Lemmy's gaze is fixed to the machine's speeding dials, but that doesn't stop him from sticking out his right leg to send the reporter – and all his pint glasses – crashing to what is already a sticky floor. 'The lesson,' growls Lemmy, still focused on the spinning oranges and lemons in front of him, 'is to always be on your guard.' The journalist thanks the veteran vocalist for the valuable advice and quietly disappears into a dark corner.

On the wall in the main bar, there's a framed triple gold disc in honour of Guns N' Roses' mega-selling *Appetite For Destruction* album. And Guns guitarist Slash, who has indeed visited the club, would surely approve of some of the bad-boy behaviour that occasionally takes place. Something suspicious is being chopped out on the table in the darkest alcove in the deepest corner one night when nobody notices the new barman approaching. On any other night, you'd expect bodies to be hastily ejected or the police to be called. But our man, as calm as you like, gathers up the empties, grabs the rolled-up £5 note from somebody's hand and snorts the stuff off the table. He hands back the note and walks off without so much as a backwards glance. He doesn't work there again.

Alice is part of the furniture at the St Moritz club. She's certainly much older than most of it. Indeed, she's something of an antique. With her fur coat, big earrings and wiry blonde-grey hair, she resembles a cross between veteran actresses Diana Dors and Yootha Joyce. Which means she looks a bit out of place when surrounded by groups of hairy young rockers, who take advantage of her generous spirit.

It's almost four in the morning. And Alice is on all fours in her front garden. Her knickers are down and stretched from one muddy knee to the other. Oh well, it's a bit late to turn back now . . . The next morning is one of those chew-your-arm-off moments when one's head hurts like hell, but is still in much better shape than one's self-esteem. Word quickly gets out and the inevitable abuse starts the following evening in the Moritz. Yet they've nearly *all* been there, as they are quickly reminded.

Normal standards of conduct are frequently forgotten in the club. Take a photograph of the regular crowd and use a marker pen to indicate who has been with whom and you'll end up with a flurry of lines zigzagging all over the place. Caroline quickly proves her popularity. She popped up on the scene as if from nowhere – and disappeared just as quickly. Half a dozen chaps are sitting around a table in the St Moritz one evening when Nick, one of the DJs at the Marquee, starts talking about a new girl he got off with. She starts to sound a bit familiar. Dave picks up the thread and describes a similar tale. The young lady starts to sound even more familiar. It soon transpires that five of the six guys around the table have enjoyed/endured one-night stands with Caroline over the previous ten days. There's a moment of reflection as drinks are quietly sipped. 'What I remember most,' says Lea, after some consideration, 'is that she had legs like upside-down beer bottles.' Everybody laughs, except Nick, that is. Because he went last . . .

At least Caroline goes home with her gentlemen, which is more than can be said for one friendly female in the Moritz one evening. There's at least an inch of piss on the floor of the gents' toilets and, while Julie is clearly all woman, her behaviour is anything but lady-like. The girl is not the only thing being banged, with the locked door coming under increasing pressure from the queue of men outside.

Megadeth frontman Dave Mustaine, making a very rare appearance, is among the blokes outside and literally hopping up and down as he clutches his trouser zip in desperation. 'It's my turn!' he spits, although whether he's talking about the bog or the bird is anyone's guess.

The St Moritz toilets clearly have several functions. However, sleeping in them is not to be advised, as is discovered one evening when dozing off in the upstairs cubicle and waking up at 6:00am with the club in darkness. I inch my way downstairs but the club exit is bolted on the outside and so I'm forced to make my way back to the restaurant at pavement level.

Dawn is starting to break, but any hope that there might be light at the end of the tunnel is dashed when I discover the front door cannot be opened from the inside. Still drunk and half asleep, the idea of ringing the police for help fails to occur to me and I decide to launch an escape bid. The front window is made up of small squares of glass and so I look around for something heavy to throw.

I pick up one of the heavy plant pots and hurl it at the window, only to send a shower of soil flying across the restaurant. I try again with a second pot and the explosion of earth is even greater, leaving every one of the white tablecloths covered in a thick layer of dirt. Meanwhile, the window remains intact.

The solution is eventually found in the shape of a square, silver flight-case. Inside is Sweety's treasured accordion which, when the mood takes him, allows him to mince around (in traditional costume) and serenade his customers – even though it's fake and relies on pre-recorded music for its jolly (irritating) sounds. I chuck the metal box with all the force I can muster and, feeling at one with Nick Lowe, rejoice in the sound of breaking glass. Sadly, the impact has triggered the club's alarm and so bells are now loudly ringing. Quite what the young couple walking up Wardour Street make of the man climbing out of the St Moritz window and rushing off up the road is anybody's guess.

Later that evening, a major inquest is taking place in the club. It's revealed that the management had reported a break-in until the police told them that it had been a break-*out* – as the glass was on the *wrong* side of the window. 'We have one clue to suggest who it might have been,' says Sweety, with a knowing look. 'In the toilet, they left behind a copy of *Metal Hammer*, the magazine you work for . . .'

THE SOHO
SCENE